Anonymus

# Agricultural Statistics of Ireland 1895

Anonymus

**Agricultural Statistics of Ireland 1895**

ISBN/EAN: 9783741196591

Manufactured in Europe, USA, Canada, Australia, Japa

Cover: Foto ©knipser5 / pixelio.de

Manufactured and distributed by brebook publishing software
(www.brebook.com)

Anonymus

# Agricultural Statistics of Ireland 1895

# AGRICULTURAL STATISTICS

OF

# IRELAND,

WITH

## DETAILED REPORT ON AGRICULTURE,

FOR THE YEAR

## 1895.

DIVISION OF LAND; ACREAGE UNDER CROPS; NUMBER AND SIZE OF HOLDINGS; NUMBER OF OCCUPIERS OF LAND; WOODS AND PLANTATIONS; RATES OF PRODUCE; NOXIOUS INSECTS, FUNGI, WEEDS; NUMBER, AGES, &c., OF LIVE STOCK; ENTIRE HORSES; BULLS; DISEASES OF ANIMALS; EXPORTS AND IMPORTS OF LIVE STOCK; DAIRY INDUSTRIES; HONEY PRODUCED; AGRICULTURAL MACHINES; NUMBER OF SCUTCHING MILLS; NUMBER OF CORN MILLS; SILOS AND ENSILAGE; FORESTRY OPERATIONS; WAGES OF AGRICULTURAL LABOURERS; OBSERVATIONS ON THE PRODUCE OF THE CROPS BY SUPERINTENDENTS OF ENUMERATION; THE WEATHER.

*Presented to both Houses of Parliament by Command of Her Majesty.*

DUBLIN:
PRINTED FOR HER MAJESTY'S STATIONERY OFFICE,
BY ALEXANDER THOM & CO. (LIMITED).

And to be purchased, either directly or through any Bookseller, from
Hodges, Figgis, and Co. (Limited), 104, Grafton-street, Dublin; or
Eyre and Spottiswoode, East Harding-street, Fleet-street, E.C.; or
John Menzies and Co., 12, Hanover-street, Edinburgh, and 90, West Nile-street, Glasgow.

1896.

# CONTENTS.


INTRODUCTORY REMARKS:— Page

DIVISIONS OF LAND, TILLAGE, &c.:

TABLE I.—Acreage under Crops in 1884 and 1885, and the Increase or Decrease in the latter year, with proportionate Area under each Crop, . . . . . . . . 5
" II.—Extent of Land and proportional Area under Cereal Crops, Green Crops, Flax, Grass, Woods and Plantations, Fallow and Bog, Waste, Water, &c., in each year from 1875 to 1885, and Averages for the ten years 1875-84; also the number of Holdings exceeding One Acre, . 8
" III.—Number of Holdings, by Classes, for each County and Province, in 1884 and 1885, and the Increase or Decrease in the latter year, . . . . . . . . 11
" IV.—Return of the Number of Occupiers resident in each County and Province in 1885, classified according to the total extent of land held, . . . . . . . 13
" V.—Number of Holdings above One Acre, in each Province in 1841, 1851, 1861, 1871, 1881, 1884, and 1885, according to the classification of the Census Commissioners of 1841, . . . 13
Woods and Plantations, . . . . . . . . . . 14

PRODUCE OF THE CROPS:

DATES OF COMMENCEMENT OF HARVESTING; CONDITIONS INFLUENCING THE PRODUCE OF THE CROPS; THE WEATHER, . . . . . . . . . . 15
[illegible], . . . . . . . . . . 15
TABLE VI.—Total Produce of the principal Crops in 1884 and 1885, and the Increase or Decrease in the latter year, . . . . . . . . . . 16
" VII.—Estimated Average Produce per Statute Acre of the principal Crops in 1884 and 1885, and the Increase or Decrease in the latter year, . . . . . . . 17
" VIII.—Extent under each of the principal Crops, and the Total Produce, for all Ireland, in each year from 1875 to 1885 inclusive; with the average yield per Statute Acre for the ten years 1875-84, 18

LIVE STOCK:

" IX.—Number and Ages of Live Stock in 1884 and 1885, and the Increase or Decrease in each description for the latter year, . . . . . . . . . 18
" X.—Number of Live Stock in each year from 1875 to 1885, with averages for the ten years 1875-84, . 19
" XI.—The proportion per cent. of Horses, Cattle, Sheep, and Pigs according to age, from 1880 to 1885, and averages for the ten years 1875-84, . . . . . . . . 19
Entire Horses, . . . . . . . . . . 20
TABLE XII.—Number of Milch Cows in each year from 1875 to 1885, . . . . . . 20
Bulls, . . . . . . . . . . 21
Diseases of Animals, . . . . . . . . . . 21

TABLE XIII.—Showing the number of Dairy Factories and Condensed Milk Factories, with number of Milk Separators in use, the number of hands permanently employed, the quantity of Butter, Cream, &c., produced, and other details, . . . . . . . . 22
Dairy Instruction, . . . . . . . . . . 23
Exports and Imports of Live Stock, . . . . . . . . . 23
TABLE XIV.—Exports of Live Stock from Ireland to Great Britain in the 11 years, 1875-85, . . 24
Honey produced in 1885, . . . . . . . . . . 24
TABLE XV.—Showing for each of the ten years, 1875-84, the quantity of Honey produced in Ireland, &c., &c., . . . . . . . . . . 25
Agricultural Machines, . . . . . . . . . . 25
Number of Scutching Mills, and Number of Scutches, . . . . . . . 26
TABLE XVI.—Number of Scutching Mills in 1885, classified according to the Number of Scutches in each Mill, and the Power used in working them, with the total number of Scutches in each County. 26
Number of Corn Mills, . . . . . . . . . . 26
TABLE XVII.—Number of Corn Mills in 1885, by Counties and Provinces, classified according to the Power used, the kind of Corn chiefly ground, &c., &c., . . . . . . 27
Silos and Ensilage, . . . . . . . . . . 28
TABLE XVIII.—Showing, by Counties and Provinces, the Number of Silos or Stacks, &c., &c., . 29
Forestry Operations, . . . . . . . . . . 29
Wages of Agricultural Labourers, . . . . . . . . . 30
TABLE XIX.—Labourers' Wages in Ireland by Constabulary Division, . . . . . 30-34


A 2

CONTENTS.

## SUMMARY TABLES.

Tillage; Meadow and Clover, &c.:


| | | Page |
|---|---|---|
| Table 1.—Number of Holdings, their Size in Statute Acres, and the Division of Land in each County and Province in [illegible], | . . . | [illegible] |
| " 2.—Proportion per cent. of Total Area under Crops, Grass, Fallow, Woods and Plantations, Turf Bog, Marsh, Barren Mountain Land and Water, Roads, Fences, &c., in each County and Province, in [illegible], | . . . | [illegible] |
| " 3.—Number of Holdings, their Size in Statute Acres, and the Division of Land in [illegible], by Poor Law Unions, | . . . | [illegible] |
| " 4.—Proportion per cent. under Crops, Grass, Fallow, &c., by Poor Law Unions, in [illegible], | . . . | [illegible] |
| " 5.—Extent of Land under Crops in [illegible], Valuation in [illegible], and Population in [illegible], by Counties and Provinces, | . . . | [illegible] |
| " 6.—Produce of the Crops in [illegible], by Counties and Provinces, | . . . | [illegible] |
| " 7.—Extent of Land under Crops in [illegible], Valuation in [illegible], and Population in [illegible], by Poor Law Unions, | . . . | [illegible] |
| " 8.—Produce of the Crops in [illegible], by Poor Law Unions, | . . . | [illegible] |
| " 9.—Number of Holdings exceeding One Acre, and the extent of Land under Crops in each year, from [illegible] to [illegible], by Counties and Provinces, | . . . | [illegible] |
| " 10.—Average Rates of Produce of Crops per Statute Acre, in each year from [illegible] to [illegible], by Counties and Provinces, | . . . | [illegible] |


Live Stock:


| | | |
|---|---|---|
| " 11.—Number of Stockholders, and Quantity of Live Stock in [illegible], by Counties and Provinces, | . . . | [illegible] |
| " 12.—Number of Stockholders and Quantity of Live Stock in [illegible], by Poor Law Unions, | . . . | [illegible] |
| " 13.—The Quantity of Live Stock in each year from [illegible] to [illegible], by Counties and Provinces, | . . . | [illegible] |


---


| | | |
|---|---|---|
| " 14.—Total Area under Potatoes, and the Extent in Statute Acres under each description of that Crop planted in [illegible], by Counties and Provinces, | . . . | [illegible] |
| " 15.—Total Area under Potatoes, and the Extent planted of each description of that Crop in [illegible], by Poor Law Unions, | . . . | [illegible] |
| " 16.—The Average Rate of Produce per Acre of each description of Potato planted in Ireland in [illegible], by Counties, | . . . | [illegible] |
| " 17.—Number of Silos serving Mass in Ireland in [illegible], by Counties and Provinces, | . . . | [illegible] |
| " 18.—Number of Bolls of the Principal Seeds, &c., in Ireland in [illegible], by Counties and Provinces, | . . . | [illegible] |
| " 19.—Agricultural Machinery, | . . . | [illegible] |
| Observations of District-Inspectors of the Royal Irish Constabulary, and of Sergeants of the Metropolitan Police, on the probable cause of the good or bad yield of the Crops in each of their Districts, | . . . | [illegible] |


---

## APPENDIX.


| | | |
|---|---|---|
| Details concerning Seeds and Manures furnished by Owners and Occupiers of Land, | . . . | [illegible] |
| Abstract of the Meteorological Observations registered at the Ordnance Survey Office, Phœnix Park, Dublin, during the year [illegible], | . . . | [illegible] |
| Remarks on the Weather of the year [illegible], by J. W. Moore, Esq., M.D., F.R.C.P.I., with Summary Tables of Meteorological Observations for the twenty-one years, [illegible], | . . . | [illegible] |

# AGRICULTURAL STATISTICS OF IRELAND,

## FOR THE YEAR 1895.

TO HIS EXCELLENCY GEORGE HENRY, EARL CADOGAN, K.G.,

&c. &c. &c.,

LORD LIEUTENANT-GENERAL AND GENERAL GOVERNOR OF IRELAND.

MAY IT PLEASE YOUR EXCELLENCY,

I have the honour to submit to your Excellency the following Report and detailed Tables concerning Agriculture in Ireland for the year 1895.

A review of the detailed Tables confirms the observations I made when presenting the General Abstracts in August, 1895, and the Produce Returns in December last.

## DIVISION OF LAND, TILLAGE, &c.

The acreage under Crops, Grass, Fallow, Woods and Plantations, and Bog, Waste, Water, &c., in 1894 and 1895, was as follows:— *Division of land, 1894 and 1895.*

| — | 1894. | 1895. | Increase or Decrease between 1894 and 1895. | |
|---|---|---|---|---|
| | | | Increase. | Decrease. |
| | Acres. | Acres. | Acres. | Acres. |
| Under Crops, including Meadow and Clover, | 4,831,011 | 4,800,527 | — | 30,484 |
| „ Grass, or Pasture, | 10,211,056 | 10,280,184 | 68,328 | — |
| „ Fallow, | 19,566 | 18,471 | — | 1,187 |
| „ Woods and Plantations, | 309,374 | 308,969 | — | 348 |
| „ Bog, Waste, Water, &c.,* | 4,830,363 | 4,845,034 | — | 14,356 |
| Total,† | 20,313,466 | 20,333,314 | — | — |

The area under Crops in 1895, compared with 1894, shows a net decrease of 30,484 acres—there being a decrease of 82,365 acres in tillage, an increase of 17,830 acres in the area under hay on permanent pasture or grass not broken up in rotation, and a decrease of 5,472 acres under hay on clover, sainfoin, and grasses under rotation. There is an increase of 66,328 acres in the area under Grass; a decrease of 1,187 acres of Fallow land; a decrease of 348 acres under Woods and Plantations; and a decrease of 14,359 acres under Bog, Waste, Water, &c.

Of the 4,845,034 acres given as under "Bog, Waste, Water, &c.," in 1895, 1,210,391 acres were enumerated as "Turf Bog," 428,975 acres as "Marsh," 2,264,840 acres as "Barren Mountain Land," and 942,829 acres as "Water, Roads, Fences, &c." Compared with 1894, "Bog and Marsh" appears to have decreased by 44,076 acres (following an increase of 35,177 acres in 1894, as compared with 1893), while "Barren Mountain Land" increased by 26,436 acres, following a decrease of 2,581 acres in 1894.

The area and proportionate extent of each crop in 1894 and 1895, with the increase or decrease in the latter year, are given in the following Table (I.), from which it appears that, compared with 1894, there was, last year, a net decrease of 44,963 acres, or 3·0 per cent. in cereals, as wheat decreased by 12,606 acres, oats by 36,436 acres, bere and rye by 443 acres, and beans and pease by 833 acres, while barley increased by 7,055 acres. *Acreage under crops 1894 and 1895.*

In green crops there was a net decrease of 11,521 acres, or 1·0 per cent., turnips having increased by 1,971 acres, and mangel wurzel and beet root by 986 acres, while potatoes decreased by 6,601 acres, cabbage by 4,766 acres, vetches and rape by 1,004 acres, and carrots, parsnips, and other green crops by 2,084 acres.

Flax shows a decrease of 3,878 acres, or 5·6 per cent., and meadow and clover an increase of 11,878 acres, or 0·5 per cent.

In 1895, 29·5 acres in every 100 under crops were under cereals, 23·6 under green crops, 1·9 under flax, and 45·0 under meadow and clover.

POTATOES.—The tables relating to the potato crop point to several important conclusions. It will be observed (see Table 14, page 78) that of the 710,486 acres planted *Varieties of Potatoes.*

* Including [illegible] acres under water. † Exclusive of [illegible] acres under the larger rivers, lakes, and tideways.

with potatoes, 77·7 per cent. were under one variety, namely, "Champions," showing a slight decline in the percentage of this variety as compared with the previous year. Of the total number of acres under potatoes 7·4 per cent. were under Flounders, 3·5 per cent. under Irish Whites, 3·3 per cent. under Magnum Bonums, 1·8 per cent. under Skerry Blues, 1·5 per cent. under White Rocks, 0·9 per cent. under Kemps, 0·6 per cent. under Scotch Downs, and 4·3 per cent. under all other varieties exclusive of Champions. It will be seen by a reference to Table 16, page 75, that not only was the Champion variety the one planted in greatest quantity, but that it was generally the most prolific in its yield.

Table 16 also points out the best potato-growing districts in Ireland, and the varieties which appear to thrive best in particular counties.

Of the total extent under crops in 1895, 84·5 per cent., or over five-sixths, were under three crops—oats (24·9 per cent.), potatoes (14·6), and meadow and clover (45·0).

(TABLE I.)—The Acreage under Crops in 1894 and 1895, and the Increase or Decrease in the latter year:—

| Crops. | 1894. | 1895. | Increase in 1895. | | Decrease in 1895. | |
|---|---|---|---|---|---|---|
| | | | Extent. | Per Centage. | Extent. | Per Centage. |
| | Acres. | Acres. | Acres. | | Acres. | |
| Wheat, | 48,330 | 36,337 | — | — | 12,[illegible] | [illegible] |
| Oats, | 1,234,837 | 1,216,401 | — | — | [illegible] | 3·1 |
| Barley, | 164,328 | 171,440 | 7,085 | 4·3 | — | — |
| Bere and Rye, | 12,103 | 11,480 | — | — | 623 | 5·7 |
| Beans and Pease, | 3,180 | 2,833 | — | — | 323 | 10·4 |
| TOTAL EXTENT under CEREAL CROPS, | 1,484,837 | 1,438,934 | — | — | 44,963 | 3·0 |
| Potatoes, | 717,280 | 710,486 | — | — | 6,804 | 0·9 |
| Turnips, | 311,310 | 313,[illegible] | 1,771 | 0·6 | — | — |
| Mangel Wurzel and Beet Root, | 41,020 | 42,377 | 1,353 | 3·0 | — | — |
| Cabbage, | 44,448 | 38,718 | — | — | 4,730 | 10·9 |
| Vetches and Rape, | 10,533 | 9,316 | — | — | 1,[illegible] | [illegible] |
| Carrots, Parsnips, and other Green Crops, | 27,425 | 25,474 | — | — | 2,[illegible] | 7·5 |
| TOTAL EXTENT under GREEN CROPS, | 1,152,573 | 1,141,794 | — | — | 11,[illegible] | 1·0 |
| Flax, | 101,081 | 95,[illegible] | — | — | 6,[illegible] | 4·4 |
| TOTAL under TILLAGE, | 2,748,433 | 2,[illegible] | — | — | 63,[illegible] | 2·3 |
| Meadow and Clover:— | | | | | | |
| Clover, Sainfoin, and Grasses under Rotation, | 641,[illegible] | 634,[illegible] | — | — | 8,477 | 0·9 |
| Permanent Pasture or Grass not broken up in Rotation, | 1,541,649 | 1,[illegible] | 17,[illegible] | 1·1 | — | — |
| TOTAL EXTENT under CROPS, | 4,931,018 | 4,880,837 | — | — | 60,484 | 1·0 |

The Proportionate Area under each Crop in 1894 and 1895:—

| Crops. | Proportion per cent. 1894. | Proportion per cent. 1895. | Crops. | Proportion per cent. 1894. | Proportion per cent. 1895. |
|---|---|---|---|---|---|
| Wheat, | 1·0 | 0·8 | Cabbage, | 0·9 | 0·8 |
| Oats, | 25·4 | 24·9 | Vetches and Rape, | 0·2 | 0·2 |
| Barley, | 3·3 | 3·5 | Carrots, Parsnips, and other Green Crops, | 0·6 | 0·5 |
| Bere and Rye, | 0·3 | 0·2 | | | |
| Beans and Pease, | 0·1 | 0·1 | TOTAL GREEN CROPS, | 23·6 | 23·4 |
| TOTAL CEREAL CROPS, | 30·1 | 29·5 | | | |
| | | | Flax, | 2·0 | 1·9 |
| Potatoes, | 14·6 | 14·6 | Meadow and Clover, | 44·3 | 45·0 |
| Turnips, | 6·3 | 6·4 | | | |
| Mangel Wurzel and Beet Root, | 1·1 | 1·1 | TOTAL, | 100·0 | 100·0 |

Tables showing the extent of land under crops in 1895 by Counties and Provinces, and by Poor Law Unions, and from 1856 to 1895 by Counties and Provinces, are given at pages 40, 44, and 52, respectively.

The extent of land under grass in 1895 (*exclusive of that under meadow and clover*) was 10,280,424 acres, or 50·6 in every 100 of the entire country. In 1894 the extent was 10,214,098 acres or 50·2 per cent. Of the 10,280,424 acres under grass, not for hay, last year 649,792 were under clover, sainfoin and grasses under rotation, and 9,630,632 under permanent pasture or grass not broken up in rotation. The relative proportions under grass in each Province were—in Leinster 55·4 per cent. in 1895, and 55·0 per cent. in 1894; Munster 54·6 per cent. in 1895, and 54·1 per cent. in 1894; Connaught 49·0 per cent. in 1895, and 48·8 per cent. in 1894; and Ulster 42·9 per cent. in 1895, and 42·8 per cent. in 1894. Grazing Land, 1894 and 1895.

There appears to have been an increase of pasture land in 1895, in Ulster of 0·1 per cent. of the total area of the province, in Connaught of 0·2 per cent., in Leinster of 0·4, and in Munster of 0·5 per cent.

Of the counties—Clare, Limerick, Meath, and Westmeath had each 60 acres or upwards in every 100 of their entire area under grass (pasture) in 1895; Fermanagh, Kildare, Kilkenny, Roscommon, and Tipperary, had above 55 and under 60 acres; Carlow, Cavan, Cork, Dublin, Galway, Leitrim, Longford, Queen's, Sligo, Waterford, and Wexford had from 50 to 55 acres; Antrim, Armagh, Kerry, King's, Louth, Monaghan, Tyrone, and Wicklow, had above 40 and under 50 acres; and Donegal, Down, Londonderry, and Mayo had over 30 and under 40 acres in every 100 acres under grass in 1895. Only 33·8 per cent. of the total area of Donegal was enumerated in 1895 as under grass. Meath shows the highest percentage, 71·1. Grazing Land in 1895.

The area of each County and Province, and the extent and percentage under grass in 1895, are given at page 96.

As already stated, the land under grass in 1895 formed a little more than half of the total area (20,333,344 statute acres) of the country. It will be observed from the succeeding Table (Table II.) that the area under grass in 1895 is slightly in excess of the average for the preceding ten years, and also somewhat more than the extent for the year 1894, the proportion of the total area having increased from 50·2 per cent. in 1894, to 50·6 in 1895. Division of Land, 1885–1895.

In Cereal Crops a continuous decrease is shown for all the years covered by the Table, except 1888 and 1892, in each of which there was a slight increase as compared with the extent for the year immediately preceding. The average area under cereals in the ten years 1885–94 was 1,532,932 acres, and the extent in 1895 was 1,439,094 acres, being a decline of 93,838 acres or 6·1 per cent.

The average area under Green Crops in the ten years was 1,202,134 acres, and in 1895 the area was 1,151,754 acres, being 50,380 acres or 4·2 per cent. under the average. The extent under Green Crops in 1894 was 1,163,275 acres.

The area under Flax fell from 101,081 acres in 1894 to 95,203 acres in 1895, and the latter extent shows a decrease of 5,230 acres as compared with the average for the ten years 1885–94.

There were 2,168,598 acres under Meadow and Clover in 1894, and 2,194,478 acres in 1895: the average extent for the ten years 1885–94 was 2,129,834 acres, the yearly extent varying from 2,034,768 acres in 1885 to 2,271,930 acres in 1888.

The extent of Fallow or uncropped arable land in 1895 was 18,431 acres, being a decline of 1,187 acres as compared with the preceding year, but 540 acres over the average extent for the ten years 1885–94.

The area returned under "Bog, Waste, Barren Mountain, Water, &c." in 1895 was 4,645,084 acres, being 14,359 acres less than the corresponding extent for the preceding year, and 11,415 acres below the average for the ten years 1885–94.

[TABLE II

Division of Land.

TABLE 11.—The Extent of Land in Statute Acres, and the proportional Area, under Cereal Crops, Green Crops, Flax, Meadow and Clover, Grass, Woods and Plantations, Fallow, Bog, Waste, Water, &c., in each Year from 1885 to 1895, with averages for the ten years, 1885-94; also the Number of Holdings exceeding 1 acre.

| Years. | Number of Holdings exceeding 1 Acre. | Extent of Land in Statute Acres under— | | | | | | | | | |
|---|---|---|---|---|---|---|---|---|---|---|---|
| | | Cereal Crops. | Green Crops. | Flax. | Meadow and Clover. | Grass. | All Land in use for Agriculture. | Woods and Plantations. | Fallow. | Bog, Waste, Water, Roads, &c. | Total. |
| | | Acres. | Acres. | Acres. | Acres. | Acres. | Acres. | Acres. | Acres. | Acres. | |
| 1885, | [illegible] | [illegible] | [illegible] | [illegible] | [illegible] | [illegible] | [illegible] | [illegible] | [illegible] | [illegible] | [illegible] |
| 1886, | [illegible] | [illegible] | [illegible] | [illegible] | [illegible] | [illegible] | [illegible] | [illegible] | [illegible] | [illegible] | [illegible] |
| 1887, | [illegible] | [illegible] | [illegible] | [illegible] | [illegible] | [illegible] | [illegible] | [illegible] | [illegible] | [illegible] | [illegible] |
| 1888, | [illegible] | [illegible] | [illegible] | [illegible] | [illegible] | [illegible] | [illegible] | [illegible] | [illegible] | [illegible] | [illegible] |
| 1889, | [illegible] | [illegible] | [illegible] | [illegible] | [illegible] | [illegible] | [illegible] | [illegible] | [illegible] | [illegible] | [illegible] |
| 1890, | [illegible] | [illegible] | [illegible] | [illegible] | [illegible] | [illegible] | [illegible] | [illegible] | [illegible] | [illegible] | [illegible] |
| 1891, | [illegible] | [illegible] | [illegible] | [illegible] | [illegible] | [illegible] | [illegible] | [illegible] | [illegible] | [illegible] | [illegible] |
| 1892, | [illegible] | [illegible] | [illegible] | [illegible] | [illegible] | [illegible] | [illegible] | [illegible] | [illegible] | [illegible] | [illegible] |
| 1893, | [illegible] | [illegible] | [illegible] | [illegible] | [illegible] | [illegible] | [illegible] | [illegible] | [illegible] | [illegible] | [illegible] |
| 1894, | [illegible] | [illegible] | [illegible] | [illegible] | [illegible] | [illegible] | [illegible] | [illegible] | [illegible] | [illegible] | [illegible] |
| Average 1885-94, | [illegible] | [illegible] | [illegible] | [illegible] | [illegible] | [illegible] | [illegible] | [illegible] | [illegible] | [illegible] | [illegible] |
| 1895, | [illegible] | [illegible] | [illegible] | [illegible] | [illegible] | [illegible] | [illegible] | [illegible] | [illegible] | [illegible] | [illegible] |

| Years. | — | Proportion per Cent. under— | | | | | | | | | |
|---|---|---|---|---|---|---|---|---|---|---|---|
| | | Cereal Crops. | Green Crops. | Flax. | Meadow and Clover. | Grass. | All Land in use for Agriculture. | Woods and Plantations. | Fallow. | Bog, Waste, Water, Roads, &c. | Total. |
| 1885, | – | [illegible] | [illegible] | [illegible] | [illegible] | [illegible] | [illegible] | [illegible] | [illegible] | [illegible] | [illegible] |
| 1886, | – | [illegible] | [illegible] | [illegible] | [illegible] | [illegible] | [illegible] | [illegible] | [illegible] | [illegible] | [illegible] |
| 1887, | – | [illegible] | [illegible] | [illegible] | [illegible] | [illegible] | [illegible] | [illegible] | [illegible] | [illegible] | [illegible] |
| 1888, | – | [illegible] | [illegible] | [illegible] | [illegible] | [illegible] | [illegible] | [illegible] | [illegible] | [illegible] | [illegible] |
| 1889, | – | [illegible] | [illegible] | [illegible] | [illegible] | [illegible] | [illegible] | [illegible] | [illegible] | [illegible] | [illegible] |
| 1890, | – | [illegible] | [illegible] | [illegible] | [illegible] | [illegible] | [illegible] | [illegible] | [illegible] | [illegible] | [illegible] |
| 1891, | – | [illegible] | [illegible] | [illegible] | [illegible] | [illegible] | [illegible] | [illegible] | [illegible] | [illegible] | [illegible] |
| 1892, | – | [illegible] | [illegible] | [illegible] | [illegible] | [illegible] | [illegible] | [illegible] | [illegible] | [illegible] | [illegible] |
| 1893, | – | [illegible] | [illegible] | [illegible] | [illegible] | [illegible] | [illegible] | [illegible] | [illegible] | [illegible] | [illegible] |
| 1894, | – | [illegible] | [illegible] | [illegible] | [illegible] | [illegible] | [illegible] | [illegible] | [illegible] | [illegible] | [illegible] |
| Average 1885-94, | – | [illegible] | [illegible] | [illegible] | [illegible] | [illegible] | [illegible] | 1·6 | [illegible] | [illegible] | [illegible] |
| 1895, | – | [illegible] | [illegible] | [illegible] | [illegible] | [illegible] | [illegible] | 1·6 | [illegible] | [illegible] | [illegible] |

Turf Bog.

Tables showing the extent and the proportionate area under Crops, Grass, Fallow, Woods and Plantations, Turf Bog, Marsh, Barren Mountain Land, and Water, Roads, Fences, &c., in 1895, by counties and provinces, will be found at page [illegible]. From these it appears that there are three counties with upwards of 100,000 acres under "Turf Bog," viz.:—Mayo, with 254,504 acres, or 19·3 per cent. of its entire area; Galway, 156,353 acres, or 10·4 per cent.; and Donegal, 113,456 acres, or [illegible] per cent. No "Turf Bog" is returned for Dublin, and of the other counties the following are those having the smallest areas under that heading, viz.:—Louth, 716 acres, or 0·4 per cent. of its entire area; Wexford, 940 acres, or 0·1 per cent.; Carlow, 1,203 acres, or 0·5 per cent.; Down, 2,717 acres, or 0·4 per cent.; Kilkenny, 3,188 acres, or 0·6 per cent.; and Waterford, 2,694 acres, or 0·6 per cent. In the province of Connaught, 357,071 acres, being [illegible] per cent. of its entire area, are returned as under "Turf Bog," including 71,699 acres, or 12·3 per cent. of the County of Roscommon, in addition to the large extent in Mayo and Galway as before mentioned.

Marsh.

In Mayo, 69,625 acres, or 5·2 per cent. of the area of the county are under Marsh; in Cork, 63,656 acres, or 3·5 per cent.; in Galway, 60,583 acres, or 4·0 per cent.; in Donegal, 37,114 acres, or 3·1 per cent., and in Kerry, 36,846 acres, or 3·9 per cent. The counties with the smallest area under "Marsh" are, Dublin with 849 acres, or 0·4 per cent. of its entire area; Louth, 1,661 or 0·8 per cent.; Meath, 1,796, or 0·3 per cent.; Fermanagh, 1,921, or 0·5 per cent.; and Monaghan, 1,969 acres, or 0·6 per cent.

* The total area adopted for 1891, 1892, 1893, 1894, and 1895, is 20,[illegible] acres.

The following statement shows in a concise manner the extent of Meadow and Clover and Pasture respectively in Ireland during the 11 years, 1885–95, and the average extents for the 10 years, 1885–94:— Meadow and Clover and Pasture.

| Year. | Meadow and Clover. | Pasture. | Total Grass Land. |
|---|---|---|---|
| | Acres. | Acres. | Acres. |
| 1885, . . . | 2,014,768 | 10,251,130 | 12,265,888 |
| 1886, . . . | 2,??1,328 | 10,148,707 | 12,??4,91? |
| 1887, . . . | 2,143,678 | 10,049,507 | 12,193,??? |
| 1888, . . . | 2,221,960 | 9,946,067 | 12,167,077 |
| 1889, . . . | 2,167,??? | 9,998,207 | 12,165,219 |
| 1890, . . . | 2,082,626 | 10,213,258 | 12,296,880 |
| 1891, . . . | 2,059,??? | 10,296,431 | 12,356,163 |
| 1892, . . . | 2,142,810 | 10,253,681 | 12,396,491 |
| 1893, . . . | 2,167,032 | 10,291,307 | 12,458,340 |
| 1894, . . . | 2,181,566 | 10,211,028 | 12,392,594 |
| Average, 1885–94, . | 2,132,834 | 10,166,667 | 12,299,501 |
| 1895, . . . | 2,194,476 | 10,280,424 | 12,474,900 |

It will be observed that the total area of grass lands has increased from 12,265,888 acres in 1885 to 12,474,900 acres in 1895, being an increase of 169,012 acres or 1·5 per cent. Comparing the area under Pasture in the two years referred to, we find that there was a slight increase in the later year; however, it will be seen further on in this Report that cattle and sheep, although somewhat less numerous than in 1894, have increased since 1885 in a much greater ratio than the pasture lands, showing that the latter are more fully stocked than they were 11 years ago.

"Barren Mountain Land"* covers an area of 100,000 acres and upwards in each of the following seven counties, viz.:—Donegal, 455,351 acres, or 38·2 per cent. of its entire area; Kerry, 295,676 acres, or 25·3 per cent.; Cork, 750,958 acres, or 16·6 per cent.; Galway, 241,673 acres, or 15·9 per cent.; Mayo, 229,800 acres, or 17·4 per cent.; Wicklow, 116,757 acres, or 23·6 per cent., and Tyrone 109,452 acres, or 14·1 per cent. Barren Mountain Land, 1895.

14·3 per cent., or 67,065 acres of Sligo, 13·8 per cent., or 71,031 acres of Londonderry, 6·8 per cent., or 71,641 acres of Tipperary, 17·6 per cent., or 80,251 acres of Waterford, and 10·7 per cent., or 83,313 acres of Clare are under "Barren Mountain Land." The counties containing the smallest areas under "Barren Mountain Land" are Longford with 401 acres, or 0·2 per cent. of its entire area; Meath, 821 acres, or 0·1 per cent.; Kildare, 1,290 acres, or 0·3 per cent.; Westmeath, 1,346 acres, or 0·3 per cent.; and Monaghan, 2,636 acres, or 0·8 per cent. Only 227,643 acres, or 4·7 per cent. of Leinster are returned as being under "Barren Mountain Land," while 803,558 acres, or 13·5 per cent. of Munster; 667,669 acres, or 15·4 per cent. of Ulster; and 873,763 acres or 15·6 per cent. of Connaught are so returned.

943,628 acres (including 139,681 acres under water), or 4·6 per cent. of the entire area of the country, were returned in 1895 as "Water, Roads, Fences, &c." In the counties the highest percentage is 7·3 in Dublin, and the lowest 3·4 in Kildare and Wicklow. These figures do not include the acreage under the larger rivers, lakes, and tideways. See note (†), page 5. Water, Roads, Fences, &c., 1895.

A table showing the division of land by Poor Law Unions is given at pages 37 and 38.

* With reference to the question whether waste land is increasing or decreasing in Ireland, the following from Part I. of Dr. Grimshaw's "Facts and Figures about Ireland" (Hodges, Figgis & Co., Limited, Dublin, 1893), may be of interest: it shows that an immense amount of waste land has been reclaimed during the past fifty years.

Number and size of Holdings, 1894 and 1895.

According to the returns for 1895, the number of separate holdings was 574,786, being 1,068 more than in the previous year. The holdings which *decreased* in number were—those "above 1 and not exceeding 5 acres" by 506; those "above 5 and not exceeding 15 acres" by 512; those "above 15 and not exceeding 30 acres" by 143; and those "above 500 acres" by 17. The holdings which increased in number were those not exceeding 1 acre by 1,699; those "above 30 and not exceeding 50 acres" by 268; those "above 50 and not exceeding 100 acres" by 124; those "above 100 and not exceeding 200 acres" by 53; and those "above 200 and not exceeding 500 acres," by 31.

| Size of Holdings. | Number in 1894. | Number in 1895. | Increase or Decrease in 1895. | |
|---|---|---|---|---|
| | | | Increase. | Decrease. |
| Not exceeding 1 Acre, | 67,580 | 69,[illegible] | 1,699 | – |
| Above 1 and not exceeding 5 Acres, | 62,781 | 62,275 | – | 506 |
| " 5 " 15 " | 156,[illegible] | 155,[illegible] | – | 512 |
| " 15 " 30 " | 133,636 | 133,[illegible] | – | 143 |
| " 30 " 50 " | 72,[illegible] | 72,[illegible] | 268 | – |
| " 50 " 100 " | 56,[illegible] | 57,[illegible] | 124 | – |
| " 100 " 200 " | 22,9[illegible] | 23,[illegible] | 53 | – |
| " 200 " 500 " | 8,[illegible] | 8,363 | 31 | – |
| Above 500 Acres, | 1,574 | 1,557 | – | 17 |
| Total, | 573,718 | 574,786 | 1,068 | – |

A table showing the number of holdings, by classes, for each Poor Law Union, in 1895, will be found on pp. 37 and 38.

The number of separate holdings in each county and province, in 1894 and 1895, is given by classes in Table III. at page 11.

Number of separate Holdings and of Occupiers, 1894 and 1895.

As in many instances landholders occupy more than one farm, and as, in other cases, farms extend into two or more townlands—*the portion in each townland being enumerated and classified as a separate holding*—it has been considered desirable, with the view of ascertaining the number of *Occupiers*, and of classifying them according to the total extent of land held by each, to obtain a Return of the number of persons having more than one farm or holding. Each Enumerator is, therefore, required to furnish the name of every landholder residing in his district who has two or more farms, or whose farm extends into two or more townlands, together with the area of each portion, and the locality in which it is situated. The number of actual occupiers in 1895 thus arrived at is given in Table IV., page 12, by counties and provinces. On comparing the results in this Table with the figures given in Table III., it appears that in 1895 there were 574,786 holdings in the hands of [illegible] occupiers.

The number of separate holdings and the number of occupiers in each Province in 1894 and 1895, respectively, were :—

| Provinces. | Number of Separate Holdings. | | Number of Occupiers. | |
|---|---|---|---|---|
| | 1894. | 1895. | 1894. | 1895. |
| Leinster, | 153,161 | 154,[illegible] | 110,163 | 111,073 |
| Munster, | 137,740 | 138,081 | 116,094 | 118,785 |
| Ulster, | 200,150 | 199,764 | 158,325 | 157,947 |
| Connaught, | 182,757 | 182,649 | 114,464 | 114,[illegible] |
| Total, | 573,718 | 574,786 | [illegible] | [illegible] |

TABLE III.—The number of Holdings, by classes, for each County and Province, in 1894 and 1895, and the increase or decrease in the latter year:—

Number and size of Holdings, 1894 and 1895.

| COUNTIES. | Year | Not exceeding 1 acre. | Above 1 and not exceeding 5 acres. | Above 5 and not exceeding 15 acres. | Above 15 and not exceeding 30 acres. | Above 30 and not exceeding 50 acres. | Above 50 and not exceeding 100 acres. | Above 100 and not exceeding 200 acres. | Above 200 and not exceeding 500 acres. | Above 500 acres. | Total. |
|---|---|---|---|---|---|---|---|---|---|---|---|
| Antrim, | [illegible] | [illegible] | [illegible] | [illegible] | [illegible] | [illegible] | [illegible] | [illegible] | [illegible] | [illegible] | [illegible] |
| Armagh, | [illegible] | [illegible] | [illegible] | [illegible] | [illegible] | [illegible] | [illegible] | [illegible] | [illegible] | [illegible] | [illegible] |
| Carlow, | [illegible] | [illegible] | [illegible] | [illegible] | [illegible] | [illegible] | [illegible] | [illegible] | [illegible] | [illegible] | [illegible] |
| Cavan, | [illegible] | [illegible] | [illegible] | [illegible] | [illegible] | [illegible] | [illegible] | [illegible] | [illegible] | [illegible] | [illegible] |
| Clare, | [illegible] | [illegible] | [illegible] | [illegible] | [illegible] | [illegible] | [illegible] | [illegible] | [illegible] | [illegible] | [illegible] |
| Cork, | [illegible] | [illegible] | [illegible] | [illegible] | [illegible] | [illegible] | [illegible] | [illegible] | [illegible] | [illegible] | [illegible] |
| Donegal, | [illegible] | [illegible] | [illegible] | [illegible] | [illegible] | [illegible] | [illegible] | [illegible] | [illegible] | [illegible] | [illegible] |
| Down, | [illegible] | [illegible] | [illegible] | [illegible] | [illegible] | [illegible] | [illegible] | [illegible] | [illegible] | [illegible] | [illegible] |
| Dublin, | [illegible] | [illegible] | [illegible] | [illegible] | [illegible] | [illegible] | [illegible] | [illegible] | [illegible] | [illegible] | [illegible] |
| Fermanagh, | [illegible] | [illegible] | [illegible] | [illegible] | [illegible] | [illegible] | [illegible] | [illegible] | [illegible] | [illegible] | [illegible] |
| Galway, | [illegible] | [illegible] | [illegible] | [illegible] | [illegible] | [illegible] | [illegible] | [illegible] | [illegible] | [illegible] | [illegible] |
| Kerry, | [illegible] | [illegible] | [illegible] | [illegible] | [illegible] | [illegible] | [illegible] | [illegible] | [illegible] | [illegible] | [illegible] |
| Kildare, | [illegible] | [illegible] | [illegible] | [illegible] | [illegible] | [illegible] | [illegible] | [illegible] | [illegible] | [illegible] | [illegible] |
| Kilkenny, | [illegible] | [illegible] | [illegible] | [illegible] | [illegible] | [illegible] | [illegible] | [illegible] | [illegible] | [illegible] | [illegible] |
| King's, | [illegible] | [illegible] | [illegible] | [illegible] | [illegible] | [illegible] | [illegible] | [illegible] | [illegible] | [illegible] | [illegible] |
| Leitrim, | [illegible] | [illegible] | [illegible] | [illegible] | [illegible] | [illegible] | [illegible] | [illegible] | [illegible] | [illegible] | [illegible] |
| Limerick, | [illegible] | [illegible] | [illegible] | [illegible] | [illegible] | [illegible] | [illegible] | [illegible] | [illegible] | [illegible] | [illegible] |
| Londonderry, | [illegible] | [illegible] | [illegible] | [illegible] | [illegible] | [illegible] | [illegible] | [illegible] | [illegible] | [illegible] | [illegible] |
| Longford, | [illegible] | [illegible] | [illegible] | [illegible] | [illegible] | [illegible] | [illegible] | [illegible] | [illegible] | [illegible] | [illegible] |
| Louth, | [illegible] | [illegible] | [illegible] | [illegible] | [illegible] | [illegible] | [illegible] | [illegible] | [illegible] | [illegible] | [illegible] |
| [illegible] | [illegible] | [illegible] | [illegible] | [illegible] | [illegible] | [illegible] | [illegible] | [illegible] | [illegible] | [illegible] | [illegible] |
| Mayo, | [illegible] | [illegible] | [illegible] | [illegible] | [illegible] | [illegible] | [illegible] | [illegible] | [illegible] | [illegible] | [illegible] |
| Meath, | [illegible] | [illegible] | [illegible] | [illegible] | [illegible] | [illegible] | [illegible] | [illegible] | [illegible] | [illegible] | [illegible] |
| Monaghan, | [illegible] | [illegible] | [illegible] | [illegible] | [illegible] | [illegible] | [illegible] | [illegible] | [illegible] | [illegible] | [illegible] |
| Queen's, | [illegible] | [illegible] | [illegible] | [illegible] | [illegible] | [illegible] | [illegible] | [illegible] | [illegible] | [illegible] | [illegible] |
| Roscommon, | [illegible] | [illegible] | [illegible] | [illegible] | [illegible] | [illegible] | [illegible] | [illegible] | [illegible] | [illegible] | [illegible] |
| Sligo, | [illegible] | [illegible] | [illegible] | [illegible] | [illegible] | [illegible] | [illegible] | [illegible] | [illegible] | [illegible] | [illegible] |
| Tipperary, | [illegible] | [illegible] | [illegible] | [illegible] | [illegible] | [illegible] | [illegible] | [illegible] | [illegible] | [illegible] | [illegible] |
| Tyrone, | [illegible] | [illegible] | [illegible] | [illegible] | [illegible] | [illegible] | [illegible] | [illegible] | [illegible] | [illegible] | [illegible] |
| Waterford, | [illegible] | [illegible] | [illegible] | [illegible] | [illegible] | [illegible] | [illegible] | [illegible] | [illegible] | [illegible] | [illegible] |
| Westmeath, | [illegible] | [illegible] | [illegible] | [illegible] | [illegible] | [illegible] | [illegible] | [illegible] | [illegible] | [illegible] | [illegible] |
| Wexford, | [illegible] | [illegible] | [illegible] | [illegible] | [illegible] | [illegible] | [illegible] | [illegible] | [illegible] | [illegible] | [illegible] |
| Wicklow, | [illegible] | [illegible] | [illegible] | [illegible] | [illegible] | [illegible] | [illegible] | [illegible] | [illegible] | [illegible] | [illegible] |

SUMMARY OF IRELAND.

| PROVINCES. | Year | Not exceeding 1 acre. | Above 1 and not exceeding 5 acres. | Above 5 and not exceeding 15 acres. | Above 15 and not exceeding 30 acres. | Above 30 and not exceeding 50 acres. | Above 50 and not exceeding 100 acres. | Above 100 and not exceeding 200 acres. | Above 200 and not exceeding 500 acres. | Above 500 acres. | Total. |
|---|---|---|---|---|---|---|---|---|---|---|---|
| Leinster, | [illegible] | [illegible] | [illegible] | [illegible] | [illegible] | [illegible] | [illegible] | [illegible] | [illegible] | [illegible] | [illegible] |
| Munster, | [illegible] | [illegible] | [illegible] | [illegible] | [illegible] | [illegible] | [illegible] | [illegible] | [illegible] | [illegible] | [illegible] |
| Ulster, | [illegible] | [illegible] | [illegible] | [illegible] | [illegible] | [illegible] | [illegible] | [illegible] | [illegible] | [illegible] | [illegible] |
| Connaught, | [illegible] | [illegible] | [illegible] | [illegible] | [illegible] | [illegible] | [illegible] | [illegible] | [illegible] | [illegible] | [illegible] |
| Total of Ireland, | 1894 / 1895 | [illegible] | [illegible] | [illegible] | [illegible] | [illegible] | [illegible] | [illegible] | [illegible] | [illegible] | [illegible] |
| Increase or Decrease in 1895, | | Increase. [illegible] | Decrease. [illegible] | Decrease. [illegible] | Decrease. [illegible] | Increase. [illegible] | Increase. [illegible] | Increase. [illegible] | Increase. [illegible] | Decrease. [illegible] | Increase. [illegible] |

[illegible]

TABLE IV.—Return of the number of Occupiers resident in each County and Province in 1894, classified according to the total extent of land held, without reference to the Townland, Poor Law Union, County, or Province in which the portions of land are situated:—

| Counties. | Number of Occupiers holding Land | | | | | | | | | |
|---|---|---|---|---|---|---|---|---|---|---|
| | Not exceeding 1 acre. | Above 1 and not exceeding 5 acres. | Above 5 and not exceeding 15 acres. | Above 15 and not exceeding 30 acres. | Above 30 and not exceeding 50 acres. | Above 50 and not exceeding 100 acres. | Above 100 and not exceeding 200 acres. | Above 200 and not exceeding 500 acres. | Above 500 acres. | Total. |
| [illegible] | [illegible] | [illegible] | [illegible] | [illegible] | [illegible] | [illegible] | [illegible] | [illegible] | [illegible] | [illegible] |
| Wexford, | [illegible] | [illegible] | [illegible] | [illegible] | [illegible] | [illegible] | [illegible] | [illegible] | [illegible] | [illegible] |
| Wicklow, | [illegible] | [illegible] | [illegible] | [illegible] | [illegible] | [illegible] | [illegible] | [illegible] | [illegible] | [illegible] |

SUMMARY OF IRELAND.

| Provinces. | Not exceeding 1 acre. | Above 1 and not exceeding 5 acres. | Above 5 and not exceeding 15 acres. | Above 15 and not exceeding 30 acres. | Above 30 and not exceeding 50 acres. | Above 50 and not exceeding 100 acres. | Above 100 and not exceeding 200 acres. | Above 200 and not exceeding 500 acres. | Above 500 acres. | Total. |
|---|---|---|---|---|---|---|---|---|---|---|
| Leinster, | [illegible] | [illegible] | [illegible] | [illegible] | [illegible] | [illegible] | [illegible] | [illegible] | [illegible] | [illegible] |
| Munster, | [illegible] | [illegible] | [illegible] | [illegible] | [illegible] | [illegible] | [illegible] | [illegible] | [illegible] | [illegible] |
| Ulster, | [illegible] | [illegible] | [illegible] | [illegible] | [illegible] | [illegible] | [illegible] | [illegible] | [illegible] | [illegible] |
| Connaught, | [illegible] | [illegible] | [illegible] | [illegible] | [illegible] | [illegible] | [illegible] | [illegible] | [illegible] | [illegible] |
| Total of Ireland, | [illegible] | [illegible] | [illegible] | [illegible] | [illegible] | [illegible] | [illegible] | [illegible] | [illegible] | [illegible] |

Number of Occupiers of Land, 1888 to 1894.

The following statement shows the number of occupiers of land in each year from 1888 to 1894, by Provinces:—

| Provinces. | Number of Occupiers in the Year. | | | | | | |
|---|---|---|---|---|---|---|---|
| | 1888. | 1889. | 1890. | 1891. | 1892. | 1893. | 1894. |
| Leinster, | 109,701 | 109,861 | 109,640 | 109,573 | 109,916 | 110,[illegible] | 111,[illegible] |
| Munster, | 113,834 | 113,640 | 114,190 | 114,606 | 116,182 | 116,[illegible] | 116,[illegible] |
| Ulster, | 188,410 | 188,648 | 188,183 | 188,090 | 187,616 | [illegible] | 187,[illegible] |
| Connaught, | 114,628 | 113,867 | 114,467 | 114,674 | 114,632 | [illegible] | [illegible] |
| Ireland, | [illegible] | 526,210 | [illegible] | [illegible] | [illegible] | [illegible] | [illegible] |

Increase or decrease in Holdings by Classes between 1841 and 1894.

As will be seen from Table V. on the opposite page, the number of holdings "above 1 and not exceeding 5 acres" diminished greatly between 1841 and 1894. In Leinster the decrease was 64·4 per cent.; in Munster 80·9; in Ulster 77·3; in Connaught 57·6; and in all Ireland 70·3 per cent.

In the same period holdings "above 5 and not exceeding 15 acres" also diminished in number; the decrease in all Ireland was 39·4 per cent.; it was—in Leinster 44·6 per cent.; in Munster 60·1; and in Ulster 35·4; while in Connaught these holdings increased 2·6 per cent.

Holdings "above 15 and not exceeding 30 acres" increased 6·8 per cent. in Leinster; 110·6 per cent. in Ulster; and 474·1 per cent. in Connaught; they decreased 19·1 per cent. in Munster. In all Ireland they increased 61·3 per cent.

Holdings "above 30 acres" increased 119·0 per cent. in Leinster; 241·9 in Munster; 437·3 in Ulster; 486·9 in Connaught; and 236·9 per cent. in all Ireland.

The total number of holdings "above 1 acre" decreased between 1841 and 1895 by 22·2 per cent. in Leinster; 32·1 per cent. in Munster; 27·6 in Ulster; and 23·3 in Connaught.

The total number of holdings in Ireland "above 1 acre" was 691,202 in 1841; 570,338 in 1851; 568,484 in 1861; 544,163 in 1871; 526,745 in 1881; 517,013 in 1891; and 515,378 in 1895, showing a decrease of 175,824 or 25·5 per cent. in the period between 1841 and 1895.

TABLE V.—The number of Holdings above 1 acre in each Province in 1841, 1851, 1861, 1871, 1881, 1891, and 1895, according to the classification used by the Census Commissioners of 1841 (in which "above 30 acres" was the maximum); the increase or decrease in the numbers in each class, and the difference per cent. between 1841 and 1895:—

Number of Holdings in 1841, 1851, 1861, 1871, 1881, 1891, and 1895.

| Sizes or Holdings. | | Leinster. | Munster. | Ulster. | Connaught. | Total. |
|---|---|---|---|---|---|---|
| | | Number. | Number. | Number. | Number. | Number. |
| Above 1 and not exceeding 5 Acres, | 1841, | 49,130 | 57,457 | 100,218 | 100,254 | 310,436 |
| | 1851, | 25,711 | 14,870 | 59,709 | 11,683 | 84,[illegible] |
| | 1861, | 23,648 | 19,738 | [illegible] | 19,[illegible] | 84,[illegible] |
| | 1871, | 21,[illegible] | 12,297 | 24,317 | 16,[illegible] | 76,[illegible] |
| | 1881, | 19,404 | 11,498 | 21,971 | 14,[illegible] | 67,071 |
| | 1891, | 18,034 | 11,307 | 21,597 | 12,[illegible] | 63,[illegible] |
| | 1895, | 17,650 | 11,[illegible] | 20,911 | 11,[illegible] | 62,[illegible] |
| | | Decrease. | Decrease. | Decrease. | Decrease. | Decrease. |
| Decrease in number between 1841 and 1895, | | 31,[illegible] | 46,[illegible] | 81,374 | 87,793 | 248,[illegible] |
| Rate per cent., | | 64·1 | [illegible] | 79·6 | 87·6 | 79·9 |
| Above 5 and not exceeding 15 Acres, | 1841, | 40,039 | 81,763 | 99,003 | 43,403 | 252,[illegible] |
| | 1851, | 33,046 | 24,[illegible] | 85,176 | 48,[illegible] | 191,[illegible] |
| | 1861, | 29,818 | 71,858 | 63,[illegible] | 40,404 | 183,[illegible] |
| | 1871, | 27,278 | 20,409 | 73,647 | 40,[illegible] | 171,[illegible] |
| | 1881, | 25,046 | 19,717 | 64,[illegible] | 49,[illegible] | 164,[illegible] |
| | 1891, | 23,[illegible] | 19,[illegible] | 61,[illegible] | 46,[illegible] | 155,[illegible] |
| | 1895, | 23,911 | 19,107 | 64,313 | 46,[illegible] | 155,[illegible] |
| | | Decrease. | Decrease. | Decrease. | Increase. | Decrease. |
| Increase or Decrease in number between 1841 and 1895, | | 20,[illegible] | 42,[illegible] | 35,[illegible] | 1,[illegible] | 97,[illegible] |
| Rate per cent., | | 44·4 | [illegible] | [illegible] | [illegible] | [illegible] |
| Above 15 and not exceeding 30 Acres, | 1841, | 20,[illegible] | 27,411 | 20,318 | 4,[illegible] | 79,342 |
| | 1851, | [illegible] | 22,[illegible] | 37,[illegible] | 20,[illegible] | 141,[illegible] |
| | 1861, | 24,[illegible] | 74,[illegible] | 37,[illegible] | [illegible] | 141,[illegible] |
| | 1871, | 23,443 | 23,[illegible] | [illegible] | 23,[illegible] | 135,[illegible] |
| | 1881, | 22,[illegible] | [illegible] | 44,[illegible] | 23,[illegible] | 133,[illegible] |
| | 1891, | [illegible] | 34,[illegible] | 43,[illegible] | 23,[illegible] | 133,[illegible] |
| | 1895, | [illegible] | 34,[illegible] | 44,[illegible] | 23,[illegible] | 130,[illegible] |
| | | Increase. | Decrease. | Increase. | Increase. | Increase. |
| Increase or Decrease in number between 1841 and 1895, | | 1,[illegible] | 3,[illegible] | [illegible] | 27,013 | 64,371 |
| Rate per cent., | | [illegible] | 13·1 | 119·0 | 476·2 | [illegible] |
| Above 30 Acres, | 1841, | 17,[illegible] | 18,[illegible] | [illegible] | 4,[illegible] | 48,[illegible] |
| | 1851, | 38,[illegible] | 43,078 | 27,[illegible] | [illegible] | 14[illegible] |
| | 1861, | 39,[illegible] | 43,[illegible] | [illegible] | [illegible] | 157,[illegible] |
| | 1871, | 39,[illegible] | [illegible] | 41,[illegible] | 23,[illegible] | 16[illegible] |
| | 1881, | 38,[illegible] | 46,[illegible] | 42,[illegible] | 21,[illegible] | 17[illegible] |
| | 1891, | 38,[illegible] | [illegible] | 44,[illegible] | 22,[illegible] | 163,[illegible] |
| | 1895, | [illegible] | [illegible] | 44,[illegible] | 25,[illegible] | 16[illegible] |
| | | Increase. | Increase. | Increase. | Increase. | Increase. |
| Increase in number between 1841 and 1895, | | 21,[illegible] | 60,1[illegible] | 34,[illegible] | 19,144 | 114,[illegible] |
| Rate per cent., | | 119·0 | 241·7 | 437·3 | 436·9 | [illegible] |
| TOTAL ABOVE 1 ACRE, | 1841, | 134,[illegible] | 162,[illegible] | 236,[illegible] | 154,[illegible] | 691,202 |
| | 1851, | 123,971 | 1[illegible] | 210,[illegible] | 116,[illegible] | 570,338 |
| | 1861, | 116,973 | 11[illegible] | 207,[illegible] | 125,[illegible] | 568,484 |
| | 1871, | 111,[illegible] | 114,[illegible] | 1[illegible] | 12[illegible] | 544,163 |
| | 1881, | 106,[illegible] | 113,[illegible] | 1[illegible] | 118,[illegible] | 526,745 |
| | 1891, | 105,[illegible] | 111,[illegible] | 1[illegible] | 116,[illegible] | 517,013 |
| | 1895, | 104,[illegible] | 111,[illegible] | 1[illegible] | 118,[illegible] | 515,378 |
| | | Decrease. | Decrease. | Decrease. | Decrease. | Decrease. |
| Decrease in number between 1841 and 1895, | | 30,[illegible] | [illegible] | [illegible] | [illegible] | 175,824 |
| Rate per cent., | | 22·3 | 32·1 | 19·6 | 23·3 | 25·5 |

## WOODS AND PLANTATIONS.

Woods and Plantations.

In addition to the information regarding the total area under Woods and Plantations, returns were obtained in 1895, showing the proportion of the area entered under this heading occupied by each of the various kinds of trees. From these Returns it appears that of the total area (309,975 statute acres) under Woods and Plantations last year, 46,319 acres were under Larch, 35,679 under Fir, 16,611 under Spruce, 3,094 under Pine, 27,079 under Oak, 8,090 under Ash, 10,860 under Beech, 9,560 under Sycamore, 4,119 under Elm, 4,343 under Other Trees, and 149,422 were returned as under Mixed Trees. The area under Woods and Plantations in Leinster was 94,210 acres, in Munster 104,201 acres, in Ulster 58,366 acres, and in Connaught 51,531 acres.

---

## PRODUCE OF THE CROPS.

Mode of obtaining the Returns of Produce.

The Tables relating to the produce of the crops have been carefully compiled from information obtained by members of the Royal Irish Constabulary and of the Metropolitan Police from practical farmers and other persons qualified to form an opinion as to the yield in that *Poor Law Electoral Division* for which they were requested to afford the information. The names and residences of the parties so co-operating and assisting are stated by the Enumerators on the Returns.

### *Notes of Superintendents of Enumeration.*

On pp. 61 to 68 will be found the Observations of the District Inspectors of the Royal Irish Constabulary and of the Sergeants of the Metropolitan Police, who acted as Superintendents of Enumeration, in reply to a circular requesting their opinion as the probable cause to which the good or bad yield of the various crops, in each of their districts, may be attributed.

### Conditions influencing the Produce of the Crops.

### *The Weather.*

The Weather.

The Weather being a potent factor in influencing the produce of the crops, both as to quantity and quality, the following particulars, and those given on pages 113–114, are inserted by the kind permission of the Editor of the Dublin Journal of Medical Science: they have been derived from Returns of Meteorological Observations taken in Dublin City during the years 1873–95, by J. W. Moore, Esq., M.D., F.R.C.P.I., F.R. MET. SOC.; and published in the Journal during the years 1895–96. The Tables on pages 145–147 also, are founded on Dr. Moore's observations:—

The mean Atmospherical Pressure has been obtained from daily readings of the barometer at 9 A.M. and 9 P.M. corrected and reduced to 32° Fahrenheit at the mean sea level. The Mean Temperature values have been deduced from the maximal and minimal readings of the thermometer in the shade. The Rainfall is that measured daily at 9 A.M. A rainy day is one on which at least one-hundredth (·01) of an inch of rain falls within the twenty-four hours from 9 A.M. to 9 A.M.

The *Mean Height of the Barometer* during the year 1896 was [illegible] inches. The highest observed reading was [illegible] inches at 7 P.M. on January [illegible]. The lowest observed reading was [illegible] inches, at [illegible] P.M. on November [illegible]. The extreme range of atmospherical pressure was [illegible] inches compared with [illegible] inches in 1894.

The *Mean Temperature* of the year, deduced from the arithmetical mean of the maximal and minimal readings of the thermometer in the shade was [illegible]. The highest reading was [illegible] on June [illegible]; the lowest reading was [illegible] on January [illegible]. The average mean temperature for the years 1873–96 calculated in the same way was [illegible]. The mean temperature deduced from the daily readings of the dry bulb thermometer at 9 A.M. and 9 P.M. was [illegible].

Rain fell on 194 days, including snow or sleet on [illegible] days, and hail on [illegible] days. The average annual number of rainy days in the years 1873–94 was 197·[illegible]. The total rainfall measured [illegible] inches compared with an average of [illegible] inches in the twenty years 1873–94. During the first half of 1896 (January to June, inclusive) the rainfall was [illegible] inches on [illegible] days; during the second half (July to December, inclusive) [illegible] inches fell on 116 days.

As regards the *Direction of the Wind*, 730 observations were made during the year, with this result—N., 69; N.E., 61; E., 86; S.E., 71; S., 60; S.W., 94; W., 180; N.W., 89; Calms, [illegible].

*Noxious Insects; Fungi; Weeds.*

Several references to the injuries caused to crops by noxious insects, fungi, &c., are contained in the Observations of the Superintendents of Enumeration, on pages 51 to 62. Noxious Insects; Fungi; Weeds.

The following may be quoted:—

In Balbriggan District, Dublin County.—"In the district around Lusk the potato crop has suffered from fungi somewhat, the estimated damage being about 50 per cent."

In Kilkenny District, Kilkenny County.—"Turnips and mangolds suffered from insects in the early part of the season owing to the drought."

In Granard District, Longford County.—"Turnips were greatly checked after sowing, by insects, and in many cases seed had to be sown again."

In Ballynacarrigy District, Westmeath County.—"Regarding special injury to crops by insects, none suffered any save the turnips, one half of which were destroyed by the 'Fly;' if its ravages could be prevented it would be an invaluable boon to agriculturists every year. Weeds injurious to farm crops—none more so than one called by an Irish name 'Praiseagh buidh' is to the oat crop, as the seed of this weed mixes with the grain, thereby reducing its marketable value."

In Arklow District, Wicklow County.—"The yield of turnips is bad, the first sowing having failed in most cases in consequence of the long drought in early summer, at which time also the insect, commonly called "the fly" did much damage to this crop."

In Ennis District, Clare County.—"Certainly much injury must be done, particularly to the potato crop, by weeds, which in some cases strangle the crop."

In Killadyvert District, Clare County.—"Weeds, the farmers call 'crowfoot,' 'presha,' and 'scutchgrass' have been much complained of."

In Tulla District, Clare County.—"In one part of the district turnips were attacked by a disease known as the 'finger and toe' disease, and though this seems to have been confined to a few farms, the loss is estimated at from 50 to 60 tons. In another part of the district turnips suffered severely from the 'turnip fly,' which is said to have attacked the turnips sown in May. Its appearance is attributed to the warm, dry weather experienced. No efforts were made to destroy the insect."

In Mallow District, Cork County.—"Turnips are a fair crop, though some injury was sustained from the fly in the early dry weather, so much so that the farmers found it necessary to make two and even three fresh sowings. Fungi did not show much in turnips. Farmers say that they are most prevalent in fields where the same crop has been repeated."

In Queenstown District, Cork County.—"Fly attacked the turnip crop, causing farmers to resow, in some instances three times."

In Cahersiveen District, Kerry County.—"Farmers of this district pay very little attention to weeding: in fact the greater portion of them do not weed their potatoes at all. If they did weed, I believe a greater yield would be obtained annually."

In Ardara District, Donegal County.—"The crops suffer most from weeds, and little from insects or fungi. The great majority of the small farmers do not realise the injury caused to their crops by weeds."

In Newtownstewart District, Tyrone County.—"The turnip crop has been a bad yield; when first sown the dry weather and the 'fly' destroyed it, and in most cases a second and third sowing had to be made. The oats in some instances have been slightly injured by 'smut.'"

In Clifden District, Galway County.—"Turnips were attacked by a maggot which first made its appearance about 10th July. It has been examined and found to be the grub of the turnip or cabbage fly. It exists for three weeks, and after that time ceases to be able to do damage, as it turns into a fly or beetle. It did serious damage by cutting the plant across about an inch below the surface of the clay. It continued the damage to the turnips up till about 1st August. The same insect (I think) has been attacking the potatoes by cutting the stem across, which killed the plants."

In Boyle District, Roscommon County.—"The small farmers in this district seem to have a total disregard for weeds, and make no attempt to clean and improve the land. It would be beneficial to this country if farmers were compelled by law to keep down weeds. It was scandalous, in some places, to see the state the potato crop was left in in this respect."

Total produce in 1894 and 1895.

Comparing the produce of the Cereal Crops in 1895 with 1894, we find a decrease in wheat of 226,463 cwts., or 37·6 per cent.; in oats of 1,069,794 cwts., or 6·5 per cent.; in bere of 828 cwts., or 13·9 per cent.; in beans of 31,799 cwts., or 38·8 per cent.; while there was an increase in barley of 32,493 cwts., or 1·7 per cent.; in rye of 2,077 cwts., or 1·4 per cent.; and in peas of 1,020 cwts., or 18·6 per cent.

In Green Crops, potatoes show an increase of 1,598,851 tons, or 85·4 per cent. (following a decrease of 1,181,161 tons, or 38·9 per cent. in 1894, as compared with 1893); turnips an increase of 211,065 tons, or 4·9 per cent.; mangel wurzel and beet-root, of 69,477 tons, or 9·2 per cent.; while cabbage shows a decrease of 19,620 tons, or 4·6 per cent.

Flax shows a decrease of 1,490,281 stones of 14 lbs., or 43·3 per cent. (following an increase of 980,112 stones, or 39·8 per cent in 1894 as compared with 1893, and an increase of 910,632 stones, or 66·7 per cent., in 1893, as compared with 1892); hay on clover, sainfoin, and grasses under rotation, a decrease of 337,636 tons, or 23·8 per cent.; and hay on permanent pasture or grass not broken up in rotation, a decrease of 409,654 tons, or 10·7 per cent.; the entire hay crop showing a decrease of 747,290 tons, or 14·1 per cent.

Estimated average produce per acre in 1894 and 1895.

The yield per acre of Cereal Crops in 1895 compared with that of 1894 shows a decrease in wheat from 16·0 cwts. to 16·3 cwts.; in oats from 15·4 cwts. to 15·0 cwts.; in barley from 17·1 to 16·6 cwts.; in beans from 21·6 cwts. to 16·3 cwts.; and in peas from 15·7 cwts. to 13·1 cwts.; while there was an increase in bere from 13·1 cwts. to 13·9 cwts.; and in rye from 12·7 cwts. to 13·4 cwts. In other crops—potatoes show an increase from 2·6 tons to 4·9 tons; turnips from 13·7 tons to 14·3 tons; mangel wurzel and beet-root from 14·6 tons to 15·6 tons; and cabbage from 9·3 tons to 10·2 tons. Hay on clover, sainfoin, and grasses under rotation shows a decrease from 2·3 tons to 1·8 tons; and hay on permanent pasture or grass not broken up in rotation from 2·6 tons to 2·3 tons.

The yield per acre of flax was lower than in any year since 1871, except 1887, and compared with the yield in 1894, shows a decrease from 34·0 stones to 20·5 stones.

The *total produce* of the principal crops in 1894 and 1895, and the increase or decrease in the latter year, are given in Table VI.; the *average produce* per statute acre in Table VII.; and in Table VIII. are given the total extent under each of the principal crops, the *estimated average* yield per statute acre, and the total produce, for each year from 1885 to 1895, inclusive.

Produce of the Crops, 1894–95.

TABLE VI.—The *total produce* of the principal Crops in 1894 and 1895 and the increase or decrease in the latter year:—

| Crops. | Produce. | | Increase in 1895. | | Decrease in 1895. | |
|---|---|---|---|---|---|---|
| | 1894. | 1895. | Quantity. | Percentage. | Quantity. | Percentage. |
| Wheat, Cwts. of 112 lbs., . | 620,490 | 394,027 | — | — | 226,463 | 37·6 |
| Oats, . . . | 16,290,994 | 15,221,200 | — | — | 1,069,794 | 6·5 |
| Barley, . . . | 2,012,679 | 2,045,172 | 32,493 | 1·7 | — | — |
| Bere, . . . | 6,307 | 5,479 | — | — | 828 | 13·9 |
| Rye, . . . | 151,790 | 153,867 | 2,077 | 1·4 | — | — |
| Beans, . . . | 82,081 | 50,282 | — | — | 31,799 | 38·8 |
| Peas, . . . | 5,487 | 6,507 | 1,020 | 18·6 | — | — |
| Potatoes, in Tons, . | 1,873,164 | 3,472,015 | 1,598,851 | 85·4 | — | — |
| Turnips, . . . | 4,279,484 | 4,490,559 | 211,065 | 4·9 | — | — |

TABLE VII.—The *estimated average produce per statute acre* of the principal crops in 1894 and 1895, and the *increase* or *decrease* in 1895 compared with 1894:— Average produce of Crops in 1894 and 1895.

| Crops. | | Produce per Statute Acre. 1894. | 1895. | Increase in 1895. | Decrease in 1895. |
|---|---|---|---|---|---|
| Wheat, in Cwts. of 112 lbs., | | 16·6 | 16·3 | — | 0·3 |
| Oats, | " | 16·4 | 16·0 | — | 0·4 |
| Barley, | " | 17·1 | 16·8 | — | 0·3 |
| Bere, | " | 13·1 | 13·9 | 0·8 | — |
| Rye, | " | 13·7 | 13·4 | 0·7 | — |
| Beans, | " | 21·6 | 16·3 | — | 5·3 |
| Peas, | " | 13·7 | 13·3 | — | 0·4 |
| Potatoes, | in Tons, | 3·6 | 4·9 | 1·3 | — |
| Turnips, | " | 10·7 | 11·5 | 0·8 | — |
| Mangel Wurzel and Beet Root, | " | 14·6 | 15·6 | 1·0 | — |
| Cabbage, | " | 9·6 | 10·3 | 0·7 | — |
| Flax, in Stones of 14 lbs., | | 34·0 | 20·5 | — | 13·5 |
| Hay, in Tons. | Clover, Sainfoin, and Grasses under Rotation, | 2·2 | 1·8 | — | 0·6 |
| | Permanent Pasture or Grass not broken up in Rotation, | 2·6 | 2·3 | — | 0·3 |

The further statement contained in Table VIII. gives a general view of the state of agriculture during the year 1895 as compared with the preceding ten years. Extent under Crops, produce, &c., 1885–95.

Tables showing the total produce of the Crops in 1895, by counties and provinces, will be found at page 42, and by poor law unions at page 46. The average rates by counties and provinces for each year from 1886 to 1895, are given at pages 57 to 61.

TABLE VIII.—The extent under each of the principal Crops—the average Yield per Statute Acre, and the total Produce for all Ireland, in each year from 1885 to 1895, inclusive, with the averages for the ten years, 1885 to 1894.

| Years. | Wheat. | Oats. | Barley. | Bere. | Rye. | Potatoes. | Turnips. | Mangel Wurzel and Beet Root. | Cabbage. | Flax. | Hay. |
|---|---|---|---|---|---|---|---|---|---|---|---|
| | EXTENT UNDER CROPS IN STATUTE MEASURE. | | | | | | | | | | |
| [illegible] | [illegible] | [illegible] | [illegible] | [illegible] | [illegible] | [illegible] | [illegible] | [illegible] | [illegible] | [illegible] | [illegible] |
| Average 1885–94. | [illegible] | [illegible] | [illegible] | [illegible] | [illegible] | [illegible] | [illegible] | [illegible] | [illegible] | [illegible] | [illegible] |
| 1895. | [illegible] | [illegible] | [illegible] | [illegible] | [illegible] | [illegible] | [illegible] | [illegible] | [illegible] | [illegible] | [illegible] |
| | ESTIMATED AVERAGE PRODUCE PER STATUTE ACRE. | | | | | | | | | | |
| [illegible] | [illegible] | [illegible] | [illegible] | [illegible] | [illegible] | [illegible] | [illegible] | [illegible] | [illegible] | [illegible] | [illegible] |
| Average 1885–94. | [illegible] | [illegible] | [illegible] | [illegible] | [illegible] | [illegible] | [illegible] | [illegible] | [illegible] | [illegible] | [illegible] |
| 1895. | [illegible] | [illegible] | [illegible] | [illegible] | [illegible] | [illegible] | [illegible] | [illegible] | [illegible] | [illegible] | [illegible] |
| | TOTAL PRODUCE. | | | | | | | | | | |
| [illegible] | [illegible] | [illegible] | [illegible] | [illegible] | [illegible] | [illegible] | [illegible] | [illegible] | [illegible] | [illegible] | [illegible] |
| Average 1885–94. | [illegible] | [illegible] | [illegible] | [illegible] | [illegible] | [illegible] | [illegible] | [illegible] | [illegible] | [illegible] | [illegible] |
| 1895. | [illegible] | [illegible] | [illegible] | [illegible] | [illegible] | [illegible] | [illegible] | [illegible] | [illegible] | [illegible] | [illegible] |

## LIVE STOCK.

Number and Ages of Live Stock, 1894 and 1895.

TABLE IX.—The Number and Ages of the Live Stock in Ireland, in 1894 and 1895, and the Increase or Decrease in each description:—

| Description of Stock. | | Number in 1894. | Number in 1895. | Increase in 1895. | | Decrease in 1895. | |
|---|---|---|---|---|---|---|---|
| | | | | In Numbers. | Per Centage. | In Numbers. | Per Centage. |
| Horses, | Two years old and upwards, | 446,468 | 458,858 | 12,390 | 2·8 | — | — |
| | One year old and under two, | 99,794 | 96,181 | — | — | 3,613 | 3·6 |
| | Under one year, | 77,423 | 75,050 | — | — | 2,373 | 3·1 |
| Total No. of Horses, | | 623,185 | 630,287 | 7,102 | 1·1 | — | — |
| Mules, | | 29,348 | 29,860 | 512 | 1·7 | — | — |
| Asses, | | 224,611 | 224,508 | — | — | 103 | — |
| Cattle, | Two years old and upwards, | 2,517,429 | 2,450,160 | — | — | 68,269 | 2·6 |
| | One year old and under two, | 914,239 | 911,705 | — | — | 2,534 | 0·3 |
| | Under one year, | 960,185 | 1,011,171 | 50,986 | 5·3 | — | — |
| Total No. of Cattle, | | 4,391,985 | 4,358,078 | — | — | 33,907 | 0·8 |
| Sheep, | One year old and upwards, | 2,492,658 | 2,349,807 | — | — | 142,848 | 5·7 |
| | Under one year, | 1,612,513 | 1,563,603 | — | — | 48,943 | 3·0 |
| Total No. of Sheep, | | 4,105,169 | 3,913,410 | — | — | 191,759 | 4·7 |
| Pigs, | One year old and upwards, | 182,309 | 180,977 | — | — | 8,638 | 1·7 |
| | Under one year, | 1,234,116 | 1,191,957 | — | — | 44,179 | 3·6 |
| Total No. of Pigs, | | 1,389,324 | 1,338,404 | — | — | 50,920 | 3·7 |
| Goats, | | 318,997 | 304,930 | — | — | 14,067 | 4·4 |
| Poultry, | | 14,180,891 | 14,309,725 | 128,834 | 1·0 | — | — |

Number of Live Stock.

At the period of the enumeration in 1895, the total number of horses in Ireland was 630,287, being an increase of 7,102 compared with 1894. There was an increase of 12,390 in the number "two years old and upwards," but a decrease of 3,613 in the "one year old and under two," and of 2,373 in those "under one year."

The number of Mules was 29,860, being 512 more than in 1894, and asses numbered 224,508, being a decrease of 103.

Horses, Mules, and Asses taken together numbered 877,046 in 1894, and 884,555 in 1895, being an increase of 7,519 or 0·9 per cent.; compared with the average number for the ten years 1885–94, they show an increase of 64,445, or 7·9 per cent.

The number of Cattle in 1895 was 4,358,078, showing a decrease of 33,907, or 0·8 per cent. as compared with the number enumerated in 1894; there was a decrease of 68,269 in the "two years old and upwards"; a decrease of 2,534 in the "one year old and under two," but an increase of 56,986 in the number "under one year." Compared with the average number for the ten years 1885–94, Cattle show an increase of 74,098, or 1·7 per cent.

The number of Sheep in 1895, was 3,913,449, being 191,781, or 4·7 per cent. less than the number for the previous year, and 90,371, or 2·3 per cent. less than the average for the ten years 1885-94; the "one year old and upwards" decreased by 143,068, or 3·7 per cent., as compared with the number in 1894, and those "under one year" by 48,663, or 3·0 per cent. *Number of Live Stock.*

Pigs were returned as 1,338,461 in 1895, showing a *decrease* of 50,660, or 3·7 per cent., as compared with the previous year. The "one year old and upwards" *decreased* by 6,481, or 4·1 per cent., and those "under one year" by 44,179, or 3·6 per cent.

Comparing the number of pigs returned in 1895 with the average for the ten years 1885-94, we find an *increase* of 7,216, or 0·5 per cent.

Goats numbered 304,830 in 1895, being 14,087 *less* than in 1894, but 736, or 0·2 per cent., over the average for the ten years 1885-94.

The number of poultry in 1895 was 16,269,525, being 168,921 more than in 1894, and 1,323,297, or 8·8 per cent., over the average for the ten years 1885-94. Of the 16,269,525 poultry in 1895, 1,001,779 were turkeys; 2,023,970 geese; 2,826,740 ducks; and 10,315,036 ordinary fowl. *Poultry.*

Compared with 1894, turkeys *decreased* by 9,833, geese by 56,066, and ducks by 31,200, while ordinary fowl *increased* by 265,962.

TABLE X.—The Number of Live Stock in Ireland, in each year from 1885 to 1895 inclusive, with the average numbers for the ten years 1885-94:— *Number of Live Stock, 1885 to 1895.*

| Years. | Horses and Mules. | Asses. | Cattle. | Sheep. | Pigs. | Goats. | Poultry. |
|---|---|---|---|---|---|---|---|
| 1885, . . | 576,630 | 187,170 | 4,228,331 | 3,478,646 | 1,269,087 | 264,457 | 15,850,327 |
| 1886, . . | 578,299 | 191,815 | 4,183,991 | 3,366,015 | 1,263,145 | 264,176 | 15,909,723 |
| 1887, . . | 581,236 | 199,811 | 4,157,404 | 3,377,558 | 1,408,416 | 271,753 | 14,440,643 |
| 1888, . . | 585,368 | 203,158 | 4,079,195 | 3,624,648 | 1,387,833 | 270,678 | 14,646,480 |
| 1889, . . | 584,107 | 208,336 | 4,001,174 | 3,789,187 | 1,390,070 | 303,753 | 14,636,317 |
| 1890, . . | 614,894 | 213,018 | 4,240,310 | 4,323,285 | 1,570,340 | 327,114 | [illegible] |
| 1891, . . | 621,470 | 216,230 | 4,449,311 | 4,722,613 | 1,367,715 | 338,320 | 15,274,175 |
| 1892, . . | 634,913 | 217,000 | 4,531,130 | 4,677,777 | 1,113,473 | 333,159 | 15,531,746 |
| 1893, . . | 612,189 | 216,770 | 4,464,567 | 4,431,536 | 1,152,417 | 323,173 | 16,097,461 |
| 1894, . . | 602,580 | 224,613 | 4,391,033 | 4,105,180 | 1,389,124 | 318,977 | 16,100,601 |
| Average 1885-94, . | 610,867 | 209,763 | 4,253,960 | 4,003,820 | 1,331,348 | 304,094 | [illegible] |
| 1895, . . | 620,167 | 224,408 | 4,362,023 | 3,913,449 | 1,338,464 | 304,830 | 16,269,525 |

TABLE XI.—The proportion per cent. of Horses, Cattle, Sheep, and Pigs in Ireland according to Age, for the years 1885 to 1895, inclusive, and averages for the ten years 1885-94. *Number of Live Stock, 1885 to 1895.*

| Years. | Horses. | | | Cattle. | | | Sheep. | | Pigs. | |
|---|---|---|---|---|---|---|---|---|---|---|
| | Percentage at each age. | | | Percentage at each age. | | | Percentage at each age. | | Percentage at each age. | |
| | Two Years old and upwards. | One Year old and under Two. | Under One Year. | Two Years old and upwards. | One Year old and under Two. | Under One Year. | One Year old and upwards. | Under One Year. | One Year old and upwards. | Under One Year. |
| 1885, . | 76·5 | 11·9 | 11·6 | 46·0 | 20·6 | 33·4 | 61·4 | 38·6 | 13·7 | 87·3 |
| 1886, . | 76·3 | 12·3 | 11·4 | 46·7 | 31·0 | 22·3 | 61·7 | 38·3 | 12·7 | 87·3 |
| 1887, . | 74·0 | 12·9 | 11·7 | 46·7 | 30·8 | 22·4 | 60·2 | 39·8 | 12·7 | 87·3 |
| 1888, . | 74·6 | 13·1 | 12·3 | 46·9 | 31·5 | 22·5 | 59·6 | 40·4 | 12·2 | 87·8 |
| 1889, . | 74·6 | 12·4 | 12·3 | 46·8 | 31·2 | 22·0 | 59·6 | 40·4 | 12·9 | 87·1 |
| 1890, . | 73·1 | 13·7 | 13·0 | 44·7 | 21·3 | 34·1 | 58·7 | 41·3 | 13·1 | 87·1 |
| 1891, . | 73·3 | 14·6 | 16·3 | 44·1 | 22·0 | 33·9 | 57·6 | 41·9 | 11·7 | 88·3 |
| 1892, . | 71·1 | 15·3 | 13·4 | 43·1 | 27·4 | 29·5 | 59·7 | 40·3 | 12·0 | 88·0 |
| 1893, . | 71·2 | 15·9 | 13·9 | 46·0 | 21·7 | 32·4 | 60·6 | 39·4 | 12·1 | 87·9 |
| 1894, . | 71·7 | 13·9 | 14·4 | 37·5 | 30·0 | 31·9 | 60·7 | 39·3 | 11·8 | 88·2 |
| Average 1885-94, | 72·7 | 13·9 | 13·4 | 45·0 | 31·3 | 23·0 | 60·1 | 39·9 | 12·3 | 87·6 |
| 1895, . | 75·0 | 14·1 | 11·9 | 45·7 | 30·9 | 23·4 | 60·0 | 40·0 | 11·7 | 88·3 |

## ENTIRE HORSES.

Entire Horses.

In connexion with the Agricultural Statistics for 1895, a return of the number of Entire Horses serving mares in his district, was obtained from each Enumerator, and the information thus arrived at will be found set forth by Provinces and Counties in Table 17, pages 76–7.

The total number of sires returned in 1895 is 2,332, against 1,925 in 1890 (the last previous occasion on which statistics relating to this subject were compiled), being an increase of 407.

The number for 1895 comprises 793 Thoroughbreds, 582 Half-breds, 111 Hackneys, 49 Shires, 249 Clydesdales, 470 Agricultural, and 79 of all other breeds.* 1,834 were bred in Ireland, and 498 were imported.

The number of "Thoroughbred" horses (793) exhibits an increase of 193 between 1890 and 1895, those returned as Half-bred (582) show an increase of 98.

Hackneys rose from 23 to 111, Shires from 6 to 49, those returned as Agricultural (470) show a decrease of 2, and all other breeds increased from 50 to 79.

## MILCH COWS.

Milch Cows.

The following statement (Table XII.) shows the number of Milch Cows in Ireland in each year from 1854—the first year in which Milch Cows were separately enumerated—to 1895. The average number for the first five years of the period was 1,579,851, and for the last five years 1,443,217, being a decline of 136,634 or 8·6 per cent. The highest number in any one year was 1,690,389 in 1859, and the lowest 1,348,886 in 1864.

| Years. | No. of Milch Cows. | Years. | No. of Milch Cows. | Years. | No. of Milch Cows. | Years. | No. of Milch Cows. |
|---|---|---|---|---|---|---|---|
| 1854, . | 1,517,673 | 1865, . | 1,397,148 | 1876, . | 1,032,974 | 1887, . | [illegible] |
| 1855, . | [illegible] | 1866, . | 1,483,610 | 1877, . | 1,073,311 | 1888, . | 1,384,771 |
| 1856, . | 1,578,835 | 1867, . | 1,531,063 | 1878, . | 1,484,816 | 1889, . | [illegible] |
| 1857, . | 1,606,230 | 1868, . | 1,674,899 | 1879, . | 1,464,818 | 1890, . | [illegible] |
| 1858, . | 1,422,409 | 1869, . | [illegible] | 1880, . | 1,380,043 | 1891, . | [illegible] |
| 1859, . | [illegible] | 1870, . | [illegible] | 1881, . | 1,392,015 | 1892, . | [illegible] |
| 1860, . | 1,620,452 | 1871, . | [illegible] | 1882, . | [illegible] | 1893, . | [illegible] |
| 1861, . | 1,543,160 | 1872, . | 1,531,744 | 1883, . | [illegible] | 1894, . | 1,467,441 |
| 1862, . | 1,467,838 | 1873, . | [illegible] | 1884, . | [illegible] | 1895, . | [illegible] |
| 1863, . | 1,394,094 | 1874, . | 1,471,373 | 1885, . | 1,417,429 | | |
| 1864, . | 1,348,886 | 1875, . | 1,310,344 | 1886, . | 1,418,646 | | |

* Under the heading "all other Breeds" in this Return are included—One Shetland and 1 Arab in Carlow; 1 Trotter, 1 American Fast Trotter, 1 Unspecified, and 1 Half-bred Cob in Dublin; 9 Suffolk Punch in Kildare; 1 Cleveland in Kilkenny; 1 Thoroughbred Norwegian Pony, 1 Suffolk Punch, 1 Half-bred Norwegian Pony, and 1 Shetland Ponies in King's County; 1 Cleveland in Longford; 1 Shetland Pony, 1 Thoroughbred Suffolk Punch, and 1 "Suffolk" in Louth; 1 Thoroughbred Shetland and 1 Thoroughbred Arabian Pony in Meath; 1 Suffolk Punch in Queen's County; 1 American Breed, 1 "Unknown," 1 Half-bred Pony, and 1 Suffolk Punch in Wexford; 1 Suffolk Punch in Wicklow; 4 Suffolk Punch, 1 Half-bred "Suffolk" and 1 Half-bred Hunter in Cork, E.R.; 1 Half-bred Norman Punch, 1 Suffolk Punch, 1 American Breed, and 1 Half-bred "Suffolk" in Cork, W.R.; 1 Suffolk Punch, 1 Common Breed, and 1 "Yorkshire Coach Horse" in Kerry; 1 Common Breed in Limerick; 1 Half-bred Pony in Tipperary, N.R.; 1 Shetland and 1 Hunter in Waterford; 1 Trotting, 1 "Yorkshire Coaching Horse", and 1 Suffolk Punch in Antrim; 1 Norfolk and 1 Cushendall in Armagh; 1 Suffolk Stallion in Cavan; 1 "Suffolk" in Donegal, 1 Pure Bred Arab in Fermanagh; 1 Arabian, 1 "Coaching", 1 Suffolk Punch, and 1 Pony in Londonderry; 1 "Suffolk" in Monaghan; 1 Black Stallion in Tyrone; 6 Connemara Ponies, 2 Welsh Cobs, 1 Half-bred Connemara, and 1 Hunter in Galway; 1 "Unknown" in Leitrim, 1 Half-bred or ½ Bred Hunter, 1 Arab, 1 "Barb," 1 Welsh Cob, and 1 Half-bred Welsh Pony in Mayo; 1 "Suffolk" in Roscommon.

## BULLS.

It having been considered desirable to ascertain the number of Bulls of each of the principal breeds in Ireland in 1895, a form was issued asking for the following particulars:—Breed—whether "Shorthorn," "Hereford," "Aberdeen Angus," "Norfolk and Suffolk Red Polled," "Kerry," "Dexter," "Channel Islands Cattle," ("Jersey," "Guernsey or Alderney"), "Cross-bred," &c.; and whether imported or bred in Ireland. Bulls.

Table 16 (pages 78-9) shows by counties and provinces the information forwarded on these points.

It will be seen from this Table that the total number of Bulls returned was 14,310, of these 2,537 were in Leinster, 6,349 in Munster, 3,338 in Ulster, and 1,243 in Connaught.

The numbers of the various breeds are as follow:—"Shorthorn," 8,390; "Hereford," 206; "Aberdeen-Angus," 365; "Norfolk and Suffolk Red Polled," 64; "Kerry," 440; "Dexter," 56; "Channel Island Cattle (Jersey, Guernsey or Alderney)," 81; "Cross-bred," or not included in the foregoing breeds, 4,578.

---

Tables showing the number of Live Stock in 1895, by counties and provinces, will be found at page 62; by Poor Law Unions at pages 63-6; and by counties and provinces, for each year from 1886 to 1895, at pages 67-71.

---

## DISEASES OF ANIMALS.

The following information has been derived from Returns compiled in pursuance of the provisions of the 50th section of the Diseases of Animals Act, 1894, for the year ended the 31st December, 1895. Diseases of Animals.

No case of Pleuro-Pneumonia occurred during the year 1895. No outbreaks occurred in 1894 or in 1893. The numbers for four previous years were 84 for 1892, 133 for 1891, 85 for 1890, and 108 for 1889.

Ireland continues to be free from Foot-and-Mouth Disease. No case has occurred since the year 1884.

As regards Swine Fever, during the year 1895, 8,903 suspected outbreaks were reported. The existence of disease was confirmed in 5,045 of these cases by the Veterinary Officers of the Privy Council Department, who examined the internal organs of the dead or slaughtered swine. There were 7,619 outbreaks in the preceding year. In the year 1893 the number was 306, and in 1892, [illegible].

Five outbreaks of Glanders were reported during the year.

There were 4 outbreaks of Anthrax during the year, as compared with 5 in the previous year, 22 in 1893, 6 in 1892, 29 in 1891, 17 in 1890, and 21 in 1889.

The Returns show that 771 cases of Rabies were reported in 1895, as compared with 179 in 1894, 424 in 1893, 446 in 1892, 670 in 1891, and 333 in 1890.

[Table XIII.

ed image digitised by the University of Southampton Library Digitisation Unit

## DAIRY INDUSTRIES.

> Dairy Industries.

As the increase during recent years in the number of Dairy Factories appeared to render it desirable that some particulars should be obtained regarding what is now an important Agricultural industry, information on several points connected with the subject was collected through the medium of the Enumerators in 1891, 1892, 1893, 1894, and 1895. Statistics were also had respecting the number of Milk Separators used in private establishments.

The Table on the opposite page shows, *inter alia*, that the number of Factories from which statistics were obtained in 1895 was 255, being an increase of 29 as compared with the number returned in 1894, and that the number of hands permanently employed amounted to 1,962, or 254 more than the number for 1894. Of the 255 factories, 119 were owned by individual proprietors, 74 were the property of Joint Stock Companies, and 62 belonging to Co-operative Farmers. In the 255 Factories there were 539 milk separators, of which 426, or 61·6 per cent., were worked by steam-power. Four-fifths of the total number of Factories were in Munster, the number for that province being 205; in Leinster there were 39, in Ulster 6, and in Connaught 5. The quantity of Butter produced during the year ended 30th September, 1895, was 206,068 cwts. (against 268,425 cwts. in the preceding year), and of Cheese 324 cwts., and the number of lbs. of Condensed Milk amounted to 21,126,820.

---

## EXPORTS AND IMPORTS OF LIVE STOCK.

> Exports of Live Stock.

With the view of giving a more accurate idea of the number of live stock produced in Ireland, the statement (TABLE XIV.) on page 24 has been compiled from Statistical Returns prepared under the "Diseases of Animals Act, 1894," by the Veterinary Department of the Privy Council.

From the Table referred to it is evident that some of the younger animals included in the Statistics of Exports must of necessity escape enumeration in June of each year when the returns of live stock are collected for this Department. Viewing the number of animals exported to Great Britain in relation to those enumerated, it is found that the cattle exported bears a relation of 15·2 per cent. to those enumerated in 1895, as compared with 16·8 per cent. in 1894; of sheep 16·7 per cent. as compared with 23·3 per cent. in 1894; and of pigs 40·9 per cent. as compared with 42·1 per cent. in 1894.

From the same Returns it appears that the number of horses exported to Great Britain in 1895 amounted to 34,560, equal to 5·5 per cent. of those enumerated.

> Imports of Live Stock.

It also appears that during the same period there were imported into Ireland, 4,556 horses, 352 cattle (including 32 calves), and 17,486 sheep, and that no pigs were imported.

Exports of Live Stock.

TABLE XIV.—Number of Cattle, Sheep, and Swine, exported from Ireland to Great Britain during each of the twenty-one years, 1875–95:—

| Years. | Cattle. | | | | | | Sheep. | | | Swine. | | | [illegible] |
|---|---|---|---|---|---|---|---|---|---|---|---|---|---|
| | Cows, Bulls, and Oxen. | | | | Calves. | Total. | Sheep. | Lambs. | Total. | Fat Swine. | Store Swine. | Total. | |
| | Fat Cattle. | Store Cattle for Fattening or Breeding purposes. | Other Cattle. | Total. | | | | | | | | | |
| 1875, | [illegible] | [illegible] | [illegible] | [illegible] | [illegible] | [illegible] | [illegible] | [illegible] | [illegible] | [illegible] | [illegible] | [illegible] | [illegible] |
| 1876, | [illegible] | [illegible] | [illegible] | [illegible] | [illegible] | [illegible] | [illegible] | [illegible] | [illegible] | [illegible] | [illegible] | [illegible] | [illegible] |
| 1877, | [illegible] | [illegible] | [illegible] | [illegible] | [illegible] | [illegible] | [illegible] | [illegible] | [illegible] | [illegible] | [illegible] | [illegible] | [illegible] |
| 1878, | [illegible] | [illegible] | [illegible] | [illegible] | [illegible] | [illegible] | [illegible] | [illegible] | [illegible] | [illegible] | [illegible] | [illegible] | [illegible] |
| 1879, | [illegible] | [illegible] | [illegible] | [illegible] | [illegible] | [illegible] | [illegible] | [illegible] | [illegible] | [illegible] | [illegible] | [illegible] | [illegible] |
| 1880, | [illegible] | [illegible] | [illegible] | [illegible] | [illegible] | [illegible] | [illegible] | [illegible] | [illegible] | [illegible] | [illegible] | [illegible] | [illegible] |
| 1881, | [illegible] | [illegible] | [illegible] | [illegible] | [illegible] | [illegible] | [illegible] | [illegible] | [illegible] | [illegible] | [illegible] | [illegible] | [illegible] |
| 1882, | [illegible] | [illegible] | [illegible] | [illegible] | [illegible] | [illegible] | [illegible] | [illegible] | [illegible] | [illegible] | [illegible] | [illegible] | [illegible] |
| 1883, | [illegible] | [illegible] | [illegible] | [illegible] | [illegible] | [illegible] | [illegible] | [illegible] | [illegible] | [illegible] | [illegible] | [illegible] | [illegible] |
| 1884, | [illegible] | [illegible] | [illegible] | [illegible] | [illegible] | [illegible] | [illegible] | [illegible] | [illegible] | [illegible] | [illegible] | [illegible] | [illegible] |
| 1885, | [illegible] | [illegible] | [illegible] | [illegible] | [illegible] | [illegible] | [illegible] | [illegible] | [illegible] | [illegible] | [illegible] | [illegible] | [illegible] |
| 1886, | [illegible] | [illegible] | [illegible] | [illegible] | [illegible] | [illegible] | [illegible] | [illegible] | [illegible] | [illegible] | [illegible] | [illegible] | [illegible] |
| 1887, | [illegible] | [illegible] | [illegible] | [illegible] | [illegible] | [illegible] | [illegible] | [illegible] | [illegible] | [illegible] | [illegible] | [illegible] | [illegible] |
| 1888, | [illegible] | [illegible] | [illegible] | [illegible] | [illegible] | [illegible] | [illegible] | [illegible] | [illegible] | [illegible] | [illegible] | [illegible] | [illegible] |
| 1889, | [illegible] | [illegible] | [illegible] | [illegible] | [illegible] | [illegible] | [illegible] | [illegible] | [illegible] | [illegible] | [illegible] | [illegible] | [illegible] |
| 1890, | [illegible] | [illegible] | [illegible] | [illegible] | [illegible] | [illegible] | [illegible] | [illegible] | [illegible] | [illegible] | [illegible] | [illegible] | [illegible] |
| 1891, | [illegible] | [illegible] | [illegible] | [illegible] | [illegible] | [illegible] | [illegible] | [illegible] | [illegible] | [illegible] | [illegible] | [illegible] | [illegible] |
| 1892, | [illegible] | [illegible] | [illegible] | [illegible] | [illegible] | [illegible] | [illegible] | [illegible] | [illegible] | [illegible] | [illegible] | [illegible] | [illegible] |
| 1893, | [illegible] | [illegible] | [illegible] | [illegible] | [illegible] | [illegible] | [illegible] | [illegible] | [illegible] | [illegible] | [illegible] | [illegible] | [illegible] |
| 1894, | [illegible] | [illegible] | [illegible] | [illegible] | [illegible] | [illegible] | [illegible] | [illegible] | [illegible] | [illegible] | [illegible] | [illegible] | [illegible] |
| 1895, | [illegible] | [illegible] | [illegible] | [illegible] | [illegible] | [illegible] | [illegible] | [illegible] | [illegible] | [illegible] | [illegible] | [illegible] | [illegible] |

## HONEY PRODUCED IN 1894.

Honey produced in 1894.

The inquiries made in the preceding nine years relative to the extent to which bee-keeping is followed in Ireland, and the degree of success attained in this special branch of rural economy, were repeated last year with reference to the season of 1894.

According to the Returns received there would appear to have been a decrease of 3·4 per cent. in the quantity of honey produced in 1894, as compared with the preceding year, the returns for which showed an increase of 29·0 per cent. as compared with the quantity in 1892.

The quantity of honey produced, according to the Returns, was 234,838 lbs.; of this, 71,713 lbs. were produced in the province of Leinster; 77,359 lbs. in Munster; 59,743 lbs. in Ulster; and 26,023 lbs. in Connaught. Of the 234,838 lbs., 129,823 lbs. were produced "in Hives having Movable Combs," and 105,015 lbs. "in other Hives." It was stated that 112,331 lbs. was "Run Honey," and 122,507 lbs. "Section Honey."

The number of stocks brought through the Winter of 1894–95 amounted to 17,317; of which 7,810 were in hives having movable combs, and 9,507 in other hives.

According to the returns collected there were 4,949 lbs. of wax manufactured in 1894; of which 1,893 lbs. were from hives having movable combs, and 3,056 lbs. from other hives.

The Returns received in 1894 gave the number of swarms at work during the season of 1893 as 12,390; the quantity of honey as 243,363 lbs.; the number of stocks brought through the winter of 1893–94 as 16,291; and the quantity of wax manufactured in 1893 as 6,159 lbs.

The following Table shows the quantity of Honey returned as produced in Ireland during each of the ten years, 1885–94. It will be observed, that the quantity produced in 1894 was less than that for any of the preceding nine years, except 1892, and very much below the average.

TABLE XV.—Showing for each of the Ten Years 1885–94 the Quantity of HONEY Produced in Ireland, distinguishing the quantity Produced in Hives having Movable Combs from that Produced in other Hives, and RUN HONEY from SECTION HONEY :—

| YEARS. | HONEY PRODUCED, IN LBS. | | | | | | |
|---|---|---|---|---|---|---|---|
| | In Hives having Movable Combs. | | | In other Hives. | | | GENERAL TOTAL. |
| | Run. | Section. | Total. | Run. | Section. | Total. | |
| 1885 | 46,196 | 59,718 | 105,914 | 141,257 | 55,396 | 196,653 | 302,567 |
| 1886 | 57,809 | 74,352 | 132,161 | 148,157 | 56,084 | 204,238 | 331,167 |
| 1887 | 77,798 | 134,457 | 212,254 | 193,021 | 54,151 | 247,172 | 459,426 |
| 1888 | 56,758 | 62,653 | 118,411 | 107,301 | 62,350 | 170,651 | 289,062 |
| 1889 | 71,945 | 143,468 | 215,408 | 152,104 | 53,978 | 206,080 | 421,488 |
| 1890 | 47,932 | 86,128 | 134,060 | 115,599 | 48,479 | 164,078 | 298,138 |
| 1891 | 13,087 | 81,561 | 124,618 | 82,909 | 30,004 | 112,913 | 237,531 |
| 1892 | 44,707 | 60,429 | 104,836 | 55,731 | 31,388 | 89,121 | 193,957 |
| 1893 | 40,900 | 91,413 | 132,313 | 87,065 | 34,365 | 116,030 | 248,343 |
| 1894 | 43,101 | 87,644 | 128,945 | 78,150 | 84,863 | 163,013 | 294,858 |

## AGRICULTURAL MACHINES.

A return of the number of Agricultural Machines in Ireland was taken in connexion with the Agricultural Statistics for 1895. On page 80 will be found a table (10) showing the number of the different kinds of these machines in 1865, 1875, 1881, 1886, 1890, and 1895, respectively. From this table it will be seen that churning machines (3,341) show an increase of 2,593 between 1865 and 1895. Mowing machines and combined mowing and reaping machines numbered 14,704 in 1895, being an increase of 13,619 since 1865, when the number was 1,085. Reaping machines increased by 2,383 between 1865 and 1895, the respective numbers for these years being 413 and 2,795. Threshing machines numbered 9,180, in 1865, 12,410 in 1875, 10,295 in 1881, 7,063 in 1886, 7,694 in 1890, and 6,546 in 1895. Agricultural Machinery.

## SCUTCHING MILLS.

The number of Mills for scutching Flax in Ireland in 1895 was 951, being a decrease of 9 compared with 1894, and a decrease of 109 since the year 1886. Of the 951 Mills, 933 were in Ulster, 6 in Connaught, 7 in Leinster, and 5 in Munster. There were 424 Mills with from 1 to 4 stocks; 289 having 5 or 6; 215 with from 7 to 12; 23 having from 13 to 18, and 1 having above 18 stocks; 781 were worked by water power; 120 by steam; and 50 by water and steam. The total number of Stocks in Ireland in 1895 amounted to 5,623, and of this number 5,495 were in Mills situated in Ulster. Scutching Mills, 1895.

The following is the number of Scutching Mills, in each year, from 1886 to 1895, inclusive, by Provinces :— Scutching Mills, 1886 to 1895.

| Provinces. | 1886. | 1887. | 1888. | 1889. | 1890. | 1891. | 1892. | 1893. | 1894. | 1895. |
|---|---|---|---|---|---|---|---|---|---|---|
| Leinster, . . | 7 | 7 | 6 | 7 | 7 | 7 | 4 | 6 | 6 | 7 |
| Munster, . . | 5 | 5 | 5 | 6 | 6 | 6 | 6 | 4 | 4 | 5 |
| Ulster, . . | 1,053 | 1,063 | 1,058 | 1,048 | 1,048 | 993 | 979 | 954 | 948 | 933 |
| Connaught, . . | 3 | 9 | 9 | 3 | 9 | 2 | 4 | 6 | 6 | 6 |
| IRELAND, . | 1,063 | 1,076 | 1,070 | 1,060 | 1,069 | 1,008 | 993 | 970 | 960 | 951 |

Scutching Mills, 1895.

TABLE XVI.—Number of SCUTCHING MILLS in 1895, by COUNTIES and PROVINCES, classified according to the number of Stocks in each Mill, and the Power used in working them; with the Total Number of Stocks in each County:—

| PROVINCES AND COUNTIES IN WHICH THERE WERE SCUTCHING MILLS. | POWER EMPLOYED. | | | | | Total No. of Mills. | CLASSIFICATION OF MILLS. | | | | | Total No. of Stocks. |
|---|---|---|---|---|---|---|---|---|---|---|---|---|
| | Water. | Steam. | Water and Steam. | Horse. | Wind. | | [illegible] | [illegible] | [illegible] | [illegible] | [illegible] | |
| LEINSTER: | | | | | | | | | | | | |
| Louth & Drogheda, Co. of Town. | 2 | 2 | - | - | - | 4 | - | - | 3 | 1 | - | 40 |
| Meath, . . | 2 | - | - | - | - | 2 | - | 1 | 1 | - | - | 14 |
| Wexford, . . | - | 1 | - | - | - | 1 | - | 1 | - | - | - | 6 |
| Total, . . | 4 | 3 | - | - | - | 7 | - | 2 | 4 | 1 | - | 72 |
| MUNSTER: | | | | | | | | | | | | |
| Cork, . . | 4 | - | - | - | - | 4 | 3 | 1 | - | - | - | 19 |
| Tipperary, . . | - | 1 | - | - | - | 1 | - | 1 | - | - | - | 9 |
| Total, . . | 4 | 1 | - | - | - | 5 | 3 | 2 | - | - | - | 27 |
| ULSTER: | | | | | | | | | | | | |
| Antrim, . . | 118 | 7 | 7 | - | - | 132 | 65 | 44 | 17 | 1 | - | 882 |
| Armagh, . . | 61 | 18 | 4 | - | - | 83 | 15 | 41 | 23 | 3 | 1 | 613 |
| Cavan, . . | 30 | 7 | - | - | - | 37 | 7 | 18 | 11 | 1 | - | 287 |
| Donegal, . . | 126 | 1 | 3 | - | - | 130 | 38 | 80 | 11 | - | - | 844 |
| Down, . . | 70 | 60 | 15 | - | - | 145 | 19 | 64 | 63 | 7 | - | 1,186 |
| Fermanagh, . . | 19 | 5 | 3 | - | - | 27 | 13 | 6 | 6 | 2 | - | 140 |
| Londonderry, . . | 140 | 6 | 5 | - | - | 151 | 83 | 48 | 17 | 3 | - | 773 |
| Monaghan, . . | 46 | 18 | 9 | - | - | 73 | 20 | 30 | 20 | 4 | - | 432 |
| Tyrone, . . | 153 | 23 | 7 | - | - | 183 | 95 | 39 | 32 | 8 | - | 999 |
| Total, . . | 770 | 119 | 60 | - | - | 925 | 418 | 350 | 220 | 30 | 1 | 6,250 |
| CONNAUGHT: | | | | | | | | | | | | |
| Leitrim, . . | 1 | - | - | - | - | 1 | 1 | - | - | - | - | 1 |
| Mayo, . . | - | 1 | - | - | - | 1 | - | - | 1 | - | - | 11 |
| Roscommon, . . | 3 | 3 | - | - | - | 6 | 3 | - | 1 | 1 | - | 25 |
| Total, . . | 5 | 4 | - | - | - | 8 | 4 | - | 2 | 1 | - | 45 |
| TOTAL OF IRELAND, | 782 | 129 | 60 | - | - | 951 | 424 | 350 | 226 | 33 | 1 | 6,435 |

## CORN MILLS.

Corn Mills.

As in 1891, 1892, 1893, and 1894, returns were obtained showing the number of Corn Mills in Ireland, with details as to the power used, the kind of corn chiefly ground, and the average quantity ground per week when the mills are at work. The results are given, by provinces and counties, in the following table, from which it appears that the total number of mills returned in 1,804 (an increase of 25 as compared with the number for 1894) of which

1,237 were worked by water, 56 by steam, 16 by wind, and 75 by water and steam; and that wheat was the chief kind of corn ground in 217 mills, oats in 1,030, and Indian corn in 201. In 199 of the 1,504 mills the average quantity ground per week, when the mills are at work, exceeds 500 cwts.

TABLE XVII.—Number of CORN MILLS in 1855, by COUNTIES and PROVINCES, classified according to the Power used, the kind of Corn chiefly ground, and the average Quantity (in cwts.) ground per week when the Mills are at work.

| Counties and Provinces. | Total No. of Mills. | Description of Power used. | | | | Kind of Corn chiefly ground. | | | | Average Quantity ground per week when at work. | | | | | |
|---|---|---|---|---|---|---|---|---|---|---|---|---|---|---|---|
| | | Water. | Steam. | Wind. | Water and Steam. | Wheat. | Oats. | Indian Corn. | All others. | Under 50 cwts. | 50 and under 100 cwts. | 100 and under 200 cwts. | 200 and under 300 cwts. | 300 and under 500 cwts. | 500 and upwards. |
| | | Number of Mills. | | | | Number of Mills. | | | | Number of Mills. | | | | | |
| **LEINSTER:** | | | | | | | | | | | | | | | |
| Carlow, | [illegible] | [illegible] | [illegible] | [illegible] | [illegible] | [illegible] | [illegible] | [illegible] | [illegible] | [illegible] | [illegible] | [illegible] | [illegible] | [illegible] | [illegible] |
| Dublin, | [illegible] | [illegible] | [illegible] | [illegible] | [illegible] | [illegible] | [illegible] | [illegible] | [illegible] | [illegible] | [illegible] | [illegible] | [illegible] | [illegible] | [illegible] |
| Kildare, | [illegible] | [illegible] | [illegible] | [illegible] | [illegible] | [illegible] | [illegible] | [illegible] | [illegible] | [illegible] | [illegible] | [illegible] | [illegible] | [illegible] | [illegible] |
| Kilkenny, | [illegible] | [illegible] | [illegible] | [illegible] | [illegible] | [illegible] | [illegible] | [illegible] | [illegible] | [illegible] | [illegible] | [illegible] | [illegible] | [illegible] | [illegible] |
| King's, | [illegible] | [illegible] | [illegible] | [illegible] | [illegible] | [illegible] | [illegible] | [illegible] | [illegible] | [illegible] | [illegible] | [illegible] | [illegible] | [illegible] | [illegible] |
| Longford, | [illegible] | [illegible] | [illegible] | [illegible] | [illegible] | [illegible] | [illegible] | [illegible] | [illegible] | [illegible] | [illegible] | [illegible] | [illegible] | [illegible] | [illegible] |
| Louth and Drogheda, County of Town, | [illegible] | [illegible] | [illegible] | [illegible] | [illegible] | [illegible] | [illegible] | [illegible] | [illegible] | [illegible] | [illegible] | [illegible] | [illegible] | [illegible] | [illegible] |
| Meath, | [illegible] | [illegible] | [illegible] | [illegible] | [illegible] | [illegible] | [illegible] | [illegible] | [illegible] | [illegible] | [illegible] | [illegible] | [illegible] | [illegible] | [illegible] |
| Queen's, | [illegible] | [illegible] | [illegible] | [illegible] | [illegible] | [illegible] | [illegible] | [illegible] | [illegible] | [illegible] | [illegible] | [illegible] | [illegible] | [illegible] | [illegible] |
| Westmeath, | [illegible] | [illegible] | [illegible] | [illegible] | [illegible] | [illegible] | [illegible] | [illegible] | [illegible] | [illegible] | [illegible] | [illegible] | [illegible] | [illegible] | [illegible] |
| Wexford, | [illegible] | [illegible] | [illegible] | [illegible] | [illegible] | [illegible] | [illegible] | [illegible] | [illegible] | [illegible] | [illegible] | [illegible] | [illegible] | [illegible] | [illegible] |
| Wicklow, | [illegible] | [illegible] | [illegible] | [illegible] | [illegible] | [illegible] | [illegible] | [illegible] | [illegible] | [illegible] | [illegible] | [illegible] | [illegible] | [illegible] | [illegible] |
| Total, | [illegible] | [illegible] | [illegible] | [illegible] | [illegible] | [illegible] | [illegible] | [illegible] | [illegible] | [illegible] | [illegible] | [illegible] | [illegible] | [illegible] | [illegible] |
| **MUNSTER:** | | | | | | | | | | | | | | | |
| Clare, | [illegible] | [illegible] | [illegible] | [illegible] | [illegible] | [illegible] | [illegible] | [illegible] | [illegible] | [illegible] | [illegible] | [illegible] | [illegible] | [illegible] | [illegible] |
| Cork, | [illegible] | [illegible] | [illegible] | [illegible] | [illegible] | [illegible] | [illegible] | [illegible] | [illegible] | [illegible] | [illegible] | [illegible] | [illegible] | [illegible] | [illegible] |
| Kerry, | [illegible] | [illegible] | [illegible] | [illegible] | [illegible] | [illegible] | [illegible] | [illegible] | [illegible] | [illegible] | [illegible] | [illegible] | [illegible] | [illegible] | [illegible] |
| Limerick, | [illegible] | [illegible] | [illegible] | [illegible] | [illegible] | [illegible] | [illegible] | [illegible] | [illegible] | [illegible] | [illegible] | [illegible] | [illegible] | [illegible] | [illegible] |
| Tipperary, | [illegible] | [illegible] | [illegible] | [illegible] | [illegible] | [illegible] | [illegible] | [illegible] | [illegible] | [illegible] | [illegible] | [illegible] | [illegible] | [illegible] | [illegible] |
| Waterford, | [illegible] | [illegible] | [illegible] | [illegible] | [illegible] | [illegible] | [illegible] | [illegible] | [illegible] | [illegible] | [illegible] | [illegible] | [illegible] | [illegible] | [illegible] |
| Total, | [illegible] | [illegible] | [illegible] | [illegible] | [illegible] | [illegible] | [illegible] | [illegible] | [illegible] | [illegible] | [illegible] | [illegible] | [illegible] | [illegible] | [illegible] |
| **ULSTER:** | | | | | | | | | | | | | | | |
| Antrim, | [illegible] | [illegible] | [illegible] | [illegible] | [illegible] | [illegible] | [illegible] | [illegible] | [illegible] | [illegible] | [illegible] | [illegible] | [illegible] | [illegible] | [illegible] |
| Armagh, | [illegible] | [illegible] | [illegible] | [illegible] | [illegible] | [illegible] | [illegible] | [illegible] | [illegible] | [illegible] | [illegible] | [illegible] | [illegible] | [illegible] | [illegible] |
| Cavan, | [illegible] | [illegible] | [illegible] | [illegible] | [illegible] | [illegible] | [illegible] | [illegible] | [illegible] | [illegible] | [illegible] | [illegible] | [illegible] | [illegible] | [illegible] |
| Donegal, | [illegible] | [illegible] | [illegible] | [illegible] | [illegible] | [illegible] | [illegible] | [illegible] | [illegible] | [illegible] | [illegible] | [illegible] | [illegible] | [illegible] | [illegible] |
| Down, | [illegible] | [illegible] | [illegible] | [illegible] | [illegible] | [illegible] | [illegible] | [illegible] | [illegible] | [illegible] | [illegible] | [illegible] | [illegible] | [illegible] | [illegible] |
| Fermanagh, | [illegible] | [illegible] | [illegible] | [illegible] | [illegible] | [illegible] | [illegible] | [illegible] | [illegible] | [illegible] | [illegible] | [illegible] | [illegible] | [illegible] | [illegible] |
| Londonderry, | [illegible] | [illegible] | [illegible] | [illegible] | [illegible] | [illegible] | [illegible] | [illegible] | [illegible] | [illegible] | [illegible] | [illegible] | [illegible] | [illegible] | [illegible] |
| Monaghan, | [illegible] | [illegible] | [illegible] | [illegible] | [illegible] | [illegible] | [illegible] | [illegible] | [illegible] | [illegible] | [illegible] | [illegible] | [illegible] | [illegible] | [illegible] |
| Tyrone, | [illegible] | [illegible] | [illegible] | [illegible] | [illegible] | [illegible] | [illegible] | [illegible] | [illegible] | [illegible] | [illegible] | [illegible] | [illegible] | [illegible] | [illegible] |
| Total, | [illegible] | [illegible] | [illegible] | [illegible] | [illegible] | [illegible] | [illegible] | [illegible] | [illegible] | [illegible] | [illegible] | [illegible] | [illegible] | [illegible] | [illegible] |
| **CONNAUGHT:** | | | | | | | | | | | | | | | |
| Galway, | [illegible] | [illegible] | [illegible] | [illegible] | [illegible] | [illegible] | [illegible] | [illegible] | [illegible] | [illegible] | [illegible] | [illegible] | [illegible] | [illegible] | [illegible] |
| Leitrim, | [illegible] | [illegible] | [illegible] | [illegible] | [illegible] | [illegible] | [illegible] | [illegible] | [illegible] | [illegible] | [illegible] | [illegible] | [illegible] | [illegible] | [illegible] |
| Mayo, | [illegible] | [illegible] | [illegible] | [illegible] | [illegible] | [illegible] | [illegible] | [illegible] | [illegible] | [illegible] | [illegible] | [illegible] | [illegible] | [illegible] | [illegible] |
| Roscommon, | [illegible] | [illegible] | [illegible] | [illegible] | [illegible] | [illegible] | [illegible] | [illegible] | [illegible] | [illegible] | [illegible] | [illegible] | [illegible] | [illegible] | [illegible] |
| Sligo, | [illegible] | [illegible] | [illegible] | [illegible] | [illegible] | [illegible] | [illegible] | [illegible] | [illegible] | [illegible] | [illegible] | [illegible] | [illegible] | [illegible] | [illegible] |
| Total, | [illegible] | [illegible] | [illegible] | [illegible] | [illegible] | [illegible] | [illegible] | [illegible] | [illegible] | [illegible] | [illegible] | [illegible] | [illegible] | [illegible] | [illegible] |
| TOTAL OF IRELAND, | [illegible] | [illegible] | [illegible] | [illegible] | [illegible] | [illegible] | [illegible] | [illegible] | [illegible] | [illegible] | [illegible] | [illegible] | [illegible] | [illegible] | [illegible] |

* One—Water and Wind. † Two—Wind and Steam. ‡ One—Wind and Steam.

## SILOS AND ENSILAGE.

Silos and Ensilage.

Following the course adopted in the eight previous years relative to Ensilage, I communicated with those Landed Proprietors and Landholders, throughout the country, reported to me as having Silos or otherwise making Ensilage, requesting them to favour me with certain details regarding the methods followed and the results obtained in the year 1895. I received replies to 192 out of 219 circulars issued by me, and I beg to express my obligations to my correspondents for the valuable and interesting information afforded. It will be found set forth in the Appendix, pp. 94 to 117. Many of the replies stated that no ensilage was made during the season of 1895, owing to the weather being so favourable for the saving of hay.

The following Table (XVIII.) shows, by Counties and Provinces, for the years 1894 and 1895, the number of Silos or Stacks mentioned in the communications received from the persons who forwarded replies to the circular above referred to:—

| Counties. | Number in 1894. | Number in 1895. | Counties. | Number in 1894. | Number in 1895. |
|---|---|---|---|---|---|
| Antrim, | 11 | 16 | Mayo, | 10 | 8 |
| Armagh, | — | — | Meath, | 25 | 26 |
| Carlow, | 5 | 1 | Monaghan, | 2 | 3 |
| Cavan, | 1 | 3 | Queen's, | 4 | 3 |
| Clare, | 6 | 6 | Roscommon, | 11 | 7 |
| Cork, | 4 | 6 | Sligo, | 5 | 3 |
| Donegal, | 4 | 4 | Tipperary, | 14 | 15 |
| Down, | 5 | 8 | Tyrone, | 5 | 7 |
| Dublin, | 6 | 9 | Waterford, | 1 | 8 |
| Fermanagh, | 7 | 6 | Westmeath, | 13 | 15 |
| Galway, | 15 | 7 | Wexford, | 3 | 3 |
| Kerry, | 5 | 2 | Wicklow, | 9 | 10 |
| Kildare, | 1 | 3 | | | |
| Kilkenny, | 7 | 6 | PROVINCES. | | |
| King's, | 12 | 12 | Leinster, | 98 | 87 |
| Leitrim, | 6 | 5 | Munster, | 33 | 40 |
| Limerick, | 8 | 11 | Ulster, | 45 | 52 |
| Londonderry, | 12 | 11 | Connaught, | 43 | 35 |
| Longford, | 5 | 4 | | | |
| Louth, | 1 | 3 | TOTAL OF IRELAND, | 220 | [illegible] |

## FORESTRY OPERATIONS.

Forestry Operations.

The inquiries into Forestry Operations instituted in 1890, and continued in 1891, 1892, 1893, and 1894, were repeated in 1895. The details are set forth in the GENERAL ABSTRACT of FORESTRY OPERATIONS in IRELAND during the year ended 30th June, 1895. The subjects dealt with in the Abstract are—I. Planting—The area planted during the year ended 30th June, 1895, the total number of trees planted in that period, and the number of each description; II. Felling—The area cleared and the number of trees of each description felled; III. Ages of trees felled; IV. Disposal of timber. The inquiry did not extend to the planting or felling of isolated trees.

It appears that during the period 1851–95 there were some slight fluctuations in the acreage, and that comparing 1895 with 1851 there has been an increase of about 1·3 per cent., the extent under woods and plantations in 1851 being 304,906 statute acres, and in last year 308,928 acres.

During the year ended 30th June, 1895, 1,343 acres were planted with trees, against 1,491 acres in the preceding year. Larch trees constituted 53·6 per cent., fir trees 25·6 per cent., pine 8·3 per cent., and spruce trees 6·3 per cent., of the total number planted.

In connection with this subject it may be here mentioned that from the passing of the Act 39 and 40 Vic., cap. 40, to the 31st March, 1895, 125 loans for £23,050 have been sanctioned for planting for shelter, and of this number three, amounting to £765, were sanctioned in the last year of the period.

The number of trees felled both for clearance and for thinning plantations amounted to 537,101. The area returned as cleared is 809 acres.

Of the 537,101 trees felled, 149,585 were used for "propping," which appears to have been the chief purpose to which the timber of almost all descriptions was applied. The numbers applied to the principal specified uses comprise also:—57,553 trees for sleepers, 46,411 for paling, 5,430 for spools, &c., 15,796 for fuel, 35,930 for furniture and building purposes, 9,870 for carts, wagons, &c., 1,615 for clog soles, and 1,897 for ship-building.

# WAGES OF AGRICULTURAL LABOURERS IN 1893.

Enquiries were made as to the Wages paid per day to Agricultural Labourers in 1893, and the information received from the District Inspectors of the Royal Irish Constabulary with reference to their respective districts is shown in the following Table (XIX.) and notes appended thereto.

## I.—PROVINCE OF LEINSTER.

| Counties and Constabulary Districts. | Summer. | | | | | | | | Winter. | | | | | | | |
|---|---|---|---|---|---|---|---|---|---|---|---|---|---|---|---|---|
| | Men. | | Boys. | | Women. | | Girls. | | Men. | | Boys. | | Women. | | Girls. | |
| | From | To | From | To | From | To | From | To | From | To | From | To | From | To | From | To |
| | s. d. | s. d. | s. d. | s. d. | s. d. | s. d. | s. d. | s. d. | s. d. | s. d. | s. d. | s. d. | s. d. | s. d. | s. d. | s. d. |
| CARLOW COUNTY. | | | | | | | | | | | | | | | | |
| [illegible] | [illegible] | [illegible] | [illegible] | [illegible] | [illegible] | [illegible] | [illegible] | [illegible] | [illegible] | [illegible] | [illegible] | [illegible] | [illegible] | [illegible] | [illegible] | [illegible] |
| [illegible] | [illegible] | [illegible] | [illegible] | [illegible] | [illegible] | [illegible] | [illegible] | [illegible] | [illegible] | [illegible] | [illegible] | [illegible] | [illegible] | [illegible] | [illegible] | [illegible] |
| [illegible] COUNTY. | | | | | | | | | | | | | | | | |
| [illegible] | [illegible] | [illegible] | [illegible] | [illegible] | [illegible] | [illegible] | [illegible] | [illegible] | [illegible] | [illegible] | [illegible] | [illegible] | [illegible] | [illegible] | [illegible] | [illegible] |
| [illegible] | [illegible] | [illegible] | [illegible] | [illegible] | [illegible] | [illegible] | [illegible] | [illegible] | [illegible] | [illegible] | [illegible] | [illegible] | [illegible] | [illegible] | [illegible] | [illegible] |
| [illegible] | [illegible] | [illegible] | [illegible] | [illegible] | [illegible] | [illegible] | [illegible] | [illegible] | [illegible] | [illegible] | [illegible] | [illegible] | [illegible] | [illegible] | [illegible] | [illegible] |
| [illegible] | [illegible] | [illegible] | [illegible] | [illegible] | [illegible] | [illegible] | [illegible] | [illegible] | [illegible] | [illegible] | [illegible] | [illegible] | [illegible] | [illegible] | [illegible] | [illegible] |
| [illegible] COUNTY. | | | | | | | | | | | | | | | | |
| [illegible] | [illegible] | [illegible] | [illegible] | [illegible] | [illegible] | [illegible] | [illegible] | [illegible] | [illegible] | [illegible] | [illegible] | [illegible] | [illegible] | [illegible] | [illegible] | [illegible] |
| [illegible] | [illegible] | [illegible] | [illegible] | [illegible] | [illegible] | [illegible] | [illegible] | [illegible] | [illegible] | [illegible] | [illegible] | [illegible] | [illegible] | [illegible] | [illegible] | [illegible] |
| [illegible] | [illegible] | [illegible] | [illegible] | [illegible] | [illegible] | [illegible] | [illegible] | [illegible] | [illegible] | [illegible] | [illegible] | [illegible] | [illegible] | [illegible] | [illegible] | [illegible] |
| [illegible] | [illegible] | [illegible] | [illegible] | [illegible] | [illegible] | [illegible] | [illegible] | [illegible] | [illegible] | [illegible] | [illegible] | [illegible] | [illegible] | [illegible] | [illegible] | [illegible] |
| [illegible] COUNTY. | | | | | | | | | | | | | | | | |
| [illegible] | [illegible] | [illegible] | [illegible] | [illegible] | [illegible] | [illegible] | [illegible] | [illegible] | [illegible] | [illegible] | [illegible] | [illegible] | [illegible] | [illegible] | [illegible] | [illegible] |
| [illegible] | [illegible] | [illegible] | [illegible] | [illegible] | [illegible] | [illegible] | [illegible] | [illegible] | [illegible] | [illegible] | [illegible] | [illegible] | [illegible] | [illegible] | [illegible] | [illegible] |
| [illegible] | [illegible] | [illegible] | [illegible] | [illegible] | [illegible] | [illegible] | [illegible] | [illegible] | [illegible] | [illegible] | [illegible] | [illegible] | [illegible] | [illegible] | [illegible] | [illegible] |
| [illegible] | [illegible] | [illegible] | [illegible] | [illegible] | [illegible] | [illegible] | [illegible] | [illegible] | [illegible] | [illegible] | [illegible] | [illegible] | [illegible] | [illegible] | [illegible] | [illegible] |
| [illegible] | [illegible] | [illegible] | [illegible] | [illegible] | [illegible] | [illegible] | [illegible] | [illegible] | [illegible] | [illegible] | [illegible] | [illegible] | [illegible] | [illegible] | [illegible] | [illegible] |
| [illegible] | [illegible] | [illegible] | [illegible] | [illegible] | [illegible] | [illegible] | [illegible] | [illegible] | [illegible] | [illegible] | [illegible] | [illegible] | [illegible] | [illegible] | [illegible] | [illegible] |
| KING'S COUNTY. | | | | | | | | | | | | | | | | |
| [illegible] | [illegible] | [illegible] | [illegible] | [illegible] | [illegible] | [illegible] | [illegible] | [illegible] | [illegible] | [illegible] | [illegible] | [illegible] | [illegible] | [illegible] | [illegible] | [illegible] |
| [illegible] | [illegible] | [illegible] | [illegible] | [illegible] | [illegible] | [illegible] | [illegible] | [illegible] | [illegible] | [illegible] | [illegible] | [illegible] | [illegible] | [illegible] | [illegible] | [illegible] |
| [illegible] | [illegible] | [illegible] | [illegible] | [illegible] | [illegible] | [illegible] | [illegible] | [illegible] | [illegible] | [illegible] | [illegible] | [illegible] | [illegible] | [illegible] | [illegible] | [illegible] |
| [illegible] | [illegible] | [illegible] | [illegible] | [illegible] | [illegible] | [illegible] | [illegible] | [illegible] | [illegible] | [illegible] | [illegible] | [illegible] | [illegible] | [illegible] | [illegible] | [illegible] |
| [illegible] | [illegible] | [illegible] | [illegible] | [illegible] | [illegible] | [illegible] | [illegible] | [illegible] | [illegible] | [illegible] | [illegible] | [illegible] | [illegible] | [illegible] | [illegible] | [illegible] |
| LONGFORD COUNTY. | | | | | | | | | | | | | | | | |
| [illegible] | [illegible] | [illegible] | [illegible] | [illegible] | [illegible] | [illegible] | [illegible] | [illegible] | [illegible] | [illegible] | [illegible] | [illegible] | [illegible] | [illegible] | [illegible] | [illegible] |
| [illegible] | [illegible] | [illegible] | [illegible] | [illegible] | [illegible] | [illegible] | [illegible] | [illegible] | [illegible] | [illegible] | [illegible] | [illegible] | [illegible] | [illegible] | [illegible] | [illegible] |
| [illegible] | [illegible] | [illegible] | [illegible] | [illegible] | [illegible] | [illegible] | [illegible] | - | - | [illegible] | [illegible] | - | - | [illegible] | [illegible] | - | - |
| LOUTH COUNTY. | | | | | | | | | | | | | | | | |
| [illegible] | [illegible] | [illegible] | [illegible] | [illegible] | [illegible] | [illegible] | [illegible] | [illegible] | [illegible] | [illegible] | [illegible] | [illegible] | [illegible] | [illegible] | [illegible] | [illegible] |
| [illegible] | [illegible] | [illegible] | [illegible] | [illegible] | [illegible] | [illegible] | [illegible] | [illegible] | [illegible] | [illegible] | [illegible] | [illegible] | [illegible] | [illegible] | [illegible] | [illegible] |
| [illegible] | [illegible] | [illegible] | [illegible] | [illegible] | [illegible] | [illegible] | [illegible] | [illegible] | [illegible] | [illegible] | [illegible] | [illegible] | [illegible] | [illegible] | [illegible] | [illegible] |
| [illegible] | [illegible] | [illegible] | [illegible] | [illegible] | [illegible] | [illegible] | [illegible] | [illegible] | [illegible] | [illegible] | [illegible] | [illegible] | [illegible] | [illegible] | [illegible] | [illegible] |

[illegible]

## I.—PROVINCE OF LEINSTER—continued.

| Counties and Constabulary Districts | Summer: Men, From | Summer: Men, To | Summer: Boys, From | Summer: Boys, To | Summer: Women, From | Summer: Women, To | Summer: Girls, From | Summer: Girls, To | Winter: Men, From | Winter: Men, To | Winter: Boys, From | Winter: Boys, To | Winter: Women, From | Winter: Women, To | Winter: Girls, From | Winter: Girls, To |
|---|---|---|---|---|---|---|---|---|---|---|---|---|---|---|---|---|
| [illegible] County. | s. d. | s. d. | s. d. | s. d. | s. d. | s. d. | s. d. | s. d. | s. d. | s. d. | s. d. | s. d. | s. d. | s. d. | s. d. | s. d. |
| [illegible] | [illegible] | [illegible] | [illegible] | [illegible] | [illegible] | [illegible] | [illegible] | [illegible] | [illegible] | [illegible] | [illegible] | [illegible] | - | - | . | . |
| [illegible] | [illegible] | [illegible] | [illegible] | [illegible] | [illegible] | [illegible] | [illegible] | [illegible] | [illegible] | [illegible] | [illegible] | [illegible] | [illegible] | [illegible] | [illegible] | [illegible] |
| [illegible] | [illegible] | [illegible] | [illegible] | [illegible] | [illegible] | [illegible] | [illegible] | [illegible] | [illegible] | [illegible] | [illegible] | [illegible] | [illegible] | [illegible] | [illegible] | [illegible] |
| [illegible] | [illegible] | [illegible] | [illegible] | [illegible] | [illegible] | [illegible] | [illegible] | [illegible] | [illegible] | [illegible] | [illegible] | [illegible] | [illegible] | [illegible] | [illegible] | [illegible] |
| [illegible] | [illegible] | [illegible] | [illegible] | [illegible] | [illegible] | [illegible] | [illegible] | [illegible] | [illegible] | [illegible] | [illegible] | [illegible] | [illegible] | [illegible] | [illegible] | [illegible] |
| [illegible] | [illegible] | [illegible] | [illegible] | [illegible] | [illegible] | [illegible] | [illegible] | [illegible] | [illegible] | [illegible] | [illegible] | [illegible] | [illegible] | [illegible] | [illegible] | [illegible] |
| [illegible] County. | | | | | | | | | | | | | | | | |
| [illegible] | [illegible] | [illegible] | [illegible] | [illegible] | [illegible] | [illegible] | [illegible] | [illegible] | [illegible] | [illegible] | [illegible] | [illegible] | [illegible] | [illegible] | [illegible] | [illegible] |
| [illegible] | [illegible] | [illegible] | [illegible] | [illegible] | [illegible] | [illegible] | [illegible] | [illegible] | [illegible] | [illegible] | [illegible] | [illegible] | [illegible] | [illegible] | [illegible] | [illegible] |
| [illegible] | [illegible] | [illegible] | [illegible] | [illegible] | [illegible] | [illegible] | [illegible] | [illegible] | [illegible] | [illegible] | [illegible] | [illegible] | [illegible] | [illegible] | [illegible] | [illegible] |
| [illegible] | [illegible] | [illegible] | [illegible] | [illegible] | [illegible] | [illegible] | [illegible] | [illegible] | [illegible] | [illegible] | [illegible] | [illegible] | [illegible] | [illegible] | [illegible] | [illegible] |
| [illegible] County. | | | | | | | | | | | | | | | | |
| [illegible] | [illegible] | [illegible] | [illegible] | [illegible] | [illegible] | [illegible] | [illegible] | [illegible] | [illegible] | [illegible] | [illegible] | [illegible] | [illegible] | [illegible] | [illegible] | [illegible] |
| [illegible] | [illegible] | [illegible] | [illegible] | [illegible] | [illegible] | [illegible] | [illegible] | [illegible] | [illegible] | [illegible] | [illegible] | [illegible] | [illegible] | [illegible] | [illegible] | [illegible] |
| [illegible] | [illegible] | [illegible] | [illegible] | [illegible] | [illegible] | [illegible] | [illegible] | [illegible] | [illegible] | [illegible] | [illegible] | [illegible] | [illegible] | [illegible] | [illegible] | [illegible] |
| [illegible] | [illegible] | [illegible] | [illegible] | [illegible] | [illegible] | [illegible] | [illegible] | [illegible] | [illegible] | [illegible] | [illegible] | [illegible] | [illegible] | [illegible] | [illegible] | [illegible] |
| [illegible] | [illegible] | [illegible] | [illegible] | [illegible] | [illegible] | [illegible] | [illegible] | [illegible] | [illegible] | [illegible] | [illegible] | [illegible] | [illegible] | [illegible] | [illegible] | [illegible] |
| [illegible] | [illegible] | [illegible] | [illegible] | [illegible] | [illegible] | [illegible] | [illegible] | [illegible] | [illegible] | [illegible] | [illegible] | [illegible] | [illegible] | [illegible] | [illegible] | [illegible] |
| [illegible] County. | | | | | | | | | | | | | | | | |
| [illegible] | [illegible] | [illegible] | [illegible] | [illegible] | [illegible] | [illegible] | [illegible] | [illegible] | [illegible] | [illegible] | [illegible] | [illegible] | [illegible] | [illegible] | [illegible] | [illegible] |
| [illegible] | [illegible] | [illegible] | [illegible] | [illegible] | [illegible] | [illegible] | [illegible] | [illegible] | [illegible] | [illegible] | [illegible] | [illegible] | [illegible] | [illegible] | [illegible] | [illegible] |
| [illegible] | [illegible] | [illegible] | [illegible] | [illegible] | [illegible] | [illegible] | [illegible] | [illegible] | [illegible] | [illegible] | [illegible] | [illegible] | [illegible] | [illegible] | [illegible] | [illegible] |
| [illegible] | [illegible] | [illegible] | [illegible] | [illegible] | [illegible] | [illegible] | [illegible] | [illegible] | [illegible] | [illegible] | [illegible] | [illegible] | [illegible] | [illegible] | [illegible] | [illegible] |
| [illegible] | [illegible] | [illegible] | [illegible] | [illegible] | [illegible] | [illegible] | [illegible] | [illegible] | [illegible] | [illegible] | [illegible] | [illegible] | [illegible] | [illegible] | [illegible] | [illegible] |
| [illegible] County. | | | | | | | | | | | | | | | | |
| [illegible] | [illegible] | [illegible] | [illegible] | [illegible] | [illegible] | [illegible] | [illegible] | [illegible] | [illegible] | [illegible] | [illegible] | [illegible] | [illegible] | [illegible] | [illegible] | [illegible] |
| [illegible] | [illegible] | [illegible] | [illegible] | [illegible] | [illegible] | [illegible] | [illegible] | [illegible] | [illegible] | [illegible] | [illegible] | [illegible] | [illegible] | [illegible] | [illegible] | [illegible] |
| [illegible] | [illegible] | [illegible] | [illegible] | [illegible] | [illegible] | [illegible] | [illegible] | [illegible] | [illegible] | [illegible] | [illegible] | [illegible] | [illegible] | [illegible] | [illegible] | [illegible] |
| [illegible] | [illegible] | [illegible] | [illegible] | [illegible] | [illegible] | [illegible] | [illegible] | [illegible] | [illegible] | [illegible] | [illegible] | [illegible] | [illegible] | [illegible] | [illegible] | [illegible] |

## II.—PROVINCE OF MUNSTER.

| Counties and Constabulary Districts | Summer: Men, From | Summer: Men, To | Summer: Boys, From | Summer: Boys, To | Summer: Women, From | Summer: Women, To | Summer: Girls, From | Summer: Girls, To | Winter: Men, From | Winter: Men, To | Winter: Boys, From | Winter: Boys, To | Winter: Women, From | Winter: Women, To | Winter: Girls, From | Winter: Girls, To |
|---|---|---|---|---|---|---|---|---|---|---|---|---|---|---|---|---|
| Clare County. | | | | | | | | | | | | | | | | |
| [illegible] | [illegible] | [illegible] | [illegible] | [illegible] | [illegible] | [illegible] | [illegible] | [illegible] | [illegible] | [illegible] | [illegible] | [illegible] | [illegible] | [illegible] | [illegible] | [illegible] |
| [illegible] | [illegible] | [illegible] | [illegible] | [illegible] | [illegible] | [illegible] | [illegible] | [illegible] | [illegible] | [illegible] | [illegible] | [illegible] | [illegible] | [illegible] | [illegible] | [illegible] |
| [illegible] | [illegible] | [illegible] | [illegible] | [illegible] | [illegible] | [illegible] | [illegible] | [illegible] | [illegible] | [illegible] | [illegible] | [illegible] | [illegible] | [illegible] | [illegible] | [illegible] |
| [illegible] | [illegible] | [illegible] | [illegible] | [illegible] | [illegible] | [illegible] | [illegible] | [illegible] | [illegible] | [illegible] | [illegible] | [illegible] | [illegible] | [illegible] | [illegible] | [illegible] |
| [illegible] | [illegible] | [illegible] | [illegible] | [illegible] | [illegible] | [illegible] | [illegible] | [illegible] | [illegible] | [illegible] | [illegible] | [illegible] | [illegible] | [illegible] | [illegible] | [illegible] |
| [illegible] | [illegible] | [illegible] | [illegible] | [illegible] | [illegible] | [illegible] | [illegible] | [illegible] | [illegible] | [illegible] | [illegible] | [illegible] | [illegible] | [illegible] | [illegible] | [illegible] |
| [illegible] | [illegible] | [illegible] | [illegible] | [illegible] | [illegible] | [illegible] | [illegible] | [illegible] | [illegible] | [illegible] | [illegible] | [illegible] | [illegible] | [illegible] | [illegible] | [illegible] |
| [illegible] | [illegible] | [illegible] | [illegible] | [illegible] | [illegible] | [illegible] | [illegible] | [illegible] | [illegible] | [illegible] | [illegible] | [illegible] | [illegible] | [illegible] | [illegible] | [illegible] |
| [illegible] | [illegible] | [illegible] | [illegible] | [illegible] | [illegible] | [illegible] | [illegible] | [illegible] | [illegible] | [illegible] | [illegible] | [illegible] | [illegible] | [illegible] | [illegible] | [illegible] |

[illegible]

II.—PROVINCE OF MUNSTER—continued.

| Counties and Constabulary Districts. | Summer. | | | | | | | | Winter. | | | | | | | |
|---|---|---|---|---|---|---|---|---|---|---|---|---|---|---|---|---|
| | Men. | | Boys. | | Women. | | Girls. | | Men. | | Boys. | | Women. | | Girls. | |
| | From | To | From | To | From | To | From | To | From | To | From | To | From | To | From | To |
| | s. d. | s. d. | s. d. | s. d. | s. d. | s. d. | s. d. | s. d. | s. d. | s. d. | s. d. | s. d. | s. d. | s. d. | s. d. | s. d. |
| Cork County (E.R.) | | | | | | | | | | | | | | | | |
| [illegible] | [illegible] | [illegible] | [illegible] | [illegible] | [illegible] | [illegible] | [illegible] | [illegible] | [illegible] | [illegible] | [illegible] | [illegible] | [illegible] | [illegible] | [illegible] | [illegible] |
| [illegible] | [illegible] | [illegible] | [illegible] | [illegible] | [illegible] | [illegible] | [illegible] | [illegible] | [illegible] | [illegible] | [illegible] | [illegible] | [illegible] | [illegible] | [illegible] | [illegible] |
| [illegible] | [illegible] | [illegible] | [illegible] | [illegible] | [illegible] | [illegible] | [illegible] | [illegible] | [illegible] | [illegible] | [illegible] | [illegible] | [illegible] | [illegible] | [illegible] | [illegible] |
| [illegible] | [illegible] | [illegible] | [illegible] | [illegible] | [illegible] | [illegible] | [illegible] | [illegible] | [illegible] | [illegible] | [illegible] | [illegible] | [illegible] | [illegible] | [illegible] | [illegible] |
| [illegible] | [illegible] | [illegible] | [illegible] | [illegible] | [illegible] | [illegible] | [illegible] | [illegible] | [illegible] | [illegible] | [illegible] | [illegible] | [illegible] | [illegible] | [illegible] | [illegible] |
| [illegible] | [illegible] | [illegible] | [illegible] | [illegible] | [illegible] | [illegible] | [illegible] | [illegible] | [illegible] | [illegible] | [illegible] | [illegible] | [illegible] | [illegible] | [illegible] | [illegible] |
| [illegible] | [illegible] | [illegible] | [illegible] | [illegible] | [illegible] | [illegible] | [illegible] | [illegible] | [illegible] | [illegible] | [illegible] | [illegible] | [illegible] | [illegible] | [illegible] | [illegible] |
| [illegible] | [illegible] | [illegible] | [illegible] | [illegible] | [illegible] | [illegible] | [illegible] | [illegible] | [illegible] | [illegible] | [illegible] | [illegible] | [illegible] | [illegible] | [illegible] | [illegible] |
| [illegible] | [illegible] | [illegible] | [illegible] | [illegible] | [illegible] | [illegible] | [illegible] | [illegible] | [illegible] | [illegible] | [illegible] | [illegible] | [illegible] | [illegible] | [illegible] | [illegible] |
| [illegible] | [illegible] | [illegible] | [illegible] | [illegible] | [illegible] | [illegible] | [illegible] | [illegible] | [illegible] | [illegible] | [illegible] | [illegible] | [illegible] | [illegible] | [illegible] | [illegible] |
| [illegible] | [illegible] | [illegible] | [illegible] | [illegible] | [illegible] | [illegible] | [illegible] | [illegible] | [illegible] | [illegible] | [illegible] | [illegible] | [illegible] | [illegible] | [illegible] | [illegible] |
| [illegible] | [illegible] | [illegible] | [illegible] | [illegible] | [illegible] | [illegible] | [illegible] | [illegible] | [illegible] | [illegible] | [illegible] | [illegible] | [illegible] | [illegible] | [illegible] | [illegible] |
| [illegible] | [illegible] | [illegible] | [illegible] | [illegible] | [illegible] | [illegible] | [illegible] | [illegible] | [illegible] | [illegible] | [illegible] | [illegible] | [illegible] | [illegible] | [illegible] | [illegible] |
| Cork County (W.R.) | | | | | | | | | | | | | | | | |
| [illegible] | [illegible] | [illegible] | [illegible] | [illegible] | [illegible] | [illegible] | [illegible] | [illegible] | [illegible] | [illegible] | [illegible] | [illegible] | [illegible] | [illegible] | [illegible] | [illegible] |
| [illegible] | [illegible] | [illegible] | [illegible] | [illegible] | [illegible] | [illegible] | [illegible] | [illegible] | [illegible] | [illegible] | [illegible] | [illegible] | [illegible] | [illegible] | [illegible] | [illegible] |
| [illegible] | [illegible] | [illegible] | [illegible] | [illegible] | [illegible] | [illegible] | [illegible] | [illegible] | [illegible] | [illegible] | [illegible] | [illegible] | [illegible] | [illegible] | - | - |
| [illegible] | [illegible] | [illegible] | [illegible] | [illegible] | [illegible] | [illegible] | [illegible] | [illegible] | [illegible] | [illegible] | [illegible] | [illegible] | [illegible] | [illegible] | [illegible] | [illegible] |
| [illegible] | [illegible] | [illegible] | [illegible] | [illegible] | [illegible] | - | [illegible] | - | [illegible] | [illegible] | [illegible] | [illegible] | - | - | - | - |
| [illegible] | [illegible] | [illegible] | [illegible] | [illegible] | [illegible] | [illegible] | [illegible] | [illegible] | [illegible] | [illegible] | [illegible] | [illegible] | - | - | - | - |
| [illegible] | [illegible] | [illegible] | [illegible] | [illegible] | [illegible] | [illegible] | [illegible] | [illegible] | [illegible] | [illegible] | [illegible] | [illegible] | [illegible] | [illegible] | [illegible] | [illegible] |
| [illegible] | [illegible] | [illegible] | [illegible] | [illegible] | [illegible] | [illegible] | [illegible] | [illegible] | [illegible] | [illegible] | [illegible] | [illegible] | [illegible] | [illegible] | [illegible] | [illegible] |
| [illegible] | [illegible] | [illegible] | [illegible] | [illegible] | [illegible] | [illegible] | [illegible] | [illegible] | [illegible] | [illegible] | [illegible] | [illegible] | [illegible] | [illegible] | [illegible] | [illegible] |
| Kerry County. | | | | | | | | | | | | | | | | |
| [illegible] | [illegible] | [illegible] | [illegible] | [illegible] | [illegible] | [illegible] | [illegible] | [illegible] | [illegible] | [illegible] | [illegible] | [illegible] | [illegible] | [illegible] | [illegible] | [illegible] |
| [illegible] | [illegible] | [illegible] | [illegible] | [illegible] | [illegible] | [illegible] | [illegible] | [illegible] | [illegible] | [illegible] | [illegible] | [illegible] | [illegible] | [illegible] | [illegible] | [illegible] |
| [illegible] | [illegible] | [illegible] | [illegible] | [illegible] | [illegible] | [illegible] | [illegible] | [illegible] | [illegible] | [illegible] | [illegible] | [illegible] | [illegible] | [illegible] | [illegible] | [illegible] |
| [illegible] | [illegible] | [illegible] | [illegible] | [illegible] | [illegible] | [illegible] | [illegible] | [illegible] | [illegible] | [illegible] | [illegible] | [illegible] | [illegible] | [illegible] | - | - |
| [illegible] | [illegible] | [illegible] | [illegible] | [illegible] | [illegible] | [illegible] | [illegible] | [illegible] | [illegible] | [illegible] | [illegible] | [illegible] | [illegible] | [illegible] | [illegible] | [illegible] |
| [illegible] | [illegible] | [illegible] | [illegible] | [illegible] | [illegible] | [illegible] | [illegible] | [illegible] | [illegible] | [illegible] | [illegible] | [illegible] | [illegible] | [illegible] | [illegible] | [illegible] |
| [illegible] | [illegible] | [illegible] | [illegible] | [illegible] | [illegible] | [illegible] | [illegible] | [illegible] | [illegible] | [illegible] | [illegible] | [illegible] | [illegible] | [illegible] | [illegible] | [illegible] |
| [illegible] | [illegible] | [illegible] | [illegible] | [illegible] | [illegible] | [illegible] | [illegible] | [illegible] | [illegible] | [illegible] | [illegible] | [illegible] | [illegible] | [illegible] | [illegible] | [illegible] |
| [illegible] County. | | | | | | | | | | | | | | | | |
| [illegible] | [illegible] | [illegible] | [illegible] | [illegible] | [illegible] | [illegible] | [illegible] | [illegible] | [illegible] | [illegible] | [illegible] | [illegible] | [illegible] | [illegible] | [illegible] | [illegible] |
| [illegible] | [illegible] | [illegible] | [illegible] | [illegible] | [illegible] | [illegible] | [illegible] | [illegible] | [illegible] | [illegible] | [illegible] | - | [illegible] | [illegible] | [illegible] | [illegible] |
| [illegible] | [illegible] | [illegible] | [illegible] | [illegible] | [illegible] | [illegible] | [illegible] | [illegible] | [illegible] | [illegible] | [illegible] | [illegible] | [illegible] | [illegible] | [illegible] | [illegible] |
| [illegible] | [illegible] | [illegible] | [illegible] | [illegible] | [illegible] | [illegible] | - | - | [illegible] | [illegible] | [illegible] | [illegible] | - | - | - | - |
| [illegible] | [illegible] | [illegible] | [illegible] | [illegible] | [illegible] | [illegible] | [illegible] | [illegible] | [illegible] | [illegible] | [illegible] | [illegible] | [illegible] | [illegible] | [illegible] | [illegible] |
| [illegible] | [illegible] | [illegible] | [illegible] | [illegible] | [illegible] | [illegible] | [illegible] | [illegible] | [illegible] | [illegible] | [illegible] | [illegible] | [illegible] | [illegible] | - | - |
| [illegible] | [illegible] | [illegible] | [illegible] | [illegible] | [illegible] | [illegible] | [illegible] | [illegible] | [illegible] | [illegible] | [illegible] | [illegible] | [illegible] | [illegible] | [illegible] | [illegible] |
| [illegible] | [illegible] | [illegible] | [illegible] | [illegible] | [illegible] | [illegible] | [illegible] | [illegible] | [illegible] | [illegible] | [illegible] | [illegible] | [illegible] | [illegible] | [illegible] | [illegible] |

[illegible]

## II.—PROVINCE OF MUNSTER—continued.

| [illegible] | Summer: Men, From | Men, To | Boys, From | Boys, To | Women, From | Women, To | Girls, From | Girls, To | Winter: Men, From | Men, To | Boys, From | Boys, To | Women, From | Women, To | Girls, From | Girls, To |
|---|---|---|---|---|---|---|---|---|---|---|---|---|---|---|---|---|
| | s. d. | s. d. | s. d. | s. d. | s. d. | s. d. | s. d. | s. d. | s. d. | s. d. | s. d. | s. d. | s. d. | s. d. | s. d. | s. d. |
| Tipperary Co., N.R. | | | | | | | | | | | | | | | | |
| [illegible] | [illegible] | [illegible] | [illegible] | [illegible] | [illegible] | [illegible] | [illegible] | [illegible] | [illegible] | [illegible] | [illegible] | [illegible] | [illegible] | [illegible] | [illegible] | [illegible] |
| Nenagh (a), | [illegible] | [illegible] | [illegible] | [illegible] | [illegible] | [illegible] | [illegible] | [illegible] | [illegible] | [illegible] | [illegible] | [illegible] | [illegible] | [illegible] | [illegible] | [illegible] |
| [illegible] (b), | [illegible] | [illegible] | [illegible] | [illegible] | [illegible] | [illegible] | [illegible] | [illegible] | [illegible] | [illegible] | [illegible] | [illegible] | [illegible] | [illegible] | [illegible] | [illegible] |
| Roscrea, | [illegible] | [illegible] | [illegible] | [illegible] | [illegible] | [illegible] | [illegible] | [illegible] | [illegible] | [illegible] | [illegible] | [illegible] | [illegible] | [illegible] | [illegible] | [illegible] |
| Templemore, | [illegible] | [illegible] | [illegible] | [illegible] | [illegible] | [illegible] | [illegible] | [illegible] | [illegible] | [illegible] | [illegible] | [illegible] | [illegible] | [illegible] | [illegible] | [illegible] |
| Thurles, | [illegible] | [illegible] | [illegible] | [illegible] | [illegible] | [illegible] | [illegible] | [illegible] | [illegible] | [illegible] | [illegible] | [illegible] | [illegible] | [illegible] | [illegible] | [illegible] |
| Tipperary Co., S.R. | | | | | | | | | | | | | | | | |
| Cahir (c), | [illegible] | [illegible] | [illegible] | [illegible] | [illegible] | [illegible] | [illegible] | [illegible] | [illegible] | [illegible] | [illegible] | [illegible] | [illegible] | [illegible] | [illegible] | [illegible] |
| [illegible] (d), | [illegible] | [illegible] | [illegible] | [illegible] | [illegible] | [illegible] | [illegible] | [illegible] | [illegible] | [illegible] | [illegible] | [illegible] | [illegible] | [illegible] | [illegible] | [illegible] |
| Carrick-on-Suir (e), | [illegible] | [illegible] | [illegible] | [illegible] | [illegible] | [illegible] | [illegible] | [illegible] | [illegible] | [illegible] | [illegible] | [illegible] | [illegible] | [illegible] | [illegible] | [illegible] |
| Cashel, | [illegible] | [illegible] | [illegible] | [illegible] | [illegible] | [illegible] | [illegible] | [illegible] | [illegible] | [illegible] | [illegible] | [illegible] | [illegible] | [illegible] | [illegible] | [illegible] |
| Clonmel, | [illegible] | [illegible] | [illegible] | [illegible] | [illegible] | [illegible] | [illegible] | [illegible] | [illegible] | [illegible] | [illegible] | [illegible] | [illegible] | [illegible] | [illegible] | [illegible] |
| [illegible] (f), | [illegible] | [illegible] | [illegible] | [illegible] | [illegible] | [illegible] | [illegible] | [illegible] | [illegible] | [illegible] | [illegible] | [illegible] | [illegible] | [illegible] | [illegible] | [illegible] |
| Tipperary, | [illegible] | [illegible] | [illegible] | [illegible] | [illegible] | [illegible] | [illegible] | [illegible] | [illegible] | [illegible] | [illegible] | [illegible] | [illegible] | [illegible] | [illegible] | [illegible] |
| Waterford Co. | | | | | | | | | | | | | | | | |
| [illegible] | [illegible] | [illegible] | [illegible] | [illegible] | [illegible] | [illegible] | - | - | [illegible] | [illegible] | [illegible] | [illegible] | [illegible] | - | - | - |
| Dungarvan, | [illegible] | [illegible] | [illegible] | [illegible] | [illegible] | [illegible] | [illegible] | [illegible] | [illegible] | [illegible] | [illegible] | [illegible] | [illegible] | [illegible] | [illegible] | [illegible] |
| [illegible] | [illegible] | [illegible] | [illegible] | [illegible] | [illegible] | [illegible] | [illegible] | [illegible] | [illegible] | [illegible] | [illegible] | [illegible] | [illegible] | [illegible] | [illegible] | [illegible] |
| Waterford, | [illegible] | [illegible] | [illegible] | [illegible] | [illegible] | [illegible] | [illegible] | [illegible] | [illegible] | [illegible] | [illegible] | [illegible] | [illegible] | [illegible] | [illegible] | [illegible] |

## III.—PROVINCE OF ULSTER.

| [illegible] | Summer: Men, From | Men, To | Boys, From | Boys, To | Women, From | Women, To | Girls, From | Girls, To | Winter: Men, From | Men, To | Boys, From | Boys, To | Women, From | Women, To | Girls, From | Girls, To |
|---|---|---|---|---|---|---|---|---|---|---|---|---|---|---|---|---|
| Antrim County. | | | | | | | | | | | | | | | | |
| Antrim, | [illegible] | [illegible] | [illegible] | [illegible] | [illegible] | [illegible] | [illegible] | [illegible] | [illegible] | [illegible] | [illegible] | [illegible] | [illegible] | [illegible] | [illegible] | [illegible] |
| [illegible] (g), | [illegible] | [illegible] | [illegible] | [illegible] | [illegible] | [illegible] | [illegible] | [illegible] | [illegible] | [illegible] | [illegible] | [illegible] | [illegible] | [illegible] | [illegible] | [illegible] |
| Ballymoney, | [illegible] | [illegible] | [illegible] | [illegible] | [illegible] | [illegible] | [illegible] | [illegible] | [illegible] | [illegible] | [illegible] | [illegible] | [illegible] | [illegible] | [illegible] | [illegible] |
| Belfast East, | [illegible] | [illegible] | [illegible] | [illegible] | [illegible] | [illegible] | - | - | [illegible] | [illegible] | [illegible] | [illegible] | [illegible] | [illegible] | - | - |
| Belfast North (h), | [illegible] | [illegible] | [illegible] | [illegible] | [illegible] | [illegible] | [illegible] | [illegible] | [illegible] | [illegible] | [illegible] | [illegible] | [illegible] | [illegible] | [illegible] | [illegible] |
| Belfast South West, | [illegible] | [illegible] | [illegible] | [illegible] | [illegible] | [illegible] | [illegible] | [illegible] | [illegible] | [illegible] | [illegible] | [illegible] | [illegible] | [illegible] | [illegible] | [illegible] |
| Belfast South (i), | [illegible] | [illegible] | [illegible] | [illegible] | [illegible] | [illegible] | [illegible] | [illegible] | [illegible] | [illegible] | [illegible] | [illegible] | [illegible] | [illegible] | [illegible] | [illegible] |
| Belfast West (j), | - | - | - | - | - | - | - | - | - | - | - | - | - | - | - | - |
| Larne (k), | [illegible] | [illegible] | [illegible] | [illegible] | [illegible] | [illegible] | [illegible] | [illegible] | [illegible] | [illegible] | [illegible] | [illegible] | [illegible] | [illegible] | [illegible] | [illegible] |
| Lisburn, | [illegible] | [illegible] | [illegible] | [illegible] | [illegible] | [illegible] | [illegible] | [illegible] | [illegible] | [illegible] | [illegible] | [illegible] | [illegible] | [illegible] | [illegible] | [illegible] |
| Armagh County. | | | | | | | | | | | | | | | | |
| Armagh, | [illegible] | [illegible] | [illegible] | [illegible] | [illegible] | [illegible] | [illegible] | [illegible] | [illegible] | [illegible] | [illegible] | [illegible] | [illegible] | [illegible] | [illegible] | [illegible] |
| Lurgan, | [illegible] | [illegible] | [illegible] | [illegible] | [illegible] | [illegible] | [illegible] | [illegible] | [illegible] | [illegible] | [illegible] | [illegible] | [illegible] | [illegible] | [illegible] | [illegible] |
| Newry, | [illegible] | [illegible] | [illegible] | [illegible] | [illegible] | [illegible] | [illegible] | [illegible] | [illegible] | [illegible] | [illegible] | [illegible] | [illegible] | [illegible] | [illegible] | [illegible] |
| [illegible] | [illegible] | [illegible] | [illegible] | [illegible] | [illegible] | [illegible] | [illegible] | [illegible] | [illegible] | [illegible] | [illegible] | [illegible] | [illegible] | [illegible] | [illegible] | [illegible] |
| Cavan County. | | | | | | | | | | | | | | | | |
| Bailieborough, | [illegible] | [illegible] | [illegible] | [illegible] | [illegible] | [illegible] | [illegible] | [illegible] | [illegible] | [illegible] | [illegible] | [illegible] | [illegible] | [illegible] | [illegible] | [illegible] |
| Cavan, | [illegible] | [illegible] | [illegible] | [illegible] | [illegible] | [illegible] | [illegible] | [illegible] | [illegible] | [illegible] | [illegible] | [illegible] | [illegible] | [illegible] | [illegible] | [illegible] |
| [illegible] (l), | [illegible] | [illegible] | [illegible] | [illegible] | [illegible] | [illegible] | [illegible] | [illegible] | [illegible] | [illegible] | [illegible] | [illegible] | [illegible] | [illegible] | [illegible] | [illegible] |
| [illegible] | [illegible] | [illegible] | [illegible] | [illegible] | [illegible] | [illegible] | [illegible] | [illegible] | [illegible] | [illegible] | [illegible] | [illegible] | [illegible] | [illegible] | [illegible] | [illegible] |
| Virginia, | [illegible] | [illegible] | [illegible] | [illegible] | [illegible] | [illegible] | [illegible] | [illegible] | [illegible] | [illegible] | [illegible] | [illegible] | [illegible] | [illegible] | [illegible] | [illegible] |

[illegible]

## III.—PROVINCE OF ULSTER—continued.

| Counties and Poor Law Unions | Summer | | | | | | | | Winter | | | | | | | |
|---|---|---|---|---|---|---|---|---|---|---|---|---|---|---|---|---|
| | Men. | | Boys. | | Women. | | Girls. | | Men. | | Boys. | | Women. | | Girls. | |
| | From | To | From | To | From | To | From | To | From | To | From | To | From | To | From | To |
| | s. d. | s. d. | s. d. | s. d. | s. d. | s. d. | s. d. | s. d. | s. d. | s. d. | s. d. | s. d. | s. d. | s. d. | s. d. | s. d. |
| [illegible] County. | | | | | | | | | | | | | | | | |
| [illegible] | [illegible] | [illegible] | [illegible] | [illegible] | [illegible] | [illegible] | [illegible] | [illegible] | [illegible] | [illegible] | [illegible] | [illegible] | [illegible] | [illegible] | [illegible] | [illegible] |
| [illegible] | [illegible] | [illegible] | [illegible] | [illegible] | [illegible] | [illegible] | [illegible] | [illegible] | [illegible] | [illegible] | [illegible] | [illegible] | [illegible] | [illegible] | [illegible] | [illegible] |
| [illegible] | [illegible] | [illegible] | [illegible] | [illegible] | [illegible] | [illegible] | [illegible] | [illegible] | [illegible] | [illegible] | [illegible] | [illegible] | [illegible] | [illegible] | [illegible] | [illegible] |
| [illegible] | [illegible] | [illegible] | [illegible] | [illegible] | [illegible] | [illegible] | [illegible] | [illegible] | [illegible] | [illegible] | [illegible] | [illegible] | [illegible] | [illegible] | [illegible] | [illegible] |
| [illegible] | [illegible] | [illegible] | [illegible] | [illegible] | [illegible] | [illegible] | [illegible] | [illegible] | [illegible] | [illegible] | [illegible] | [illegible] | [illegible] | [illegible] | [illegible] | [illegible] |
| [illegible] | [illegible] | [illegible] | [illegible] | [illegible] | [illegible] | [illegible] | [illegible] | [illegible] | [illegible] | [illegible] | [illegible] | [illegible] | [illegible] | [illegible] | [illegible] | [illegible] |
| [illegible] | [illegible] | [illegible] | [illegible] | [illegible] | [illegible] | [illegible] | [illegible] | [illegible] | [illegible] | [illegible] | [illegible] | [illegible] | [illegible] | [illegible] | [illegible] | [illegible] |
| [illegible] | [illegible] | [illegible] | [illegible] | [illegible] | [illegible] | [illegible] | [illegible] | [illegible] | [illegible] | [illegible] | [illegible] | [illegible] | [illegible] | [illegible] | [illegible] | [illegible] |
| [illegible] | [illegible] | [illegible] | [illegible] | [illegible] | [illegible] | [illegible] | [illegible] | [illegible] | [illegible] | [illegible] | [illegible] | [illegible] | [illegible] | [illegible] | [illegible] | [illegible] |
| [illegible] County. | | | | | | | | | | | | | | | | |
| [illegible] | [illegible] | [illegible] | [illegible] | [illegible] | [illegible] | [illegible] | [illegible] | [illegible] | [illegible] | [illegible] | [illegible] | [illegible] | [illegible] | [illegible] | [illegible] | [illegible] |
| [illegible] | [illegible] | [illegible] | [illegible] | [illegible] | [illegible] | [illegible] | [illegible] | [illegible] | [illegible] | [illegible] | [illegible] | [illegible] | [illegible] | [illegible] | [illegible] | [illegible] |
| [illegible] | [illegible] | [illegible] | [illegible] | [illegible] | [illegible] | [illegible] | [illegible] | [illegible] | [illegible] | [illegible] | [illegible] | [illegible] | [illegible] | [illegible] | [illegible] | [illegible] |
| [illegible] | [illegible] | [illegible] | [illegible] | [illegible] | [illegible] | [illegible] | [illegible] | [illegible] | [illegible] | [illegible] | [illegible] | [illegible] | [illegible] | [illegible] | [illegible] | [illegible] |
| [illegible] County. | | | | | | | | | | | | | | | | |
| [illegible] | [illegible] | [illegible] | [illegible] | [illegible] | [illegible] | [illegible] | [illegible] | [illegible] | [illegible] | [illegible] | [illegible] | [illegible] | [illegible] | [illegible] | [illegible] | [illegible] |
| [illegible] | [illegible] | [illegible] | [illegible] | [illegible] | [illegible] | [illegible] | [illegible] | [illegible] | [illegible] | [illegible] | [illegible] | [illegible] | [illegible] | [illegible] | [illegible] | [illegible] |
| [illegible] | [illegible] | [illegible] | [illegible] | [illegible] | [illegible] | [illegible] | [illegible] | [illegible] | [illegible] | [illegible] | [illegible] | [illegible] | [illegible] | [illegible] | [illegible] | [illegible] |
| [illegible] | [illegible] | [illegible] | [illegible] | [illegible] | [illegible] | [illegible] | [illegible] | [illegible] | [illegible] | [illegible] | [illegible] | [illegible] | [illegible] | [illegible] | [illegible] | [illegible] |
| [illegible] Co. | | | | | | | | | | | | | | | | |
| [illegible] | [illegible] | [illegible] | [illegible] | [illegible] | [illegible] | [illegible] | [illegible] | [illegible] | [illegible] | [illegible] | [illegible] | [illegible] | [illegible] | [illegible] | [illegible] | [illegible] |
| [illegible] | [illegible] | [illegible] | [illegible] | [illegible] | [illegible] | [illegible] | [illegible] | [illegible] | [illegible] | [illegible] | [illegible] | [illegible] | [illegible] | [illegible] | [illegible] | [illegible] |
| [illegible] | [illegible] | [illegible] | [illegible] | [illegible] | [illegible] | [illegible] | [illegible] | [illegible] | [illegible] | [illegible] | [illegible] | [illegible] | [illegible] | [illegible] | [illegible] | [illegible] |
| [illegible] | [illegible] | [illegible] | [illegible] | [illegible] | [illegible] | [illegible] | [illegible] | [illegible] | [illegible] | [illegible] | [illegible] | [illegible] | [illegible] | [illegible] | [illegible] | [illegible] |
| [illegible] County. | | | | | | | | | | | | | | | | |
| [illegible] | [illegible] | [illegible] | [illegible] | [illegible] | [illegible] | [illegible] | [illegible] | [illegible] | [illegible] | [illegible] | [illegible] | [illegible] | [illegible] | [illegible] | [illegible] | [illegible] |
| [illegible] | [illegible] | [illegible] | [illegible] | [illegible] | [illegible] | [illegible] | [illegible] | [illegible] | [illegible] | [illegible] | [illegible] | [illegible] | [illegible] | [illegible] | [illegible] | [illegible] |
| [illegible] | [illegible] | [illegible] | [illegible] | [illegible] | [illegible] | [illegible] | [illegible] | [illegible] | [illegible] | [illegible] | [illegible] | [illegible] | [illegible] | [illegible] | [illegible] | [illegible] |
| Tyrone County. | | | | | | | | | | | | | | | | |
| [illegible] | [illegible] | [illegible] | [illegible] | [illegible] | [illegible] | [illegible] | [illegible] | [illegible] | [illegible] | [illegible] | [illegible] | [illegible] | [illegible] | [illegible] | [illegible] | [illegible] |
| [illegible] | [illegible] | [illegible] | [illegible] | [illegible] | [illegible] | [illegible] | [illegible] | [illegible] | [illegible] | [illegible] | [illegible] | [illegible] | [illegible] | [illegible] | [illegible] | [illegible] |
| [illegible] | [illegible] | [illegible] | [illegible] | [illegible] | [illegible] | [illegible] | [illegible] | [illegible] | [illegible] | [illegible] | [illegible] | [illegible] | [illegible] | [illegible] | [illegible] | [illegible] |
| [illegible] | [illegible] | [illegible] | [illegible] | [illegible] | [illegible] | [illegible] | [illegible] | [illegible] | [illegible] | [illegible] | [illegible] | [illegible] | [illegible] | [illegible] | [illegible] | [illegible] |
| [illegible] | [illegible] | [illegible] | [illegible] | [illegible] | [illegible] | [illegible] | [illegible] | [illegible] | [illegible] | [illegible] | [illegible] | [illegible] | [illegible] | [illegible] | [illegible] | [illegible] |
| [illegible] | [illegible] | [illegible] | [illegible] | [illegible] | [illegible] | [illegible] | [illegible] | [illegible] | [illegible] | [illegible] | [illegible] | [illegible] | [illegible] | [illegible] | [illegible] | [illegible] |

[illegible]

## IV.—PROVINCE OF CONNAUGHT.

| Counties and Poor Law Unions. | Summer. | | | | | | | | Winter. | | | | | | | |
|---|---|---|---|---|---|---|---|---|---|---|---|---|---|---|---|---|
| | Men. | | Boys. | | Women. | | Girls. | | Men. | | Boys. | | Women. | | Girls. | |
| | From | To | From | To | From | To | From | To | From | To | From | To | From | To | From | To |
| | s. d. | s. d. | s. d. | s. d. | s. d. | s. d. | s. d. | s. d. | s. d. | s. d. | s. d. | s. d. | s. d. | s. d. | s. d. | s. d. |
| GALWAY COUNTY. | | | | | | | | | | | | | | | | |
| [illegible] | [illegible] | [illegible] | [illegible] | [illegible] | [illegible] | [illegible] | [illegible] | [illegible] | [illegible] | [illegible] | [illegible] | [illegible] | [illegible] | [illegible] | [illegible] | [illegible] |
| [illegible] | [illegible] | [illegible] | [illegible] | [illegible] | [illegible] | [illegible] | [illegible] | [illegible] | [illegible] | [illegible] | [illegible] | [illegible] | [illegible] | [illegible] | [illegible] | [illegible] |
| [illegible] | [illegible] | [illegible] | [illegible] | [illegible] | [illegible] | [illegible] | [illegible] | [illegible] | [illegible] | [illegible] | [illegible] | [illegible] | [illegible] | [illegible] | [illegible] | [illegible] |
| [illegible] | [illegible] | [illegible] | [illegible] | [illegible] | [illegible] | [illegible] | [illegible] | [illegible] | [illegible] | [illegible] | [illegible] | [illegible] | [illegible] | [illegible] | [illegible] | [illegible] |
| [illegible] | [illegible] | [illegible] | [illegible] | [illegible] | [illegible] | [illegible] | [illegible] | [illegible] | [illegible] | [illegible] | [illegible] | [illegible] | [illegible] | [illegible] | [illegible] | [illegible] |
| [illegible] | [illegible] | [illegible] | [illegible] | [illegible] | [illegible] | [illegible] | [illegible] | [illegible] | [illegible] | [illegible] | [illegible] | [illegible] | [illegible] | [illegible] | [illegible] | [illegible] |
| [illegible] | [illegible] | [illegible] | [illegible] | [illegible] | [illegible] | [illegible] | [illegible] | [illegible] | [illegible] | [illegible] | [illegible] | [illegible] | [illegible] | [illegible] | [illegible] | [illegible] |
| [illegible] | [illegible] | [illegible] | [illegible] | [illegible] | [illegible] | [illegible] | [illegible] | [illegible] | [illegible] | [illegible] | [illegible] | [illegible] | [illegible] | [illegible] | [illegible] | [illegible] |
| [illegible] | [illegible] | [illegible] | [illegible] | [illegible] | [illegible] | [illegible] | [illegible] | [illegible] | [illegible] | [illegible] | [illegible] | [illegible] | [illegible] | [illegible] | [illegible] | [illegible] |
| [illegible] | [illegible] | [illegible] | [illegible] | [illegible] | [illegible] | [illegible] | [illegible] | [illegible] | [illegible] | [illegible] | [illegible] | [illegible] | [illegible] | [illegible] | [illegible] | [illegible] |
| [illegible] | [illegible] | [illegible] | [illegible] | [illegible] | [illegible] | [illegible] | [illegible] | [illegible] | [illegible] | [illegible] | [illegible] | [illegible] | [illegible] | [illegible] | [illegible] | [illegible] |
| [illegible] | [illegible] | [illegible] | [illegible] | [illegible] | [illegible] | [illegible] | [illegible] | [illegible] | [illegible] | [illegible] | [illegible] | [illegible] | [illegible] | [illegible] | [illegible] | [illegible] |
| [illegible] | [illegible] | [illegible] | [illegible] | [illegible] | [illegible] | [illegible] | [illegible] | [illegible] | [illegible] | [illegible] | [illegible] | [illegible] | [illegible] | [illegible] | [illegible] | [illegible] |
| [illegible] | [illegible] | [illegible] | [illegible] | [illegible] | [illegible] | [illegible] | [illegible] | [illegible] | [illegible] | [illegible] | [illegible] | [illegible] | [illegible] | [illegible] | [illegible] | [illegible] |
| [illegible] | [illegible] | [illegible] | [illegible] | [illegible] | [illegible] | [illegible] | [illegible] | [illegible] | [illegible] | [illegible] | [illegible] | [illegible] | [illegible] | [illegible] | [illegible] | [illegible] |
| LEITRIM COUNTY. | | | | | | | | | | | | | | | | |
| [illegible] | [illegible] | [illegible] | [illegible] | [illegible] | [illegible] | [illegible] | [illegible] | [illegible] | [illegible] | [illegible] | [illegible] | [illegible] | [illegible] | [illegible] | [illegible] | [illegible] |
| [illegible] | [illegible] | [illegible] | [illegible] | [illegible] | [illegible] | [illegible] | [illegible] | [illegible] | [illegible] | [illegible] | [illegible] | [illegible] | [illegible] | [illegible] | [illegible] | [illegible] |
| [illegible] | [illegible] | [illegible] | [illegible] | [illegible] | [illegible] | [illegible] | [illegible] | [illegible] | [illegible] | [illegible] | [illegible] | [illegible] | [illegible] | [illegible] | [illegible] | [illegible] |
| [illegible] | [illegible] | [illegible] | [illegible] | [illegible] | [illegible] | [illegible] | [illegible] | [illegible] | [illegible] | [illegible] | [illegible] | [illegible] | [illegible] | [illegible] | [illegible] | [illegible] |
| [illegible] | [illegible] | [illegible] | [illegible] | [illegible] | [illegible] | [illegible] | [illegible] | [illegible] | [illegible] | [illegible] | [illegible] | [illegible] | [illegible] | [illegible] | [illegible] | [illegible] |
| MAYO COUNTY. | | | | | | | | | | | | | | | | |
| [illegible] | [illegible] | [illegible] | [illegible] | [illegible] | [illegible] | [illegible] | [illegible] | [illegible] | [illegible] | [illegible] | [illegible] | [illegible] | [illegible] | [illegible] | [illegible] | [illegible] |
| [illegible] | [illegible] | [illegible] | [illegible] | [illegible] | [illegible] | [illegible] | [illegible] | [illegible] | [illegible] | [illegible] | [illegible] | [illegible] | [illegible] | [illegible] | [illegible] | [illegible] |
| [illegible] | [illegible] | [illegible] | [illegible] | [illegible] | [illegible] | [illegible] | [illegible] | [illegible] | [illegible] | [illegible] | [illegible] | [illegible] | [illegible] | [illegible] | [illegible] | [illegible] |
| [illegible] | [illegible] | [illegible] | [illegible] | [illegible] | [illegible] | [illegible] | [illegible] | [illegible] | [illegible] | [illegible] | [illegible] | [illegible] | [illegible] | [illegible] | [illegible] | [illegible] |
| [illegible] | [illegible] | [illegible] | [illegible] | [illegible] | [illegible] | [illegible] | [illegible] | [illegible] | [illegible] | [illegible] | [illegible] | [illegible] | [illegible] | [illegible] | [illegible] | [illegible] |
| [illegible] | [illegible] | [illegible] | [illegible] | [illegible] | [illegible] | [illegible] | [illegible] | [illegible] | [illegible] | [illegible] | [illegible] | [illegible] | [illegible] | [illegible] | [illegible] | [illegible] |
| [illegible] | [illegible] | [illegible] | [illegible] | [illegible] | [illegible] | [illegible] | [illegible] | [illegible] | [illegible] | [illegible] | [illegible] | [illegible] | [illegible] | [illegible] | [illegible] | [illegible] |
| [illegible] | [illegible] | [illegible] | [illegible] | [illegible] | [illegible] | [illegible] | [illegible] | [illegible] | [illegible] | [illegible] | [illegible] | [illegible] | [illegible] | [illegible] | [illegible] | [illegible] |
| [illegible] | [illegible] | [illegible] | [illegible] | [illegible] | [illegible] | [illegible] | [illegible] | [illegible] | [illegible] | [illegible] | [illegible] | [illegible] | [illegible] | [illegible] | [illegible] | [illegible] |
| ROSCOMMON COUNTY. | | | | | | | | | | | | | | | | |
| [illegible] | [illegible] | [illegible] | [illegible] | [illegible] | [illegible] | [illegible] | [illegible] | [illegible] | [illegible] | [illegible] | [illegible] | [illegible] | [illegible] | [illegible] | [illegible] | [illegible] |
| [illegible] | [illegible] | [illegible] | [illegible] | [illegible] | [illegible] | [illegible] | [illegible] | [illegible] | [illegible] | [illegible] | [illegible] | [illegible] | [illegible] | [illegible] | [illegible] | [illegible] |
| [illegible] | [illegible] | [illegible] | [illegible] | [illegible] | [illegible] | [illegible] | [illegible] | [illegible] | [illegible] | [illegible] | [illegible] | [illegible] | [illegible] | [illegible] | [illegible] | [illegible] |
| [illegible] | [illegible] | [illegible] | [illegible] | [illegible] | [illegible] | [illegible] | [illegible] | [illegible] | [illegible] | [illegible] | [illegible] | [illegible] | [illegible] | [illegible] | [illegible] | [illegible] |
| [illegible] | [illegible] | [illegible] | [illegible] | [illegible] | [illegible] | [illegible] | [illegible] | [illegible] | [illegible] | [illegible] | [illegible] | [illegible] | [illegible] | [illegible] | [illegible] | [illegible] |
| SLIGO COUNTY. | | | | | | | | | | | | | | | | |
| [illegible] | [illegible] | [illegible] | [illegible] | [illegible] | [illegible] | [illegible] | [illegible] | [illegible] | [illegible] | [illegible] | [illegible] | [illegible] | [illegible] | [illegible] | [illegible] | [illegible] |
| [illegible] | [illegible] | [illegible] | [illegible] | [illegible] | [illegible] | [illegible] | [illegible] | [illegible] | [illegible] | [illegible] | [illegible] | [illegible] | [illegible] | [illegible] | [illegible] | [illegible] |
| [illegible] | [illegible] | [illegible] | [illegible] | [illegible] | [illegible] | [illegible] | [illegible] | [illegible] | [illegible] | [illegible] | [illegible] | [illegible] | [illegible] | [illegible] | [illegible] | [illegible] |
| [illegible] | [illegible] | [illegible] | [illegible] | [illegible] | [illegible] | [illegible] | [illegible] | [illegible] | [illegible] | [illegible] | [illegible] | [illegible] | [illegible] | [illegible] | [illegible] | [illegible] |
| [illegible] | [illegible] | [illegible] | [illegible] | [illegible] | [illegible] | [illegible] | [illegible] | [illegible] | [illegible] | [illegible] | [illegible] | [illegible] | [illegible] | [illegible] | [illegible] | [illegible] |

[illegible]

In conclusion I have to thank the occupiers and owners of land in general, and also the proprietors and managers of Scutching Mills, Corn Mills, and Dairy Factories, for their courtesy in supplying the information required for the various Returns to the Enumerators. I have also to express my thanks to the District Inspectors of the Royal Irish Constabulary and the Sergeants of the Metropolitan Police, who have furnished the valuable notes on the local circumstances affecting agriculture in the various parts of the country, which will be found at pages 61 to 63; and to add, as I do, with much pleasure, that the Enumerators discharged their duty with their usual efficiency.

I have the honour to remain

Your Excellency's faithful servant,

T. W. GRIMSHAW,

*Registrar-General.*

General Register Office,

Charlemont House, Dublin,

21st *April* 1896.

TABLE 1.—Showing, by Counties and Provinces, the Number of Holdings, their Size in Statute Acres, and the Division of Land in the Year [illegible].

| COUNTIES. | [illegible] |
|---|---|
| [illegible] | [illegible] |
| PROVINCES. | [illegible] |
| TOTAL OF IRELAND. | [illegible] |

[illegible]
[illegible]
[illegible]
[illegible]
[illegible]
[illegible]
[illegible]
[illegible]
[illegible]
[illegible]
[illegible]
[illegible]
[illegible]
[illegible]
[illegible]

Table [illegible].—Showing, by Poor Law Unions, the Number of Holdings, their Size in Statute Acres, and the Division of Land in the Year [illegible]—continued.

| [illegible] |
| --- |
| [illegible] |

| | | | | | | | | | | | | | | | | |
|---|---|---|---|---|---|---|---|---|---|---|---|---|---|---|---|---|
| [illegible] | [illegible] | [illegible] | [illegible] | [illegible] | [illegible] | [illegible] | [illegible] | [illegible] | [illegible] | [illegible] | [illegible] | [illegible] | [illegible] | [illegible] | [illegible] | [illegible] |
| [illegible] | [illegible] | [illegible] | [illegible] | [illegible] | [illegible] | [illegible] | [illegible] | [illegible] | [illegible] | [illegible] | [illegible] | [illegible] | [illegible] | [illegible] | [illegible] | [illegible] |
| [illegible] | [illegible] | [illegible] | [illegible] | [illegible] | [illegible] | [illegible] | [illegible] | [illegible] | [illegible] | [illegible] | [illegible] | [illegible] | [illegible] | [illegible] | [illegible] | [illegible] |
| [illegible] | [illegible] | [illegible] | [illegible] | [illegible] | [illegible] | [illegible] | [illegible] | [illegible] | [illegible] | [illegible] | [illegible] | [illegible] | [illegible] | [illegible] | [illegible] | [illegible] |
| [illegible] | [illegible] | [illegible] | [illegible] | [illegible] | [illegible] | [illegible] | [illegible] | [illegible] | [illegible] | [illegible] | [illegible] | [illegible] | [illegible] | [illegible] | [illegible] | [illegible] |
| [illegible] | [illegible] | [illegible] | [illegible] | [illegible] | [illegible] | [illegible] | [illegible] | [illegible] | [illegible] | [illegible] | [illegible] | [illegible] | [illegible] | [illegible] | [illegible] | [illegible] |
| [illegible] | [illegible] | [illegible] | [illegible] | [illegible] | [illegible] | [illegible] | [illegible] | [illegible] | [illegible] | [illegible] | [illegible] | [illegible] | [illegible] | [illegible] | [illegible] | [illegible] |

Table [illegible].—[illegible], by Counties and Provinces, [illegible]

| Counties. | [illegible] | | | | | | | | [illegible] | | |
|---|---|---|---|---|---|---|---|---|---|---|---|
| | Wheat. | [illegible] | [illegible] | [illegible] | [illegible] | [illegible] | [illegible] | [illegible] | [illegible] | [illegible] | [illegible] |
| Antrim, | 143 | [illegible] | [illegible] | - | 6 | [illegible] | [illegible] | [illegible] | [illegible] | [illegible] | [illegible] |
| Armagh, | [illegible] | [illegible] | [illegible] | [illegible] | [illegible] | [illegible] | [illegible] | [illegible] | [illegible] | [illegible] | [illegible] |
| Carlow, | [illegible] | [illegible] | [illegible] | [illegible] | [illegible] | - | - | [illegible] | [illegible] | [illegible] | [illegible] |
| Cavan, | [illegible] | [illegible] | 7 | - | [illegible] | 7 | [illegible] | [illegible] | [illegible] | [illegible] | [illegible] |
| Clare, | [illegible] | [illegible] | [illegible] | [illegible] | [illegible] | [illegible] | - | [illegible] | [illegible] | [illegible] | [illegible] |
| Cork, | [illegible] | [illegible] | [illegible] | [illegible] | [illegible] | 6 | 4 | [illegible] | [illegible] | [illegible] | [illegible] |
| Donegal, | [illegible] | [illegible] | [illegible] | [illegible] | [illegible] | [illegible] | [illegible] | [illegible] | [illegible] | [illegible] | [illegible] |
| Down, | [illegible] | [illegible] | [illegible] | [illegible] | [illegible] | [illegible] | [illegible] | [illegible] | [illegible] | [illegible] | [illegible] |
| Dublin, | [illegible] | [illegible] | [illegible] | [illegible] | [illegible] | 4 | [illegible] | [illegible] | [illegible] | [illegible] | [illegible] |
| Fermanagh, | [illegible] | [illegible] | [illegible] | [illegible] | [illegible] | [illegible] | [illegible] | [illegible] | [illegible] | [illegible] | [illegible] |
| Galway, | [illegible] | [illegible] | [illegible] | [illegible] | [illegible] | [illegible] | [illegible] | [illegible] | [illegible] | [illegible] | [illegible] |
| Kerry, | [illegible] | [illegible] | [illegible] | [illegible] | [illegible] | [illegible] | - | [illegible] | [illegible] | [illegible] | [illegible] |
| Kildare, | [illegible] | [illegible] | [illegible] | [illegible] | [illegible] | [illegible] | [illegible] | [illegible] | [illegible] | [illegible] | [illegible] |
| Kilkenny, | [illegible] | [illegible] | [illegible] | [illegible] | [illegible] | [illegible] | [illegible] | [illegible] | [illegible] | [illegible] | [illegible] |
| King's, | [illegible] | [illegible] | [illegible] | [illegible] | [illegible] | [illegible] | [illegible] | [illegible] | [illegible] | [illegible] | [illegible] |
| Leitrim, | 7 | [illegible] | [illegible] | [illegible] | [illegible] | [illegible] | - | [illegible] | [illegible] | [illegible] | [illegible] |
| Limerick, | [illegible] | [illegible] | [illegible] | [illegible] | [illegible] | [illegible] | [illegible] | [illegible] | [illegible] | [illegible] | [illegible] |
| Londonderry, | [illegible] | [illegible] | [illegible] | - | [illegible] | [illegible] | [illegible] | [illegible] | [illegible] | [illegible] | [illegible] |
| Longford, | [illegible] | [illegible] | [illegible] | [illegible] | [illegible] | - | - | [illegible] | [illegible] | [illegible] | [illegible] |
| Louth and [illegible], County of [illegible] | [illegible] | [illegible] | [illegible] | [illegible] | [illegible] | [illegible] | [illegible] | [illegible] | [illegible] | [illegible] | [illegible] |
| Mayo, | [illegible] | [illegible] | [illegible] | [illegible] | [illegible] | 7 | [illegible] | [illegible] | [illegible] | [illegible] | [illegible] |
| Meath, | [illegible] | [illegible] | [illegible] | - | [illegible] | [illegible] | [illegible] | [illegible] | [illegible] | [illegible] | [illegible] |
| Monaghan, | [illegible] | [illegible] | [illegible] | [illegible] | [illegible] | [illegible] | - | [illegible] | [illegible] | [illegible] | [illegible] |
| Queen's, | [illegible] | [illegible] | [illegible] | [illegible] | [illegible] | [illegible] | - | [illegible] | [illegible] | [illegible] | [illegible] |
| Roscommon, | [illegible] | [illegible] | [illegible] | [illegible] | [illegible] | [illegible] | [illegible] | [illegible] | [illegible] | [illegible] | [illegible] |
| Sligo, | [illegible] | [illegible] | [illegible] | [illegible] | [illegible] | - | - | [illegible] | [illegible] | [illegible] | [illegible] |
| Tipperary, | [illegible] | [illegible] | [illegible] | [illegible] | [illegible] | [illegible] | [illegible] | [illegible] | [illegible] | [illegible] | [illegible] |
| Tyrone, | [illegible] | [illegible] | [illegible] | [illegible] | [illegible] | [illegible] | - | [illegible] | [illegible] | [illegible] | [illegible] |
| Waterford, | [illegible] | [illegible] | [illegible] | [illegible] | [illegible] | - | [illegible] | [illegible] | [illegible] | [illegible] | [illegible] |
| Westmeath, | [illegible] | [illegible] | [illegible] | [illegible] | [illegible] | [illegible] | [illegible] | [illegible] | [illegible] | [illegible] | [illegible] |
| Wexford, | [illegible] | [illegible] | [illegible] | [illegible] | [illegible] | [illegible] | - | [illegible] | [illegible] | [illegible] | [illegible] |
| Wicklow, | [illegible] | [illegible] | [illegible] | - | [illegible] | - | - | [illegible] | [illegible] | [illegible] | [illegible] |
| **Provinces.** | | | | | | | | | | | |
| Leinster, | [illegible] | [illegible] | [illegible] | [illegible] | [illegible] | [illegible] | [illegible] | [illegible] | [illegible] | [illegible] | [illegible] |
| Munster, | [illegible] | [illegible] | [illegible] | [illegible] | [illegible] | [illegible] | [illegible] | [illegible] | [illegible] | [illegible] | [illegible] |
| Ulster, | [illegible] | [illegible] | [illegible] | [illegible] | [illegible] | [illegible] | [illegible] | [illegible] | [illegible] | [illegible] | [illegible] |
| Connaught, | [illegible] | [illegible] | [illegible] | [illegible] | [illegible] | [illegible] | [illegible] | [illegible] | [illegible] | [illegible] | [illegible] |
| Total, | [illegible] | [illegible] | [illegible] | [illegible] | [illegible] | [illegible] | [illegible] | [illegible] | [illegible] | [illegible] | [illegible] |

[illegible] CROPS IN THE YEAR 1856; THE VALUATION IN 1856; AND THE POPULATION IN 1851.

IN STATUTE ACRES.

| [illegible] | Green Crops. | | | | | Flax. | Meadow and Clover. | | [illegible] | Valuation in 1856. | Population in 1851. | COUNTIES. |
|---|---|---|---|---|---|---|---|---|---|---|---|---|
| [illegible] | [illegible] | [illegible] | [illegible] | [illegible] | [illegible] | | [illegible] | [illegible] | [illegible] | | | |
| [illegible] | [illegible] | [illegible] | [illegible] | [illegible] | [illegible] | [illegible] | [illegible] | [illegible] | [illegible] | [illegible] | [illegible] | Antrim. |
| [illegible] | [illegible] | [illegible] | [illegible] | [illegible] | [illegible] | [illegible] | [illegible] | [illegible] | [illegible] | [illegible] | [illegible] | Armagh. |
| [illegible] | [illegible] | [illegible] | [illegible] | [illegible] | [illegible] | [illegible] | [illegible] | [illegible] | [illegible] | [illegible] | [illegible] | Carlow. |
| [illegible] | [illegible] | [illegible] | [illegible] | [illegible] | [illegible] | [illegible] | [illegible] | [illegible] | [illegible] | [illegible] | [illegible] | Cavan. |
| [illegible] | [illegible] | [illegible] | [illegible] | [illegible] | [illegible] | [illegible] | [illegible] | [illegible] | [illegible] | [illegible] | [illegible] | Clare. |
| [illegible] | [illegible] | [illegible] | [illegible] | [illegible] | [illegible] | [illegible] | [illegible] | [illegible] | [illegible] | [illegible] | [illegible] | Cork. |
| [illegible] | [illegible] | [illegible] | [illegible] | [illegible] | [illegible] | [illegible] | [illegible] | [illegible] | [illegible] | [illegible] | [illegible] | Donegal. |
| [illegible] | [illegible] | [illegible] | [illegible] | [illegible] | [illegible] | [illegible] | [illegible] | [illegible] | [illegible] | [illegible] | [illegible] | Down. |
| [illegible] | [illegible] | [illegible] | [illegible] | [illegible] | [illegible] | [illegible] | [illegible] | [illegible] | [illegible] | [illegible] | [illegible] | Dublin. |
| [illegible] | [illegible] | [illegible] | [illegible] | [illegible] | [illegible] | [illegible] | [illegible] | [illegible] | [illegible] | [illegible] | [illegible] | Fermanagh. |
| [illegible] | [illegible] | [illegible] | [illegible] | [illegible] | [illegible] | [illegible] | [illegible] | [illegible] | [illegible] | [illegible] | [illegible] | Galway. |
| [illegible] | [illegible] | [illegible] | [illegible] | [illegible] | [illegible] | [illegible] | [illegible] | [illegible] | [illegible] | [illegible] | [illegible] | Kerry. |
| [illegible] | [illegible] | [illegible] | [illegible] | [illegible] | [illegible] | [illegible] | [illegible] | [illegible] | [illegible] | [illegible] | [illegible] | Kildare. |
| [illegible] | [illegible] | [illegible] | [illegible] | [illegible] | [illegible] | [illegible] | [illegible] | [illegible] | [illegible] | [illegible] | [illegible] | Kilkenny. |
| [illegible] | [illegible] | [illegible] | [illegible] | [illegible] | [illegible] | [illegible] | [illegible] | [illegible] | [illegible] | [illegible] | [illegible] | King's. |
| [illegible] | [illegible] | [illegible] | [illegible] | [illegible] | [illegible] | [illegible] | [illegible] | [illegible] | [illegible] | [illegible] | [illegible] | Leitrim. |
| [illegible] | [illegible] | [illegible] | [illegible] | [illegible] | [illegible] | [illegible] | [illegible] | [illegible] | [illegible] | [illegible] | [illegible] | Limerick. |
| [illegible] | [illegible] | [illegible] | [illegible] | [illegible] | [illegible] | [illegible] | [illegible] | [illegible] | [illegible] | [illegible] | [illegible] | Londonderry. |
| [illegible] | [illegible] | [illegible] | [illegible] | [illegible] | [illegible] | [illegible] | [illegible] | [illegible] | [illegible] | [illegible] | [illegible] | Longford. |
| [illegible] | [illegible] | [illegible] | [illegible] | [illegible] | [illegible] | [illegible] | [illegible] | [illegible] | [illegible] | [illegible] | [illegible] | Louth & [illegible] |
| [illegible] | [illegible] | [illegible] | [illegible] | [illegible] | [illegible] | [illegible] | [illegible] | [illegible] | [illegible] | [illegible] | [illegible] | Mayo. |
| [illegible] | [illegible] | [illegible] | [illegible] | [illegible] | [illegible] | [illegible] | [illegible] | [illegible] | [illegible] | [illegible] | [illegible] | Meath. |
| [illegible] | [illegible] | [illegible] | [illegible] | [illegible] | [illegible] | [illegible] | [illegible] | [illegible] | [illegible] | [illegible] | [illegible] | Monaghan. |
| [illegible] | [illegible] | [illegible] | [illegible] | [illegible] | [illegible] | [illegible] | [illegible] | [illegible] | [illegible] | [illegible] | [illegible] | Queen's. |
| [illegible] | [illegible] | [illegible] | [illegible] | [illegible] | [illegible] | [illegible] | [illegible] | [illegible] | [illegible] | [illegible] | [illegible] | Roscommon. |
| [illegible] | [illegible] | [illegible] | [illegible] | [illegible] | [illegible] | [illegible] | [illegible] | [illegible] | [illegible] | [illegible] | [illegible] | Sligo. |
| [illegible] | [illegible] | [illegible] | [illegible] | [illegible] | [illegible] | [illegible] | [illegible] | [illegible] | [illegible] | [illegible] | [illegible] | Tipperary. |
| [illegible] | [illegible] | [illegible] | [illegible] | [illegible] | [illegible] | [illegible] | [illegible] | [illegible] | [illegible] | [illegible] | [illegible] | Tyrone. |
| [illegible] | [illegible] | [illegible] | [illegible] | [illegible] | [illegible] | [illegible] | [illegible] | [illegible] | [illegible] | [illegible] | [illegible] | Waterford. |
| [illegible] | [illegible] | [illegible] | [illegible] | [illegible] | [illegible] | [illegible] | [illegible] | [illegible] | [illegible] | [illegible] | [illegible] | Westmeath. |
| [illegible] | [illegible] | [illegible] | [illegible] | [illegible] | [illegible] | [illegible] | [illegible] | [illegible] | [illegible] | [illegible] | [illegible] | Wexford. |
| [illegible] | [illegible] | [illegible] | [illegible] | [illegible] | [illegible] | [illegible] | [illegible] | [illegible] | [illegible] | [illegible] | [illegible] | Wicklow. |
| | | | | | | | | | | | | PROVINCES. |
| [illegible] | [illegible] | [illegible] | [illegible] | [illegible] | [illegible] | [illegible] | [illegible] | [illegible] | [illegible] | [illegible] | [illegible] | Leinster. |
| [illegible] | [illegible] | [illegible] | [illegible] | [illegible] | [illegible] | [illegible] | [illegible] | [illegible] | [illegible] | [illegible] | [illegible] | Munster. |
| [illegible] | [illegible] | [illegible] | [illegible] | [illegible] | [illegible] | [illegible] | [illegible] | [illegible] | [illegible] | [illegible] | [illegible] | Ulster. |
| [illegible] | [illegible] | [illegible] | [illegible] | [illegible] | [illegible] | [illegible] | [illegible] | [illegible] | [illegible] | [illegible] | [illegible] | Connaught. |
| [illegible] | [illegible] | [illegible] | [illegible] | [illegible] | [illegible] | [illegible] | [illegible] | [illegible] | [illegible] | [illegible] | [illegible] | Total. |

TABLE 6.—PRODUCE, BY COUNTIES AND PROVINCES, THE

| COUNTIES. | PRODUCE OF Corn, Beans, and Peas. Wheat. | Oats. | Barley. | Bere. | Rye. | Beans. | Peas. |
|---|---|---|---|---|---|---|---|
| | [illegible] | [illegible] | [illegible] | [illegible] | [illegible] | [illegible] | [illegible] |
| Antrim, | [illegible] | [illegible] | [illegible] | - | [illegible] | [illegible] | [illegible] |
| Armagh, | [illegible] | [illegible] | [illegible] | [illegible] | [illegible] | [illegible] | [illegible] |
| Carlow, | [illegible] | [illegible] | [illegible] | - | [illegible] | - | [illegible] |
| Cavan, | [illegible] | [illegible] | [illegible] | - | [illegible] | [illegible] | [illegible] |
| Clare, | [illegible] | [illegible] | [illegible] | [illegible] | [illegible] | [illegible] | [illegible] |
| Cork, | [illegible] | [illegible] | [illegible] | [illegible] | [illegible] | [illegible] | [illegible] |
| Donegal, | [illegible] | [illegible] | [illegible] | [illegible] | [illegible] | [illegible] | [illegible] |
| Down, | [illegible] | [illegible] | [illegible] | [illegible] | [illegible] | [illegible] | [illegible] |
| Dublin, | [illegible] | [illegible] | [illegible] | [illegible] | [illegible] | [illegible] | [illegible] |
| Fermanagh, | [illegible] | [illegible] | [illegible] | [illegible] | [illegible] | [illegible] | [illegible] |
| Galway, | [illegible] | [illegible] | [illegible] | [illegible] | [illegible] | [illegible] | [illegible] |
| Kerry, | [illegible] | [illegible] | [illegible] | [illegible] | [illegible] | [illegible] | - |
| Kildare, | [illegible] | [illegible] | [illegible] | [illegible] | [illegible] | [illegible] | [illegible] |
| Kilkenny, | [illegible] | [illegible] | [illegible] | [illegible] | [illegible] | [illegible] | [illegible] |
| King's, | [illegible] | [illegible] | [illegible] | [illegible] | [illegible] | [illegible] | [illegible] |
| Leitrim, | [illegible] | [illegible] | [illegible] | [illegible] | [illegible] | [illegible] | - |
| Limerick, | [illegible] | [illegible] | [illegible] | [illegible] | [illegible] | [illegible] | [illegible] |
| Londonderry, | [illegible] | [illegible] | [illegible] | - | [illegible] | [illegible] | [illegible] |
| Longford, | [illegible] | [illegible] | [illegible] | [illegible] | [illegible] | - | - |
| Louth and Drogheda, County of Town, | [illegible] | [illegible] | [illegible] | [illegible] | [illegible] | [illegible] | [illegible] |
| Mayo, | [illegible] | [illegible] | [illegible] | [illegible] | [illegible] | [illegible] | [illegible] |
| Meath, | [illegible] | [illegible] | [illegible] | - | [illegible] | [illegible] | [illegible] |
| Monaghan, | [illegible] | [illegible] | [illegible] | [illegible] | [illegible] | [illegible] | - |
| Queen's, | [illegible] | [illegible] | [illegible] | [illegible] | [illegible] | [illegible] | - |
| Roscommon, | [illegible] | [illegible] | [illegible] | [illegible] | [illegible] | [illegible] | [illegible] |
| Sligo, | [illegible] | [illegible] | [illegible] | [illegible] | [illegible] | - | - |
| Tipperary, | [illegible] | [illegible] | [illegible] | [illegible] | [illegible] | [illegible] | [illegible] |
| Tyrone, | [illegible] | [illegible] | [illegible] | [illegible] | [illegible] | [illegible] | - |
| Waterford, | [illegible] | [illegible] | [illegible] | [illegible] | [illegible] | - | [illegible] |
| Westmeath, | [illegible] | [illegible] | [illegible] | [illegible] | [illegible] | [illegible] | [illegible] |
| Wexford, | [illegible] | [illegible] | [illegible] | [illegible] | [illegible] | [illegible] | - |
| Wicklow, | [illegible] | [illegible] | [illegible] | - | [illegible] | - | - |
| PROVINCES. | | | | | | | |
| Leinster, | [illegible] | [illegible] | [illegible] | [illegible] | [illegible] | [illegible] | [illegible] |
| Munster, | [illegible] | [illegible] | [illegible] | [illegible] | [illegible] | [illegible] | [illegible] |
| Ulster, | [illegible] | [illegible] | [illegible] | [illegible] | [illegible] | [illegible] | [illegible] |
| Connaught, | [illegible] | [illegible] | [illegible] | [illegible] | [illegible] | [illegible] | [illegible] |
| Total, | [illegible] | [illegible] | [illegible] | [illegible] | [illegible] | [illegible] | [illegible] |

[illegible] of the Crops in the Year 18[illegible].

[illegible]

| [illegible] | | | | | | | [illegible] | [illegible] | | Counties. |
|---|---|---|---|---|---|---|---|---|---|---|
| [illegible] | [illegible] | [illegible] | [illegible] | [illegible] | [illegible] | [illegible] | [illegible] | [illegible] | [illegible] | |
| [illegible] | [illegible] | [illegible] | [illegible] | [illegible] | [illegible] | [illegible] | [illegible] | [illegible] | [illegible] | Antrim. |
| [illegible] | [illegible] | [illegible] | [illegible] | [illegible] | [illegible] | [illegible] | [illegible] | [illegible] | [illegible] | Armagh. |
| [illegible] | [illegible] | [illegible] | [illegible] | [illegible] | [illegible] | [illegible] | . | [illegible] | [illegible] | Carlow. |
| [illegible] | [illegible] | [illegible] | [illegible] | [illegible] | [illegible] | [illegible] | [illegible] | [illegible] | [illegible] | Cavan. |
| [illegible] | [illegible] | [illegible] | [illegible] | [illegible] | [illegible] | [illegible] | [illegible] | [illegible] | [illegible] | Clare. |
| [illegible] | [illegible] | [illegible] | [illegible] | [illegible] | [illegible] | [illegible] | [illegible] | [illegible] | [illegible] | Cork. |
| [illegible] | [illegible] | [illegible] | [illegible] | [illegible] | [illegible] | [illegible] | [illegible] | [illegible] | [illegible] | Donegal. |
| [illegible] | [illegible] | [illegible] | [illegible] | [illegible] | [illegible] | [illegible] | [illegible] | [illegible] | [illegible] | Down. |
| [illegible] | [illegible] | [illegible] | [illegible] | [illegible] | [illegible] | [illegible] | . | [illegible] | [illegible] | Dublin. |
| [illegible] | [illegible] | [illegible] | [illegible] | [illegible] | [illegible] | [illegible] | [illegible] | [illegible] | [illegible] | Fermanagh. |
| [illegible] | [illegible] | [illegible] | [illegible] | [illegible] | [illegible] | [illegible] | . | [illegible] | [illegible] | Galway. |
| [illegible] | [illegible] | [illegible] | [illegible] | [illegible] | [illegible] | [illegible] | [illegible] | [illegible] | [illegible] | Kerry. |
| [illegible] | [illegible] | [illegible] | [illegible] | [illegible] | [illegible] | [illegible] | . | [illegible] | [illegible] | Kildare. |
| [illegible] | [illegible] | [illegible] | [illegible] | [illegible] | [illegible] | [illegible] | . | [illegible] | [illegible] | Kilkenny. |
| [illegible] | [illegible] | [illegible] | [illegible] | [illegible] | [illegible] | [illegible] | . | [illegible] | [illegible] | King's. |
| [illegible] | [illegible] | [illegible] | [illegible] | [illegible] | [illegible] | . | [illegible] | [illegible] | [illegible] | Leitrim. |
| [illegible] | [illegible] | [illegible] | [illegible] | [illegible] | [illegible] | [illegible] | . | [illegible] | [illegible] | Limerick. |
| [illegible] | [illegible] | [illegible] | [illegible] | [illegible] | [illegible] | [illegible] | [illegible] | [illegible] | [illegible] | Londonderry. |
| [illegible] | [illegible] | [illegible] | [illegible] | [illegible] | [illegible] | [illegible] | [illegible] | [illegible] | [illegible] | Longford. |
| [illegible] | [illegible] | [illegible] | [illegible] | [illegible] | [illegible] | [illegible] | [illegible] | [illegible] | [illegible] | Louth and Drogheda, County of Town. |
| [illegible] | [illegible] | [illegible] | [illegible] | [illegible] | [illegible] | [illegible] | [illegible] | [illegible] | [illegible] | Mayo. |
| [illegible] | [illegible] | [illegible] | [illegible] | [illegible] | [illegible] | [illegible] | [illegible] | [illegible] | [illegible] | Meath. |
| [illegible] | [illegible] | [illegible] | [illegible] | [illegible] | [illegible] | [illegible] | [illegible] | [illegible] | [illegible] | Monaghan. |
| [illegible] | [illegible] | [illegible] | [illegible] | [illegible] | [illegible] | [illegible] | . | [illegible] | [illegible] | Queen's. |
| [illegible] | [illegible] | [illegible] | [illegible] | [illegible] | [illegible] | [illegible] | [illegible] | [illegible] | [illegible] | Roscommon. |
| [illegible] | [illegible] | [illegible] | [illegible] | [illegible] | [illegible] | . | [illegible] | [illegible] | [illegible] | Sligo. |
| [illegible] | [illegible] | [illegible] | [illegible] | [illegible] | [illegible] | [illegible] | . | [illegible] | [illegible] | Tipperary. |
| [illegible] | [illegible] | [illegible] | [illegible] | [illegible] | [illegible] | [illegible] | [illegible] | [illegible] | [illegible] | Tyrone. |
| [illegible] | [illegible] | [illegible] | [illegible] | [illegible] | [illegible] | [illegible] | [illegible] | [illegible] | [illegible] | Waterford. |
| [illegible] | [illegible] | [illegible] | [illegible] | [illegible] | [illegible] | [illegible] | . | [illegible] | [illegible] | Westmeath. |
| [illegible] | [illegible] | [illegible] | [illegible] | [illegible] | [illegible] | [illegible] | . | [illegible] | [illegible] | Wexford. |
| [illegible] | [illegible] | [illegible] | [illegible] | [illegible] | [illegible] | [illegible] | . | [illegible] | [illegible] | Wicklow. |
| | | | | | | | | | | PROVINCES. |
| [illegible] | [illegible] | [illegible] | [illegible] | [illegible] | [illegible] | [illegible] | [illegible] | [illegible] | [illegible] | Leinster. |
| [illegible] | [illegible] | [illegible] | [illegible] | [illegible] | [illegible] | [illegible] | [illegible] | [illegible] | [illegible] | Munster. |
| [illegible] | [illegible] | [illegible] | [illegible] | [illegible] | [illegible] | [illegible] | [illegible] | [illegible] | [illegible] | Ulster. |
| [illegible] | [illegible] | [illegible] | [illegible] | [illegible] | [illegible] | [illegible] | [illegible] | [illegible] | [illegible] | Connaught. |
| [illegible] | [illegible] | [illegible] | [illegible] | [illegible] | [illegible] | [illegible] | [illegible] | [illegible] | [illegible] | Total. |

| | | | | | | | | | | | | | | |
|---|---|---|---|---|---|---|---|---|---|---|---|---|---|---|
| [illegible] | [illegible] | [illegible] | [illegible] | [illegible] | [illegible] | [illegible] | [illegible] | [illegible] | [illegible] | [illegible] | [illegible] | [illegible] | [illegible] | [illegible] |
| [illegible] | [illegible] | [illegible] | [illegible] | [illegible] | [illegible] | [illegible] | [illegible] | [illegible] | [illegible] | [illegible] | [illegible] | [illegible] | [illegible] | [illegible] |
| [illegible] | [illegible] | [illegible] | [illegible] | [illegible] | [illegible] | [illegible] | [illegible] | [illegible] | [illegible] | [illegible] | [illegible] | [illegible] | [illegible] | [illegible] |
| [illegible] | [illegible] | [illegible] | [illegible] | [illegible] | [illegible] | [illegible] | [illegible] | [illegible] | [illegible] | [illegible] | [illegible] | [illegible] | [illegible] | [illegible] |

CROPS IN THE YEAR 1853; THE VALUATION IN 1853; AND THE POPULATION IN 1851.

IN STATUTE ACRES.

Green Crops.

[illegible]

# AGRICULTURAL STATISTICS FOR THE YEAR [illegible]

[illegible] the Year [illegible]; the Valuation in [illegible]; and the Population in [illegible]—continued.

| [illegible] | [illegible] | [illegible] | [illegible] | [illegible] | [illegible] | [illegible] | [illegible] | [illegible] | [illegible] | [illegible] | [illegible] | [illegible] |
|---|---|---|---|---|---|---|---|---|---|---|---|---|
| [illegible] | [illegible] | [illegible] | [illegible] | [illegible] | [illegible] | [illegible] | [illegible] | [illegible] | [illegible] | [illegible] | [illegible] | [illegible] |

[illegible]

[illegible]

[illegible]

[illegible]

[illegible]

PRODUCE OF THE CROPS IN THE YEAR 1884.

OF THE CROPS.

TABLE 6.—PRODUCE, BY POOR LAW UNIONS, THE

| [illegible] | [illegible] | [illegible] | [illegible] | [illegible] | [illegible] | [illegible] | [illegible] |
|---|---|---|---|---|---|---|---|
| [illegible] | [illegible] | [illegible] | [illegible] | [illegible] | [illegible] | [illegible] | [illegible] |

PRODUCE OF THE CROPS IN THE YEAR 18[illegible]—continued.

| [illegible] | [illegible] | [illegible] | [illegible] | [illegible] | [illegible] | [illegible] | [illegible] | [illegible] | [illegible] | POOR LAW UNIONS. |
|---|---|---|---|---|---|---|---|---|---|---|
| [illegible] | [illegible] | [illegible] | [illegible] | [illegible] | [illegible] | [illegible] | [illegible] | [illegible] | [illegible] | [illegible] |

TABLE 8.—[illegible]

TABLE [illegible].—Showing the Number of Holdings [illegible] and Extent of Land under Crops in each Year from 18[illegible] to 18[illegible], by Counties and Provinces—continued.

| Counties. | Years. | No. of Holdings [illegible] | Extent under Crops in Statute Acres in each Year from 18[illegible] to 18[illegible]. Corn, Beans, and Peas. | | | | | | | Green Crops. | | | | | | | Total [illegible] |
|---|---|---|---|---|---|---|---|---|---|---|---|---|---|---|---|---|---|
| | | | [illegible] | [illegible] | [illegible] | [illegible] | [illegible] | [illegible] | [illegible] | [illegible] | [illegible] | [illegible] | [illegible] | [illegible] | [illegible] | [illegible] | |
| [illegible]: Area, [illegible] Acres. | [illegible] | [illegible] | [illegible] | [illegible] | [illegible] | [illegible] | [illegible] | [illegible] | [illegible] | [illegible] | [illegible] | [illegible] | [illegible] | [illegible] | [illegible] | [illegible] | [illegible] |
| [illegible]: Area, [illegible] Acres. | [illegible] | [illegible] | [illegible] | [illegible] | [illegible] | [illegible] | [illegible] | [illegible] | [illegible] | [illegible] | [illegible] | [illegible] | [illegible] | [illegible] | [illegible] | [illegible] | [illegible] |
| [illegible]: Area, [illegible] Acres. | [illegible] | [illegible] | [illegible] | [illegible] | [illegible] | [illegible] | [illegible] | [illegible] | [illegible] | [illegible] | [illegible] | [illegible] | [illegible] | [illegible] | [illegible] | [illegible] | [illegible] |
| [illegible]: Area, [illegible] Acres. | [illegible] | [illegible] | [illegible] | [illegible] | [illegible] | [illegible] | [illegible] | [illegible] | [illegible] | [illegible] | [illegible] | [illegible] | [illegible] | [illegible] | [illegible] | [illegible] | [illegible] |
| [illegible]: Area, [illegible] Acres. | [illegible] | [illegible] | [illegible] | [illegible] | [illegible] | [illegible] | [illegible] | [illegible] | [illegible] | [illegible] | [illegible] | [illegible] | [illegible] | [illegible] | [illegible] | [illegible] | [illegible] |
| [illegible]: Area, [illegible] Acres. | [illegible] | [illegible] | [illegible] | [illegible] | [illegible] | [illegible] | [illegible] | [illegible] | [illegible] | [illegible] | [illegible] | [illegible] | [illegible] | [illegible] | [illegible] | [illegible] | [illegible] |
| [illegible]: Area, [illegible] Acres. | [illegible] | [illegible] | [illegible] | [illegible] | [illegible] | [illegible] | [illegible] | [illegible] | [illegible] | [illegible] | [illegible] | [illegible] | [illegible] | [illegible] | [illegible] | [illegible] | [illegible] |
| [illegible]: Area, [illegible] Acres. | [illegible] | [illegible] | [illegible] | [illegible] | [illegible] | [illegible] | [illegible] | [illegible] | [illegible] | [illegible] | [illegible] | [illegible] | [illegible] | [illegible] | [illegible] | [illegible] | [illegible] |

TABLE 5.—Showing the Number of Holdings exceeding one Acre, and Extent of Land under Crops in each Year from 1886 to 1895, by Counties and Provinces—continued.

| COUNTIES. | Years. | No. of Holdings | [illegible] | [illegible] | [illegible] |
| --- | --- | --- | --- | --- | --- |
| [illegible] | [illegible] | [illegible] | [illegible] | [illegible] | [illegible] |

Table 2.—Showing the Number of Holdings exceeding one Acre, the Extent of Land under Crops in each Year from [illegible] to [illegible], by Counties and Provinces—continued.

| Counties. | Years. | [illegible] | Corn, Beans, and Peas. | | | | | | | Green Crops. | | | | | | | [illegible] |
|---|---|---|---|---|---|---|---|---|---|---|---|---|---|---|---|---|---|
| [illegible] | [illegible] | [illegible] | [illegible] | [illegible] | [illegible] | [illegible] | [illegible] | [illegible] | [illegible] | [illegible] | [illegible] | [illegible] | [illegible] | [illegible] | [illegible] | [illegible] | [illegible] |

TABLE 2.—[illegible]

PROVINCES.

[illegible]

TOTAL OF IRELAND.

[illegible]

TABLE 10.—Showing, by Counties and Provinces, the Average Rates of Produce of Crops on the Statute Acre, in each Year, from [illegible] to [illegible].

| Counties. | [illegible] | [illegible] | [illegible] | [illegible] | [illegible] | [illegible] | [illegible] | [illegible] | [illegible] | [illegible] | [illegible] | [illegible] | [illegible] | [illegible] |
|---|---|---|---|---|---|---|---|---|---|---|---|---|---|---|
| Antrim, | [illegible] | [illegible] | [illegible] | [illegible] | [illegible] | [illegible] | [illegible] | [illegible] | [illegible] | [illegible] | [illegible] | [illegible] | [illegible] | [illegible] |
| Armagh, | [illegible] | [illegible] | [illegible] | [illegible] | [illegible] | [illegible] | [illegible] | [illegible] | [illegible] | [illegible] | [illegible] | [illegible] | [illegible] | [illegible] |
| Carlow, | [illegible] | [illegible] | [illegible] | [illegible] | [illegible] | [illegible] | [illegible] | [illegible] | [illegible] | [illegible] | [illegible] | [illegible] | [illegible] | [illegible] |
| Cavan, | [illegible] | [illegible] | [illegible] | [illegible] | [illegible] | [illegible] | [illegible] | [illegible] | [illegible] | [illegible] | [illegible] | [illegible] | [illegible] | [illegible] |
| Clare, | [illegible] | [illegible] | [illegible] | [illegible] | [illegible] | [illegible] | [illegible] | [illegible] | [illegible] | [illegible] | [illegible] | [illegible] | [illegible] | [illegible] |
| Cork, | [illegible] | [illegible] | [illegible] | [illegible] | [illegible] | [illegible] | [illegible] | [illegible] | [illegible] | [illegible] | [illegible] | [illegible] | [illegible] | [illegible] |
| Donegal, | [illegible] | [illegible] | [illegible] | [illegible] | [illegible] | [illegible] | [illegible] | [illegible] | [illegible] | [illegible] | [illegible] | [illegible] | [illegible] | [illegible] |
| Down, | [illegible] | [illegible] | [illegible] | [illegible] | [illegible] | [illegible] | [illegible] | [illegible] | [illegible] | [illegible] | [illegible] | [illegible] | [illegible] | [illegible] |

Table [illegible] — continued.

[illegible]

[illegible]

| [illegible] | [illegible] | [illegible] | [illegible] | [illegible] | [illegible] | [illegible] | [illegible] | [illegible] | [illegible] | [illegible] | [illegible] | [illegible] | [illegible] | [illegible] |
|---|---|---|---|---|---|---|---|---|---|---|---|---|---|---|
| [illegible] | [illegible] | [illegible] | [illegible] | [illegible] | [illegible] | [illegible] | [illegible] | [illegible] | [illegible] | [illegible] | [illegible] | [illegible] | [illegible] | [illegible] |
| [illegible] | [illegible] | [illegible] | [illegible] | [illegible] | [illegible] | [illegible] | [illegible] | [illegible] | [illegible] | [illegible] | [illegible] | [illegible] | [illegible] | [illegible] |
| [illegible] | [illegible] | [illegible] | [illegible] | [illegible] | [illegible] | [illegible] | [illegible] | [illegible] | [illegible] | [illegible] | [illegible] | [illegible] | [illegible] | [illegible] |
| [illegible] | [illegible] | [illegible] | [illegible] | [illegible] | [illegible] | [illegible] | [illegible] | [illegible] | [illegible] | [illegible] | [illegible] | [illegible] | [illegible] | [illegible] |
| [illegible] | [illegible] | [illegible] | [illegible] | [illegible] | [illegible] | [illegible] | [illegible] | [illegible] | [illegible] | [illegible] | [illegible] | [illegible] | [illegible] | [illegible] |
| [illegible] | [illegible] | [illegible] | [illegible] | [illegible] | [illegible] | [illegible] | [illegible] | [illegible] | [illegible] | [illegible] | [illegible] | [illegible] | [illegible] | [illegible] |
| [illegible] | [illegible] | [illegible] | [illegible] | [illegible] | [illegible] | [illegible] | [illegible] | [illegible] | [illegible] | [illegible] | [illegible] | [illegible] | [illegible] | [illegible] |
| [illegible] | [illegible] | [illegible] | [illegible] | [illegible] | [illegible] | [illegible] | [illegible] | [illegible] | [illegible] | [illegible] | [illegible] | [illegible] | [illegible] | [illegible] |

TABLE 10.—SHOWING THE AVERAGE RATE OF PRODUCE TO THE STATUTE ACRE—continued.

AVERAGE OF PROVINCES.

| Provinces. | [illegible] | [illegible] | [illegible] | [illegible] | [illegible] | [illegible] | [illegible] | [illegible] | [illegible] | [illegible] | [illegible] | [illegible] | [illegible] | [illegible] |
|---|---|---|---|---|---|---|---|---|---|---|---|---|---|---|
| Leinster, | [illegible] | [illegible] | [illegible] | [illegible] | [illegible] | [illegible] | [illegible] | [illegible] | [illegible] | [illegible] | [illegible] | [illegible] | [illegible] | [illegible] |
| Munster, | [illegible] | [illegible] | [illegible] | [illegible] | [illegible] | [illegible] | [illegible] | [illegible] | [illegible] | [illegible] | [illegible] | [illegible] | [illegible] | [illegible] |
| Ulster, | [illegible] | [illegible] | [illegible] | [illegible] | [illegible] | [illegible] | [illegible] | [illegible] | [illegible] | [illegible] | [illegible] | [illegible] | [illegible] | [illegible] |
| Connaught, | [illegible] | [illegible] | [illegible] | [illegible] | [illegible] | [illegible] | [illegible] | [illegible] | [illegible] | [illegible] | [illegible] | [illegible] | [illegible] | [illegible] |

AVERAGE OF IRELAND.

| — | [illegible] | [illegible] | [illegible] | [illegible] | [illegible] | [illegible] | [illegible] | [illegible] | [illegible] | [illegible] | [illegible] | [illegible] | [illegible] | [illegible] |
|---|---|---|---|---|---|---|---|---|---|---|---|---|---|---|
| Ireland, | [illegible] | [illegible] | [illegible] | [illegible] | [illegible] | [illegible] | [illegible] | [illegible] | [illegible] | [illegible] | [illegible] | [illegible] | [illegible] | [illegible] |

d image digitised by the University of Southampton Library Digitisation Unit

[illegible]

| [illegible] | | | | | | | | | | | | | | | | | | | | | | | | | | | |
|---|---|---|---|---|---|---|---|---|---|---|---|---|---|---|---|---|---|---|---|---|---|---|---|---|---|---|---|
| [illegible] | [illegible] | [illegible] | [illegible] | [illegible] | [illegible] | [illegible] | [illegible] | [illegible] | [illegible] | [illegible] | [illegible] | [illegible] | [illegible] | [illegible] | [illegible] | [illegible] | [illegible] | [illegible] | [illegible] | [illegible] | [illegible] | [illegible] | [illegible] | [illegible] | [illegible] | [illegible] | [illegible] |
| [illegible] | [illegible] | [illegible] | [illegible] | [illegible] | [illegible] | [illegible] | [illegible] | [illegible] | [illegible] | [illegible] | [illegible] | [illegible] | [illegible] | [illegible] | [illegible] | [illegible] | [illegible] | [illegible] | [illegible] | [illegible] | [illegible] | [illegible] | [illegible] | [illegible] | [illegible] | [illegible] | [illegible] |
| [illegible] | [illegible] | [illegible] | [illegible] | [illegible] | [illegible] | [illegible] | [illegible] | [illegible] | [illegible] | [illegible] | [illegible] | [illegible] | [illegible] | [illegible] | [illegible] | [illegible] | [illegible] | [illegible] | [illegible] | [illegible] | [illegible] | [illegible] | [illegible] | [illegible] | [illegible] | [illegible] | [illegible] |
| [illegible] | [illegible] | [illegible] | [illegible] | [illegible] | [illegible] | [illegible] | [illegible] | [illegible] | [illegible] | [illegible] | [illegible] | [illegible] | [illegible] | [illegible] | [illegible] | [illegible] | [illegible] | [illegible] | [illegible] | [illegible] | [illegible] | [illegible] | [illegible] | [illegible] | [illegible] | [illegible] | [illegible] |
| [illegible] | [illegible] | [illegible] | [illegible] | [illegible] | [illegible] | [illegible] | [illegible] | [illegible] | [illegible] | [illegible] | [illegible] | [illegible] | [illegible] | [illegible] | [illegible] | [illegible] | [illegible] | [illegible] | [illegible] | [illegible] | [illegible] | [illegible] | [illegible] | [illegible] | [illegible] | [illegible] | [illegible] |
| [illegible] | [illegible] | [illegible] | [illegible] | [illegible] | [illegible] | [illegible] | [illegible] | [illegible] | [illegible] | [illegible] | [illegible] | [illegible] | [illegible] | [illegible] | [illegible] | [illegible] | [illegible] | [illegible] | [illegible] | [illegible] | [illegible] | [illegible] | [illegible] | [illegible] | [illegible] | [illegible] | [illegible] |
| [illegible] | [illegible] | [illegible] | [illegible] | [illegible] | [illegible] | [illegible] | [illegible] | [illegible] | [illegible] | [illegible] | [illegible] | [illegible] | [illegible] | [illegible] | [illegible] | [illegible] | [illegible] | [illegible] | [illegible] | [illegible] | [illegible] | [illegible] | [illegible] | [illegible] | [illegible] | [illegible] | [illegible] |
| [illegible] | [illegible] | [illegible] | [illegible] | [illegible] | [illegible] | [illegible] | [illegible] | [illegible] | [illegible] | [illegible] | [illegible] | [illegible] | [illegible] | [illegible] | [illegible] | [illegible] | [illegible] | [illegible] | [illegible] | [illegible] | [illegible] | [illegible] | [illegible] | [illegible] | [illegible] | [illegible] | [illegible] |
| [illegible] | [illegible] | [illegible] | [illegible] | [illegible] | [illegible] | [illegible] | [illegible] | [illegible] | [illegible] | [illegible] | [illegible] | [illegible] | [illegible] | [illegible] | [illegible] | [illegible] | [illegible] | [illegible] | [illegible] | [illegible] | [illegible] | [illegible] | [illegible] | [illegible] | [illegible] | [illegible] | [illegible] |
| [illegible] | [illegible] | [illegible] | [illegible] | [illegible] | [illegible] | [illegible] | [illegible] | [illegible] | [illegible] | [illegible] | [illegible] | [illegible] | [illegible] | [illegible] | [illegible] | [illegible] | [illegible] | [illegible] | [illegible] | [illegible] | [illegible] | [illegible] | [illegible] | [illegible] | [illegible] | [illegible] | [illegible] |

Table [illegible].—Showing the Quantity of Live Stock in each Year from [illegible] to [illegible], by Counties and Provinces.

| Counties. | Years. | No. of Horses. | | | Mules and Asses. | | No. of Cattle. | | | No. of Sheep. | | No. of Pigs. | | No. of [illegible] | No. of [illegible] |
|---|---|---|---|---|---|---|---|---|---|---|---|---|---|---|---|
| | | [illegible] | [illegible] | [illegible] | No. of [illegible] | No. of [illegible] | [illegible] | [illegible] | [illegible] | [illegible] | [illegible] | [illegible] | [illegible] | | |
| Antrim: Area, [illegible] Acres. | [illegible] | [illegible] | [illegible] | [illegible] | [illegible] | [illegible] | [illegible] | [illegible] | [illegible] | [illegible] | [illegible] | [illegible] | [illegible] | [illegible] | [illegible] |
| Armagh: Area, [illegible] Acres. | [illegible] | [illegible] | [illegible] | [illegible] | [illegible] | [illegible] | [illegible] | [illegible] | [illegible] | [illegible] | [illegible] | [illegible] | [illegible] | [illegible] | [illegible] |
| Carlow: Area, [illegible] Acres. | [illegible] | [illegible] | [illegible] | [illegible] | [illegible] | [illegible] | [illegible] | [illegible] | [illegible] | [illegible] | [illegible] | [illegible] | [illegible] | [illegible] | [illegible] |
| Cavan: Area, [illegible] Acres. | [illegible] | [illegible] | [illegible] | [illegible] | [illegible] | [illegible] | [illegible] | [illegible] | [illegible] | [illegible] | [illegible] | [illegible] | [illegible] | [illegible] | [illegible] |
| Clare: Area, [illegible] Acres. | [illegible] | [illegible] | [illegible] | [illegible] | [illegible] | [illegible] | [illegible] | [illegible] | [illegible] | [illegible] | [illegible] | [illegible] | [illegible] | [illegible] | [illegible] |
| Cork: Area, [illegible] Acres. | [illegible] | [illegible] | [illegible] | [illegible] | [illegible] | [illegible] | [illegible] | [illegible] | [illegible] | [illegible] | [illegible] | [illegible] | [illegible] | [illegible] | [illegible] |
| Donegal: Area, [illegible] Acres. | [illegible] | [illegible] | [illegible] | [illegible] | [illegible] | [illegible] | [illegible] | [illegible] | [illegible] | [illegible] | [illegible] | [illegible] | [illegible] | [illegible] | [illegible] |
| Down: Area, [illegible] Acres. | [illegible] | [illegible] | [illegible] | [illegible] | [illegible] | [illegible] | [illegible] | [illegible] | [illegible] | [illegible] | [illegible] | [illegible] | [illegible] | [illegible] | [illegible] |

TABLE 1A.—Showing the Quantity of Live Stock in each Year from [illegible] to [illegible], in Counties and Provinces—continued.

| Counties. | Years. | No. of Horses. | | | Mules and Asses. | | No. of Cattle. | | | No. of Sheep. | | No. of Pigs. | | [illegible] | [illegible] |
|---|---|---|---|---|---|---|---|---|---|---|---|---|---|---|---|
| | | [illegible] | [illegible] | [illegible] | [illegible] | [illegible] | [illegible] | [illegible] | [illegible] | [illegible] | [illegible] | [illegible] | [illegible] | | |

[illegible]

Galway. [illegible]

[illegible]

Kerry. [illegible]

[illegible]

TABLE [illegible].—SHOWING THE QUANTITY OF LIVE STOCK IN EACH YEAR FROM [illegible] TO [illegible], BY COUNTIES AND PROVINCES—*continued.*

| COUNTIES. | Years. | No. of Horses. | | | Mules and Asses. | | No. of Cattle. | | | No. of Sheep. | | No. of Pigs. | | No. of Goats. | No. of Poultry. |
|---|---|---|---|---|---|---|---|---|---|---|---|---|---|---|---|
| | | [illegible] | [illegible] | [illegible] | No. of Mules. | No. of Asses. | [illegible] | [illegible] | Under one year. | [illegible] | Under one year. | [illegible] | Under one year. | | |
| LIMERICK: Area, [illegible] Acres. | [illegible] | [illegible] | [illegible] | [illegible] | [illegible] | [illegible] | [illegible] | [illegible] | [illegible] | [illegible] | [illegible] | [illegible] | [illegible] | [illegible] | [illegible] |
| LONDONDERRY: Area, [illegible] Acres. | [illegible] | [illegible] | [illegible] | [illegible] | [illegible] | [illegible] | [illegible] | [illegible] | [illegible] | [illegible] | [illegible] | [illegible] | [illegible] | [illegible] | [illegible] |
| LONGFORD: Area, [illegible] Acres. | [illegible] | [illegible] | [illegible] | [illegible] | [illegible] | [illegible] | [illegible] | [illegible] | [illegible] | [illegible] | [illegible] | [illegible] | [illegible] | [illegible] | [illegible] |
| LOUTH & DROGHEDA, Co. of Town: Area, [illegible] Acres. | [illegible] | [illegible] | [illegible] | [illegible] | [illegible] | [illegible] | [illegible] | [illegible] | [illegible] | [illegible] | [illegible] | [illegible] | [illegible] | [illegible] | [illegible] |
| MAYO: Area, [illegible] Acres. | [illegible] | [illegible] | [illegible] | [illegible] | [illegible] | [illegible] | [illegible] | [illegible] | [illegible] | [illegible] | [illegible] | [illegible] | [illegible] | [illegible] | [illegible] |
| MEATH: Area, [illegible] Acres. | [illegible] | [illegible] | [illegible] | [illegible] | [illegible] | [illegible] | [illegible] | [illegible] | [illegible] | [illegible] | [illegible] | [illegible] | [illegible] | [illegible] | [illegible] |
| MONAGHAN: Area, [illegible] Acres. | [illegible] | [illegible] | [illegible] | [illegible] | [illegible] | [illegible] | [illegible] | [illegible] | [illegible] | [illegible] | [illegible] | [illegible] | [illegible] | [illegible] | [illegible] |
| QUEEN'S: Area, [illegible] Acres. | [illegible] | [illegible] | [illegible] | [illegible] | [illegible] | [illegible] | [illegible] | [illegible] | [illegible] | [illegible] | [illegible] | [illegible] | [illegible] | [illegible] | [illegible] |

TABLE 13.—SHOWING THE QUANTITY OF LIVE STOCK IN EACH YEAR FROM 1866 TO 1885, IN COUNTIES AND PROVINCES—continued.

| COUNTIES. | Years. | No. of Horses. | | | Mules and Asses. | | No. of Cattle. | | | No. of Sheep. | | No. of Pigs. | | [illegible] | [illegible] |
|---|---|---|---|---|---|---|---|---|---|---|---|---|---|---|---|
| | | [illegible] | [illegible] | [illegible] | [illegible] | [illegible] | [illegible] | [illegible] | [illegible] | [illegible] | [illegible] | [illegible] | [illegible] | | |
| ROSCOMMON: Acres [illegible] | [illegible] | [illegible] | [illegible] | [illegible] | [illegible] | [illegible] | [illegible] | [illegible] | [illegible] | [illegible] | [illegible] | [illegible] | [illegible] | [illegible] | [illegible] |
| SLIGO: Acres [illegible] | [illegible] | [illegible] | [illegible] | [illegible] | [illegible] | [illegible] | [illegible] | [illegible] | [illegible] | [illegible] | [illegible] | [illegible] | [illegible] | [illegible] | [illegible] |
| TIPPERARY: Acres [illegible] | [illegible] | [illegible] | [illegible] | [illegible] | [illegible] | [illegible] | [illegible] | [illegible] | [illegible] | [illegible] | [illegible] | [illegible] | [illegible] | [illegible] | [illegible] |
| TYRONE: Acres [illegible] | [illegible] | [illegible] | [illegible] | [illegible] | [illegible] | [illegible] | [illegible] | [illegible] | [illegible] | [illegible] | [illegible] | [illegible] | [illegible] | [illegible] | [illegible] |
| WATERFORD: Acres [illegible] | [illegible] | [illegible] | [illegible] | [illegible] | [illegible] | [illegible] | [illegible] | [illegible] | [illegible] | [illegible] | [illegible] | [illegible] | [illegible] | [illegible] | [illegible] |
| WESTMEATH: Acres [illegible] | [illegible] | [illegible] | [illegible] | [illegible] | [illegible] | [illegible] | [illegible] | [illegible] | [illegible] | [illegible] | [illegible] | [illegible] | [illegible] | [illegible] | [illegible] |
| WEXFORD: Acres [illegible] | [illegible] | [illegible] | [illegible] | [illegible] | [illegible] | [illegible] | [illegible] | [illegible] | [illegible] | [illegible] | [illegible] | [illegible] | [illegible] | [illegible] | [illegible] |
| WICKLOW: Acres [illegible] | [illegible] | [illegible] | [illegible] | [illegible] | [illegible] | [illegible] | [illegible] | [illegible] | [illegible] | [illegible] | [illegible] | [illegible] | [illegible] | [illegible] | [illegible] |

TABLE 13.—SHOWING THE QUANTITY OF LIVE STOCK IN EACH YEAR FROM 18[illegible] TO 18[illegible], BY COUNTIES AND PROVINCES—continued.

PROVINCES.

| PROVINCES. | Years. | No. of Horses | | | Mules and Asses | | No. of Cattle | | | No. of Sheep | | No. of Pigs | | No. of Goats. | No. of Poultry. |
|---|---|---|---|---|---|---|---|---|---|---|---|---|---|---|---|
| | | [illegible] | [illegible] | [illegible] | [illegible] | [illegible] | [illegible] | [illegible] | [illegible] | [illegible] | [illegible] | [illegible] | [illegible] | | |
| LEINSTER: Area, [illegible] Acres. | [illegible] | [illegible] | [illegible] | [illegible] | [illegible] | [illegible] | [illegible] | [illegible] | [illegible] | [illegible] | [illegible] | [illegible] | [illegible] | [illegible] | [illegible] |
| MUNSTER: Area, [illegible] Acres. | [illegible] | [illegible] | [illegible] | [illegible] | [illegible] | [illegible] | [illegible] | [illegible] | [illegible] | [illegible] | [illegible] | [illegible] | [illegible] | [illegible] | [illegible] |
| ULSTER: Area, [illegible] Acres. | [illegible] | [illegible] | [illegible] | [illegible] | [illegible] | [illegible] | [illegible] | [illegible] | [illegible] | [illegible] | [illegible] | [illegible] | [illegible] | [illegible] | [illegible] |
| CONNAUGHT: Area, [illegible] Acres. | [illegible] | [illegible] | [illegible] | [illegible] | [illegible] | [illegible] | [illegible] | [illegible] | [illegible] | [illegible] | [illegible] | [illegible] | [illegible] | [illegible] | [illegible] |

TOTAL OF IRELAND.

| IRELAND. | Years. | No. of Horses | | | Mules and Asses | | No. of Cattle | | | No. of Sheep | | No. of Pigs | | No. of Goats. | No. of Poultry. |
|---|---|---|---|---|---|---|---|---|---|---|---|---|---|---|---|
| | | [illegible] | [illegible] | [illegible] | [illegible] | [illegible] | [illegible] | [illegible] | [illegible] | [illegible] | [illegible] | [illegible] | [illegible] | | |
| Total of Ireland: Area, [illegible] Acres. | [illegible] | [illegible] | [illegible] | [illegible] | [illegible] | [illegible] | [illegible] | [illegible] | [illegible] | [illegible] | [illegible] | [illegible] | [illegible] | [illegible] | [illegible] |

| | |
|---|---|
| [illegible] | [illegible] |
| [illegible] | [illegible] |
| [illegible] | [illegible] |
| [illegible] | [illegible] |
| [illegible] | [illegible] |
| [illegible] | [illegible] |
| [illegible] | [illegible] |
| [illegible] | [illegible] |
| [illegible] | [illegible] |

[illegible]

[illegible]

[illegible]

[illegible]

[illegible]

[illegible]

[illegible]

[illegible]

TABLE 16.—SHOWING, by COUNTIES, the average rate of Produce per Statute acre of the principal descriptions of POTATOES planted in Ireland in 18[illegible].

| COUNTIES. | AVERAGE RATE OF PRODUCE PER STATUTE ACRE OF | | | | | | | | | | | | | | |
|---|---|---|---|---|---|---|---|---|---|---|---|---|---|---|---|
| | [illegible] | [illegible] | [illegible] | [illegible] | [illegible] | [illegible] | [illegible] | [illegible] | [illegible] | [illegible] | [illegible] | [illegible] | [illegible] | [illegible] | [illegible] |
| | Cwts. | Cwts. | Cwts. | Cwts. | Cwts. | Cwts. | Cwts. | Cwts. | Cwts. | Cwts. | Cwts. | Cwts. | Cwts. | Cwts. | Cwts. |
| ANTRIM, | [illegible] | [illegible] | [illegible] | [illegible] | [illegible] | [illegible] | [illegible] | [illegible] | [illegible] | [illegible] | . | . | . | . | . |
| ARMAGH, | [illegible] | [illegible] | [illegible] | [illegible] | [illegible] | [illegible] | [illegible] | [illegible] | [illegible] | [illegible] | [illegible] | . | . | . | . |
| CARLOW, | [illegible] | [illegible] | [illegible] | . | [illegible] | [illegible] | [illegible] | [illegible] | . | . | . | . | . | . | . |
| CAVAN, | [illegible] | [illegible] | . | [illegible] | [illegible] | [illegible] | [illegible] | [illegible] | [illegible] | . | . | . | . | . | . |
| CLARE, | [illegible] | [illegible] | . | . | [illegible] | [illegible] | [illegible] | [illegible] | . | . | . | [illegible] | . | . | |
| CORK, | [illegible] | [illegible] | [illegible] | . | [illegible] | [illegible] | [illegible] | [illegible] | [illegible] | . | . | . | . | . | . |
| DONEGAL, | [illegible] | [illegible] | [illegible] | [illegible] | [illegible] | [illegible] | [illegible] | [illegible] | [illegible] | . | [illegible] | . | . | [illegible] | [illegible] |
| DOWN, | [illegible] | [illegible] | [illegible] | [illegible] | [illegible] | [illegible] | [illegible] | [illegible] | [illegible] | [illegible] | . | . | . | . | . |
| DUBLIN, | [illegible] | [illegible] | . | [illegible] | [illegible] | [illegible] | [illegible] | [illegible] | . | . | . | . | . | . | . |
| FERMANAGH, | [illegible] | [illegible] | [illegible] | [illegible] | [illegible] | [illegible] | [illegible] | [illegible] | [illegible] | . | . | . | . | . | . |
| GALWAY, | [illegible] | [illegible] | . | [illegible] | [illegible] | [illegible] | [illegible] | [illegible] | [illegible] | . | . | . | [illegible] | . | . |
| KERRY, | [illegible] | [illegible] | [illegible] | . | [illegible] | [illegible] | [illegible] | [illegible] | . | . | . | . | . | . | . |
| KILDARE, | [illegible] | [illegible] | . | [illegible] | [illegible] | [illegible] | [illegible] | [illegible] | [illegible] | . | . | . | . | . | . |
| KILKENNY, | [illegible] | [illegible] | [illegible] | . | . | [illegible] | [illegible] | [illegible] | [illegible] | . | . | . | . | . | . |
| KING'S, | [illegible] | [illegible] | . | . | [illegible] | [illegible] | [illegible] | [illegible] | [illegible] | . | . | . | . | . | . |
| LEITRIM, | [illegible] | [illegible] | . | [illegible] | [illegible] | [illegible] | [illegible] | [illegible] | [illegible] | . | . | . | . | [illegible] | . |
| LIMERICK, | [illegible] | [illegible] | . | . | [illegible] | [illegible] | [illegible] | [illegible] | . | . | . | [illegible] | . | . | . |
| LONDONDERRY, | [illegible] | [illegible] | [illegible] | [illegible] | [illegible] | [illegible] | [illegible] | [illegible] | [illegible] | . | [illegible] | . | . | . | . |
| LONGFORD, | [illegible] | [illegible] | . | . | [illegible] | [illegible] | [illegible] | [illegible] | [illegible] | . | . | . | . | . | . |
| LOUTH and [illegible], County of Town, | [illegible] | [illegible] | . | [illegible] | [illegible] | [illegible] | [illegible] | [illegible] | [illegible] | . | [illegible] | . | . | . | . |
| MAYO, | [illegible] | [illegible] | [illegible] | . | [illegible] | [illegible] | [illegible] | [illegible] | . | . | . | . | . | . | . |
| MEATH, | [illegible] | [illegible] | [illegible] | [illegible] | [illegible] | [illegible] | [illegible] | [illegible] | [illegible] | . | . | . | . | . | . |
| MONAGHAN, | [illegible] | [illegible] | . | [illegible] | [illegible] | [illegible] | [illegible] | [illegible] | [illegible] | . | . | . | . | . | . |
| QUEEN'S, | [illegible] | [illegible] | . | . | [illegible] | [illegible] | [illegible] | [illegible] | [illegible] | . | . | . | . | . | . |
| ROSCOMMON, | [illegible] | [illegible] | [illegible] | [illegible] | [illegible] | [illegible] | [illegible] | [illegible] | [illegible] | . | . | . | [illegible] | . | . |
| SLIGO, | [illegible] | [illegible] | [illegible] | [illegible] | [illegible] | [illegible] | . | . | . | . | . | . | . | . | . |
| TIPPERARY, | [illegible] | [illegible] | . | . | [illegible] | [illegible] | [illegible] | [illegible] | [illegible] | . | . | . | . | [illegible] | . |
| TYRONE, | [illegible] | [illegible] | [illegible] | [illegible] | [illegible] | [illegible] | [illegible] | [illegible] | [illegible] | . | [illegible] | . | . | . | . |
| WATERFORD, | [illegible] | [illegible] | . | [illegible] | [illegible] | [illegible] | [illegible] | [illegible] | . | . | . | . | . | . | . |
| WESTMEATH, | [illegible] | [illegible] | . | [illegible] | [illegible] | [illegible] | [illegible] | [illegible] | [illegible] | . | . | . | . | . | . |
| WEXFORD, | [illegible] | [illegible] | . | [illegible] | [illegible] | [illegible] | [illegible] | [illegible] | [illegible] | . | . | . | . | . | . |
| WICKLOW, | [illegible] | [illegible] | [illegible] | [illegible] | . | [illegible] | [illegible] | [illegible] | [illegible] | . | . | . | . | . | . |

Table 17.—Showing, by Counties and Provinces, the

| Counties and Provinces. | [illegible] | | | | | | | | | | | |
|---|---|---|---|---|---|---|---|---|---|---|---|---|
| | [illegible] | | | [illegible] | | | [illegible] | | | [illegible] | | |
| | Bred in Ireland. | Imported. | Total. | Bred in Ireland. | Imported. | Total. | Bred in Ireland. | Imported. | Total. | Bred in Ireland. | Imported. | Total. |
| **Leinster.** | | | | | | | | | | | | |
| Carlow, | [illegible] | [illegible] | [illegible] | [illegible] | [illegible] | [illegible] | [illegible] | [illegible] | [illegible] | [illegible] | [illegible] | [illegible] |
| Dublin, | [illegible] | [illegible] | [illegible] | [illegible] | [illegible] | [illegible] | [illegible] | [illegible] | [illegible] | [illegible] | [illegible] | [illegible] |
| Kildare, | [illegible] | [illegible] | [illegible] | [illegible] | [illegible] | [illegible] | [illegible] | [illegible] | [illegible] | [illegible] | [illegible] | [illegible] |
| Kilkenny, | [illegible] | [illegible] | [illegible] | [illegible] | [illegible] | [illegible] | [illegible] | [illegible] | [illegible] | [illegible] | [illegible] | [illegible] |
| King's, | [illegible] | [illegible] | [illegible] | [illegible] | [illegible] | [illegible] | [illegible] | [illegible] | [illegible] | [illegible] | [illegible] | [illegible] |
| Longford, | [illegible] | [illegible] | [illegible] | [illegible] | [illegible] | [illegible] | [illegible] | [illegible] | [illegible] | [illegible] | [illegible] | [illegible] |
| Louth, | [illegible] | [illegible] | [illegible] | [illegible] | [illegible] | [illegible] | [illegible] | [illegible] | [illegible] | [illegible] | [illegible] | [illegible] |
| Meath, | [illegible] | [illegible] | [illegible] | [illegible] | [illegible] | [illegible] | [illegible] | [illegible] | [illegible] | [illegible] | [illegible] | [illegible] |
| Queen's, | [illegible] | [illegible] | [illegible] | [illegible] | [illegible] | [illegible] | [illegible] | [illegible] | [illegible] | [illegible] | [illegible] | [illegible] |
| Westmeath, | [illegible] | [illegible] | [illegible] | [illegible] | [illegible] | [illegible] | [illegible] | [illegible] | [illegible] | [illegible] | [illegible] | [illegible] |
| Wexford, | [illegible] | [illegible] | [illegible] | [illegible] | [illegible] | [illegible] | [illegible] | [illegible] | [illegible] | [illegible] | [illegible] | [illegible] |
| Wicklow, | [illegible] | [illegible] | [illegible] | [illegible] | [illegible] | [illegible] | [illegible] | [illegible] | [illegible] | [illegible] | [illegible] | [illegible] |
| Total of Leinster, | [illegible] | [illegible] | [illegible] | [illegible] | [illegible] | [illegible] | [illegible] | [illegible] | [illegible] | [illegible] | [illegible] | [illegible] |
| **Munster.** | | | | | | | | | | | | |
| Clare, | [illegible] | [illegible] | [illegible] | [illegible] | [illegible] | [illegible] | [illegible] | [illegible] | [illegible] | [illegible] | [illegible] | [illegible] |
| Cork, E.R., | [illegible] | [illegible] | [illegible] | [illegible] | [illegible] | [illegible] | [illegible] | [illegible] | [illegible] | [illegible] | [illegible] | [illegible] |
| Cork, W.R., | [illegible] | [illegible] | [illegible] | [illegible] | [illegible] | [illegible] | [illegible] | [illegible] | [illegible] | [illegible] | [illegible] | [illegible] |
| Kerry, | [illegible] | [illegible] | [illegible] | [illegible] | [illegible] | [illegible] | [illegible] | [illegible] | [illegible] | [illegible] | [illegible] | [illegible] |
| Limerick, | [illegible] | [illegible] | [illegible] | [illegible] | [illegible] | [illegible] | [illegible] | [illegible] | [illegible] | [illegible] | [illegible] | [illegible] |
| Tipperary N.R., | [illegible] | [illegible] | [illegible] | [illegible] | [illegible] | [illegible] | [illegible] | [illegible] | [illegible] | [illegible] | [illegible] | [illegible] |
| Tipperary S.R., | [illegible] | [illegible] | [illegible] | [illegible] | [illegible] | [illegible] | [illegible] | [illegible] | [illegible] | [illegible] | [illegible] | [illegible] |
| Waterford, | [illegible] | [illegible] | [illegible] | [illegible] | [illegible] | [illegible] | [illegible] | [illegible] | [illegible] | [illegible] | [illegible] | [illegible] |
| Total of Munster, | [illegible] | [illegible] | [illegible] | [illegible] | [illegible] | [illegible] | [illegible] | [illegible] | [illegible] | [illegible] | [illegible] | [illegible] |
| **Ulster.** | | | | | | | | | | | | |
| Antrim, | [illegible] | [illegible] | [illegible] | [illegible] | [illegible] | [illegible] | [illegible] | [illegible] | [illegible] | [illegible] | [illegible] | [illegible] |
| Armagh, | [illegible] | [illegible] | [illegible] | [illegible] | [illegible] | [illegible] | [illegible] | [illegible] | [illegible] | [illegible] | [illegible] | [illegible] |
| Cavan, | [illegible] | [illegible] | [illegible] | [illegible] | [illegible] | [illegible] | [illegible] | [illegible] | [illegible] | [illegible] | [illegible] | [illegible] |
| Donegal, | [illegible] | [illegible] | [illegible] | [illegible] | [illegible] | [illegible] | [illegible] | [illegible] | [illegible] | [illegible] | [illegible] | [illegible] |
| Down, | [illegible] | [illegible] | [illegible] | [illegible] | [illegible] | [illegible] | [illegible] | [illegible] | [illegible] | [illegible] | [illegible] | [illegible] |
| Fermanagh, | [illegible] | [illegible] | [illegible] | [illegible] | [illegible] | [illegible] | [illegible] | [illegible] | [illegible] | [illegible] | [illegible] | [illegible] |
| Londonderry, | [illegible] | [illegible] | [illegible] | [illegible] | [illegible] | [illegible] | [illegible] | [illegible] | [illegible] | [illegible] | [illegible] | [illegible] |
| Monaghan, | [illegible] | [illegible] | [illegible] | [illegible] | [illegible] | [illegible] | [illegible] | [illegible] | [illegible] | [illegible] | [illegible] | [illegible] |
| Tyrone, | [illegible] | [illegible] | [illegible] | [illegible] | [illegible] | [illegible] | [illegible] | [illegible] | [illegible] | [illegible] | [illegible] | [illegible] |
| Total of Ulster, | [illegible] | [illegible] | [illegible] | [illegible] | [illegible] | [illegible] | [illegible] | [illegible] | [illegible] | [illegible] | [illegible] | [illegible] |
| **Connaught.** | | | | | | | | | | | | |
| Galway, | [illegible] | [illegible] | [illegible] | [illegible] | [illegible] | [illegible] | [illegible] | [illegible] | [illegible] | [illegible] | [illegible] | [illegible] |
| Leitrim, | [illegible] | [illegible] | [illegible] | [illegible] | [illegible] | [illegible] | [illegible] | [illegible] | [illegible] | [illegible] | [illegible] | [illegible] |
| Mayo, | [illegible] | [illegible] | [illegible] | [illegible] | [illegible] | [illegible] | [illegible] | [illegible] | [illegible] | [illegible] | [illegible] | [illegible] |
| Roscommon, | [illegible] | [illegible] | [illegible] | [illegible] | [illegible] | [illegible] | [illegible] | [illegible] | [illegible] | [illegible] | [illegible] | [illegible] |
| Sligo, | [illegible] | [illegible] | [illegible] | [illegible] | [illegible] | [illegible] | [illegible] | [illegible] | [illegible] | [illegible] | [illegible] | [illegible] |
| Total of Connaught, | [illegible] | [illegible] | [illegible] | [illegible] | [illegible] | [illegible] | [illegible] | [illegible] | [illegible] | [illegible] | [illegible] | [illegible] |
| Total of Ireland, | [illegible] | [illegible] | [illegible] | [illegible] | [illegible] | [illegible] | [illegible] | [illegible] | [illegible] | [illegible] | [illegible] | [illegible] |

* For a detailed statement of the [illegible]

Number of Sires serving Mares in Ireland in the Year 187[illegible]

| Horses. | | | | | | All other Breeds. | | | Total. | | | Counties and Provinces. |
|---|---|---|---|---|---|---|---|---|---|---|---|---|
| Thoroughbred. | | | Agricultural. | | | | | | | | | |
| Bred in Ireland. | Imported. | Total. | Bred in Ireland. | Imported. | Total. | Bred in Ireland. | Imported. | Total. | Bred in Ireland. | Imported. | Total. | |
| | | | | | | | | | | | | Leinster. |
| [illegible] | [illegible] | [illegible] | [illegible] | [illegible] | [illegible] | [illegible] | [illegible] | [illegible] | [illegible] | [illegible] | [illegible] | Carlow. |
| [illegible] | [illegible] | [illegible] | [illegible] | [illegible] | [illegible] | [illegible] | [illegible] | [illegible] | [illegible] | [illegible] | [illegible] | Dublin. |
| [illegible] | [illegible] | [illegible] | [illegible] | [illegible] | [illegible] | [illegible] | [illegible] | [illegible] | [illegible] | [illegible] | [illegible] | Kildare. |
| [illegible] | [illegible] | [illegible] | [illegible] | [illegible] | [illegible] | [illegible] | [illegible] | [illegible] | [illegible] | [illegible] | [illegible] | Kilkenny. |
| [illegible] | [illegible] | [illegible] | [illegible] | [illegible] | [illegible] | [illegible] | [illegible] | [illegible] | [illegible] | [illegible] | [illegible] | King's. |
| [illegible] | [illegible] | [illegible] | [illegible] | [illegible] | [illegible] | [illegible] | [illegible] | [illegible] | [illegible] | [illegible] | [illegible] | Longford. |
| [illegible] | [illegible] | [illegible] | [illegible] | [illegible] | [illegible] | [illegible] | [illegible] | [illegible] | [illegible] | [illegible] | [illegible] | Louth. |
| [illegible] | [illegible] | [illegible] | [illegible] | [illegible] | [illegible] | [illegible] | [illegible] | [illegible] | [illegible] | [illegible] | [illegible] | Meath. |
| [illegible] | [illegible] | [illegible] | [illegible] | [illegible] | [illegible] | [illegible] | [illegible] | [illegible] | [illegible] | [illegible] | [illegible] | Queen's. |
| [illegible] | [illegible] | [illegible] | [illegible] | [illegible] | [illegible] | [illegible] | [illegible] | [illegible] | [illegible] | [illegible] | [illegible] | Westmeath. |
| [illegible] | [illegible] | [illegible] | [illegible] | [illegible] | [illegible] | [illegible] | [illegible] | [illegible] | [illegible] | [illegible] | [illegible] | Wexford. |
| [illegible] | [illegible] | [illegible] | [illegible] | [illegible] | [illegible] | [illegible] | [illegible] | [illegible] | [illegible] | [illegible] | [illegible] | Wicklow. |
| [illegible] | [illegible] | [illegible] | [illegible] | [illegible] | [illegible] | [illegible] | [illegible] | [illegible] | [illegible] | [illegible] | [illegible] | Total of Leinster. |
| | | | | | | | | | | | | Munster. |
| [illegible] | [illegible] | [illegible] | [illegible] | [illegible] | [illegible] | [illegible] | [illegible] | [illegible] | [illegible] | [illegible] | [illegible] | Clare. |
| [illegible] | [illegible] | [illegible] | [illegible] | [illegible] | [illegible] | [illegible] | [illegible] | [illegible] | [illegible] | [illegible] | [illegible] | Cork, E.R. |
| [illegible] | [illegible] | [illegible] | [illegible] | [illegible] | [illegible] | [illegible] | [illegible] | [illegible] | [illegible] | [illegible] | [illegible] | Cork, W.R. |
| [illegible] | [illegible] | [illegible] | [illegible] | [illegible] | [illegible] | [illegible] | [illegible] | [illegible] | [illegible] | [illegible] | [illegible] | Kerry. |
| [illegible] | [illegible] | [illegible] | [illegible] | [illegible] | [illegible] | [illegible] | [illegible] | [illegible] | [illegible] | [illegible] | [illegible] | Limerick. |
| [illegible] | [illegible] | [illegible] | [illegible] | [illegible] | [illegible] | [illegible] | [illegible] | [illegible] | [illegible] | [illegible] | [illegible] | Tipperary, N.R. |
| [illegible] | [illegible] | [illegible] | [illegible] | [illegible] | [illegible] | [illegible] | [illegible] | [illegible] | [illegible] | [illegible] | [illegible] | Tipperary, S.R. |
| [illegible] | [illegible] | [illegible] | [illegible] | [illegible] | [illegible] | [illegible] | [illegible] | [illegible] | [illegible] | [illegible] | [illegible] | Waterford. |
| [illegible] | [illegible] | [illegible] | [illegible] | [illegible] | [illegible] | [illegible] | [illegible] | [illegible] | [illegible] | [illegible] | [illegible] | Total of Munster. |
| | | | | | | | | | | | | Ulster. |
| [illegible] | [illegible] | [illegible] | [illegible] | [illegible] | [illegible] | [illegible] | [illegible] | [illegible] | [illegible] | [illegible] | [illegible] | Antrim. |
| [illegible] | [illegible] | [illegible] | [illegible] | [illegible] | [illegible] | [illegible] | [illegible] | [illegible] | [illegible] | [illegible] | [illegible] | Armagh. |
| [illegible] | [illegible] | [illegible] | [illegible] | [illegible] | [illegible] | [illegible] | [illegible] | [illegible] | [illegible] | [illegible] | [illegible] | Cavan. |
| [illegible] | [illegible] | [illegible] | [illegible] | [illegible] | [illegible] | [illegible] | [illegible] | [illegible] | [illegible] | [illegible] | [illegible] | Donegal. |
| [illegible] | [illegible] | [illegible] | [illegible] | [illegible] | [illegible] | [illegible] | [illegible] | [illegible] | [illegible] | [illegible] | [illegible] | Down. |
| [illegible] | [illegible] | [illegible] | [illegible] | [illegible] | [illegible] | [illegible] | [illegible] | [illegible] | [illegible] | [illegible] | [illegible] | Fermanagh. |
| [illegible] | [illegible] | [illegible] | [illegible] | [illegible] | [illegible] | [illegible] | [illegible] | [illegible] | [illegible] | [illegible] | [illegible] | Londonderry. |
| [illegible] | [illegible] | [illegible] | [illegible] | [illegible] | [illegible] | [illegible] | [illegible] | [illegible] | [illegible] | [illegible] | [illegible] | Monaghan. |
| [illegible] | [illegible] | [illegible] | [illegible] | [illegible] | [illegible] | [illegible] | [illegible] | [illegible] | [illegible] | [illegible] | [illegible] | Tyrone. |
| [illegible] | [illegible] | [illegible] | [illegible] | [illegible] | [illegible] | [illegible] | [illegible] | [illegible] | [illegible] | [illegible] | [illegible] | Total of Ulster. |
| | | | | | | | | | | | | Connaught. |
| [illegible] | [illegible] | [illegible] | [illegible] | [illegible] | [illegible] | [illegible] | [illegible] | [illegible] | [illegible] | [illegible] | [illegible] | Galway. |
| [illegible] | [illegible] | [illegible] | [illegible] | [illegible] | [illegible] | [illegible] | [illegible] | [illegible] | [illegible] | [illegible] | [illegible] | Leitrim. |
| [illegible] | [illegible] | [illegible] | [illegible] | [illegible] | [illegible] | [illegible] | [illegible] | [illegible] | [illegible] | [illegible] | [illegible] | Mayo. |
| [illegible] | [illegible] | [illegible] | [illegible] | [illegible] | [illegible] | [illegible] | [illegible] | [illegible] | [illegible] | [illegible] | [illegible] | Roscommon. |
| [illegible] | [illegible] | [illegible] | [illegible] | [illegible] | [illegible] | [illegible] | [illegible] | [illegible] | [illegible] | [illegible] | [illegible] | Sligo. |
| [illegible] | [illegible] | [illegible] | [illegible] | [illegible] | [illegible] | [illegible] | [illegible] | [illegible] | [illegible] | [illegible] | [illegible] | Total of Connaught. |
| [illegible] | [illegible] | [illegible] | [illegible] | [illegible] | [illegible] | [illegible] | [illegible] | [illegible] | [illegible] | [illegible] | [illegible] | Total of Ireland. |

[illegible] under the head All other Breeds in 18[illegible], see page [illegible].

TABLE 18.—Showing, by Counties and Provinces, the number

| COUNTIES AND PROVINCES. | [illegible] | | | [illegible] | | | [illegible] | | | [illegible] | | | [illegible] | | |
|---|---|---|---|---|---|---|---|---|---|---|---|---|---|---|---|
| | [illegible] | [illegible] | [illegible] | [illegible] | [illegible] | [illegible] | [illegible] | [illegible] | [illegible] | [illegible] | [illegible] | [illegible] | [illegible] | [illegible] | [illegible] |
| LEINSTER: | | | | | | | | | | | | | | | |
| Carlow, | [illegible] | [illegible] | [illegible] | [illegible] | [illegible] | [illegible] | [illegible] | [illegible] | [illegible] | [illegible] | [illegible] | [illegible] | [illegible] | [illegible] | [illegible] |
| Dublin, | [illegible] | [illegible] | [illegible] | [illegible] | [illegible] | [illegible] | [illegible] | [illegible] | [illegible] | [illegible] | [illegible] | [illegible] | [illegible] | [illegible] | [illegible] |
| Kildare, | [illegible] | [illegible] | [illegible] | [illegible] | [illegible] | [illegible] | [illegible] | [illegible] | [illegible] | [illegible] | [illegible] | [illegible] | [illegible] | [illegible] | [illegible] |
| Kilkenny, | [illegible] | [illegible] | [illegible] | [illegible] | [illegible] | [illegible] | [illegible] | [illegible] | [illegible] | [illegible] | [illegible] | [illegible] | [illegible] | [illegible] | [illegible] |
| King's, | [illegible] | [illegible] | [illegible] | [illegible] | [illegible] | [illegible] | [illegible] | [illegible] | [illegible] | [illegible] | [illegible] | [illegible] | [illegible] | [illegible] | [illegible] |
| Longford, | [illegible] | [illegible] | [illegible] | [illegible] | [illegible] | [illegible] | [illegible] | [illegible] | [illegible] | [illegible] | [illegible] | [illegible] | [illegible] | [illegible] | [illegible] |
| Louth, | [illegible] | [illegible] | [illegible] | [illegible] | [illegible] | [illegible] | [illegible] | [illegible] | [illegible] | [illegible] | [illegible] | [illegible] | [illegible] | [illegible] | [illegible] |
| Meath, | [illegible] | [illegible] | [illegible] | [illegible] | [illegible] | [illegible] | [illegible] | [illegible] | [illegible] | [illegible] | [illegible] | [illegible] | [illegible] | [illegible] | [illegible] |
| Queen's, | [illegible] | [illegible] | [illegible] | [illegible] | [illegible] | [illegible] | [illegible] | [illegible] | [illegible] | [illegible] | [illegible] | [illegible] | [illegible] | [illegible] | [illegible] |
| Westmeath, | [illegible] | [illegible] | [illegible] | [illegible] | [illegible] | [illegible] | [illegible] | [illegible] | [illegible] | [illegible] | [illegible] | [illegible] | [illegible] | [illegible] | [illegible] |
| Wexford, | [illegible] | [illegible] | [illegible] | [illegible] | [illegible] | [illegible] | [illegible] | [illegible] | [illegible] | [illegible] | [illegible] | [illegible] | [illegible] | [illegible] | [illegible] |
| Wicklow, | [illegible] | [illegible] | [illegible] | [illegible] | [illegible] | [illegible] | [illegible] | [illegible] | [illegible] | [illegible] | [illegible] | [illegible] | [illegible] | [illegible] | [illegible] |
| Total of Leinster, | [illegible] | [illegible] | [illegible] | [illegible] | [illegible] | [illegible] | [illegible] | [illegible] | [illegible] | [illegible] | [illegible] | [illegible] | [illegible] | [illegible] | [illegible] |
| MUNSTER: | | | | | | | | | | | | | | | |
| Clare, | [illegible] | [illegible] | [illegible] | [illegible] | [illegible] | [illegible] | [illegible] | [illegible] | [illegible] | [illegible] | [illegible] | [illegible] | [illegible] | [illegible] | [illegible] |
| Cork, E.R. | [illegible] | [illegible] | [illegible] | [illegible] | [illegible] | [illegible] | [illegible] | [illegible] | [illegible] | [illegible] | [illegible] | [illegible] | [illegible] | [illegible] | [illegible] |
| Cork, W.R. | [illegible] | [illegible] | [illegible] | [illegible] | [illegible] | [illegible] | [illegible] | [illegible] | [illegible] | [illegible] | [illegible] | [illegible] | [illegible] | [illegible] | [illegible] |
| Kerry, | [illegible] | [illegible] | [illegible] | [illegible] | [illegible] | [illegible] | [illegible] | [illegible] | [illegible] | [illegible] | [illegible] | [illegible] | [illegible] | [illegible] | [illegible] |
| Limerick, | [illegible] | [illegible] | [illegible] | [illegible] | [illegible] | [illegible] | [illegible] | [illegible] | [illegible] | [illegible] | [illegible] | [illegible] | [illegible] | [illegible] | [illegible] |
| Tipperary, N.R. | [illegible] | [illegible] | [illegible] | [illegible] | [illegible] | [illegible] | [illegible] | [illegible] | [illegible] | [illegible] | [illegible] | [illegible] | [illegible] | [illegible] | [illegible] |
| Tipperary, S.R. | [illegible] | [illegible] | [illegible] | [illegible] | [illegible] | [illegible] | [illegible] | [illegible] | [illegible] | [illegible] | [illegible] | [illegible] | [illegible] | [illegible] | [illegible] |
| Waterford, | [illegible] | [illegible] | [illegible] | [illegible] | [illegible] | [illegible] | [illegible] | [illegible] | [illegible] | [illegible] | [illegible] | [illegible] | [illegible] | [illegible] | [illegible] |
| Total of Munster, | [illegible] | [illegible] | [illegible] | [illegible] | [illegible] | [illegible] | [illegible] | [illegible] | [illegible] | [illegible] | [illegible] | [illegible] | [illegible] | [illegible] | [illegible] |
| ULSTER: | | | | | | | | | | | | | | | |
| Antrim, | [illegible] | [illegible] | [illegible] | [illegible] | [illegible] | [illegible] | [illegible] | [illegible] | [illegible] | [illegible] | [illegible] | [illegible] | [illegible] | [illegible] | [illegible] |
| Armagh, | [illegible] | [illegible] | [illegible] | [illegible] | [illegible] | [illegible] | [illegible] | [illegible] | [illegible] | [illegible] | [illegible] | [illegible] | [illegible] | [illegible] | [illegible] |
| Cavan, | [illegible] | [illegible] | [illegible] | [illegible] | [illegible] | [illegible] | [illegible] | [illegible] | [illegible] | [illegible] | [illegible] | [illegible] | [illegible] | [illegible] | [illegible] |
| Donegal, | [illegible] | [illegible] | [illegible] | [illegible] | [illegible] | [illegible] | [illegible] | [illegible] | [illegible] | [illegible] | [illegible] | [illegible] | [illegible] | [illegible] | [illegible] |
| Down, | [illegible] | [illegible] | [illegible] | [illegible] | [illegible] | [illegible] | [illegible] | [illegible] | [illegible] | [illegible] | [illegible] | [illegible] | [illegible] | [illegible] | [illegible] |
| Fermanagh, | [illegible] | [illegible] | [illegible] | [illegible] | [illegible] | [illegible] | [illegible] | [illegible] | [illegible] | [illegible] | [illegible] | [illegible] | [illegible] | [illegible] | [illegible] |
| Londonderry, | [illegible] | [illegible] | [illegible] | [illegible] | [illegible] | [illegible] | [illegible] | [illegible] | [illegible] | [illegible] | [illegible] | [illegible] | [illegible] | [illegible] | [illegible] |
| Monaghan, | [illegible] | [illegible] | [illegible] | [illegible] | [illegible] | [illegible] | [illegible] | [illegible] | [illegible] | [illegible] | [illegible] | [illegible] | [illegible] | [illegible] | [illegible] |
| Tyrone, | [illegible] | [illegible] | [illegible] | [illegible] | [illegible] | [illegible] | [illegible] | [illegible] | [illegible] | [illegible] | [illegible] | [illegible] | [illegible] | [illegible] | [illegible] |
| Total of Ulster, | [illegible] | [illegible] | [illegible] | [illegible] | [illegible] | [illegible] | [illegible] | [illegible] | [illegible] | [illegible] | [illegible] | [illegible] | [illegible] | [illegible] | [illegible] |
| CONNAUGHT: | | | | | | | | | | | | | | | |
| Galway, | [illegible] | [illegible] | [illegible] | [illegible] | [illegible] | [illegible] | [illegible] | [illegible] | [illegible] | [illegible] | [illegible] | [illegible] | [illegible] | [illegible] | [illegible] |
| Leitrim, | [illegible] | [illegible] | [illegible] | [illegible] | [illegible] | [illegible] | [illegible] | [illegible] | [illegible] | [illegible] | [illegible] | [illegible] | [illegible] | [illegible] | [illegible] |
| Mayo, | [illegible] | [illegible] | [illegible] | [illegible] | [illegible] | [illegible] | [illegible] | [illegible] | [illegible] | [illegible] | [illegible] | [illegible] | [illegible] | [illegible] | [illegible] |
| Roscommon, | [illegible] | [illegible] | [illegible] | [illegible] | [illegible] | [illegible] | [illegible] | [illegible] | [illegible] | [illegible] | [illegible] | [illegible] | [illegible] | [illegible] | [illegible] |
| Sligo, | [illegible] | [illegible] | [illegible] | [illegible] | [illegible] | [illegible] | [illegible] | [illegible] | [illegible] | [illegible] | [illegible] | [illegible] | [illegible] | [illegible] | [illegible] |
| Total of Connaught, | [illegible] | [illegible] | [illegible] | [illegible] | [illegible] | [illegible] | [illegible] | [illegible] | [illegible] | [illegible] | [illegible] | [illegible] | [illegible] | [illegible] | [illegible] |
| Total of Ireland, | [illegible] | [illegible] | [illegible] | [illegible] | [illegible] | [illegible] | [illegible] | [illegible] | [illegible] | [illegible] | [illegible] | [illegible] | [illegible] | [illegible] | [illegible] |

…of Bulls of the Principal Breeds, &c., in Ireland in the year 185[illegible].

| [illegible] | | | [illegible] | | | [illegible] | | | [illegible] | | | Counties and Provinces. |
|---|---|---|---|---|---|---|---|---|---|---|---|---|
| [illegible] | [illegible] | [illegible] | [illegible] | [illegible] | [illegible] | [illegible] | [illegible] | [illegible] | [illegible] | [illegible] | [illegible] | |
| | | | | | | | | | | | | **Leinster:** |
| [illegible] | [illegible] | [illegible] | [illegible] | [illegible] | [illegible] | [illegible] | [illegible] | [illegible] | [illegible] | [illegible] | [illegible] | Carlow. |
| [illegible] | [illegible] | [illegible] | [illegible] | [illegible] | [illegible] | [illegible] | [illegible] | [illegible] | [illegible] | [illegible] | [illegible] | Dublin. |
| [illegible] | [illegible] | [illegible] | [illegible] | [illegible] | [illegible] | [illegible] | [illegible] | [illegible] | [illegible] | [illegible] | [illegible] | Kildare. |
| [illegible] | [illegible] | [illegible] | [illegible] | [illegible] | [illegible] | [illegible] | [illegible] | [illegible] | [illegible] | [illegible] | [illegible] | Kilkenny. |
| [illegible] | [illegible] | [illegible] | [illegible] | [illegible] | [illegible] | [illegible] | [illegible] | [illegible] | [illegible] | [illegible] | [illegible] | King's. |
| [illegible] | [illegible] | [illegible] | [illegible] | [illegible] | [illegible] | [illegible] | [illegible] | [illegible] | [illegible] | [illegible] | [illegible] | Longford. |
| [illegible] | [illegible] | [illegible] | [illegible] | [illegible] | [illegible] | [illegible] | [illegible] | [illegible] | [illegible] | [illegible] | [illegible] | Louth. |
| [illegible] | [illegible] | [illegible] | [illegible] | [illegible] | [illegible] | [illegible] | [illegible] | [illegible] | [illegible] | [illegible] | [illegible] | Meath. |
| [illegible] | [illegible] | [illegible] | [illegible] | [illegible] | [illegible] | [illegible] | [illegible] | [illegible] | [illegible] | [illegible] | [illegible] | Queen's. |
| [illegible] | [illegible] | [illegible] | [illegible] | [illegible] | [illegible] | [illegible] | [illegible] | [illegible] | [illegible] | [illegible] | [illegible] | Westmeath. |
| [illegible] | [illegible] | [illegible] | [illegible] | [illegible] | [illegible] | [illegible] | [illegible] | [illegible] | [illegible] | [illegible] | [illegible] | Wexford. |
| [illegible] | [illegible] | [illegible] | [illegible] | [illegible] | [illegible] | [illegible] | [illegible] | [illegible] | [illegible] | [illegible] | [illegible] | Wicklow. |
| [illegible] | [illegible] | [illegible] | [illegible] | [illegible] | [illegible] | [illegible] | [illegible] | [illegible] | [illegible] | [illegible] | [illegible] | Total of Leinster. |
| | | | | | | | | | | | | **Munster:** |
| [illegible] | [illegible] | [illegible] | [illegible] | [illegible] | [illegible] | [illegible] | [illegible] | [illegible] | [illegible] | [illegible] | [illegible] | Clare. |
| [illegible] | [illegible] | [illegible] | [illegible] | [illegible] | [illegible] | [illegible] | [illegible] | [illegible] | [illegible] | [illegible] | [illegible] | Cork, E.R. |
| [illegible] | [illegible] | [illegible] | [illegible] | [illegible] | [illegible] | [illegible] | [illegible] | [illegible] | [illegible] | [illegible] | [illegible] | Cork, W.R. |
| [illegible] | [illegible] | [illegible] | [illegible] | [illegible] | [illegible] | [illegible] | [illegible] | [illegible] | [illegible] | [illegible] | [illegible] | Kerry. |
| [illegible] | [illegible] | [illegible] | [illegible] | [illegible] | [illegible] | [illegible] | [illegible] | [illegible] | [illegible] | [illegible] | [illegible] | Limerick. |
| [illegible] | [illegible] | [illegible] | [illegible] | [illegible] | [illegible] | [illegible] | [illegible] | [illegible] | [illegible] | [illegible] | [illegible] | Tipperary, N.R. |
| [illegible] | [illegible] | [illegible] | [illegible] | [illegible] | [illegible] | [illegible] | [illegible] | [illegible] | [illegible] | [illegible] | [illegible] | Tipperary, S.R. |
| [illegible] | [illegible] | [illegible] | [illegible] | [illegible] | [illegible] | [illegible] | [illegible] | [illegible] | [illegible] | [illegible] | [illegible] | Waterford. |
| [illegible] | [illegible] | [illegible] | [illegible] | [illegible] | [illegible] | [illegible] | [illegible] | [illegible] | [illegible] | [illegible] | [illegible] | Total of Munster. |
| | | | | | | | | | | | | **[illegible]:** |
| [illegible] | [illegible] | [illegible] | [illegible] | [illegible] | [illegible] | [illegible] | [illegible] | [illegible] | [illegible] | [illegible] | [illegible] | Antrim. |
| [illegible] | [illegible] | [illegible] | [illegible] | [illegible] | [illegible] | [illegible] | [illegible] | [illegible] | [illegible] | [illegible] | [illegible] | Armagh. |
| [illegible] | [illegible] | [illegible] | [illegible] | [illegible] | [illegible] | [illegible] | [illegible] | [illegible] | [illegible] | [illegible] | [illegible] | Cavan. |
| [illegible] | [illegible] | [illegible] | [illegible] | [illegible] | [illegible] | [illegible] | [illegible] | [illegible] | [illegible] | [illegible] | [illegible] | Donegal. |
| [illegible] | [illegible] | [illegible] | [illegible] | [illegible] | [illegible] | [illegible] | [illegible] | [illegible] | [illegible] | [illegible] | [illegible] | Down. |
| [illegible] | [illegible] | [illegible] | [illegible] | [illegible] | [illegible] | [illegible] | [illegible] | [illegible] | [illegible] | [illegible] | [illegible] | Fermanagh. |
| [illegible] | [illegible] | [illegible] | [illegible] | [illegible] | [illegible] | [illegible] | [illegible] | [illegible] | [illegible] | [illegible] | [illegible] | Londonderry. |
| [illegible] | [illegible] | [illegible] | [illegible] | [illegible] | [illegible] | [illegible] | [illegible] | [illegible] | [illegible] | [illegible] | [illegible] | Monaghan. |
| [illegible] | [illegible] | [illegible] | [illegible] | [illegible] | [illegible] | [illegible] | [illegible] | [illegible] | [illegible] | [illegible] | [illegible] | Tyrone. |
| [illegible] | [illegible] | [illegible] | [illegible] | [illegible] | [illegible] | [illegible] | [illegible] | [illegible] | [illegible] | [illegible] | [illegible] | Total of [illegible]. |
| | | | | | | | | | | | | **Connaught:** |
| [illegible] | [illegible] | [illegible] | [illegible] | [illegible] | [illegible] | [illegible] | [illegible] | [illegible] | [illegible] | [illegible] | [illegible] | Galway. |
| [illegible] | [illegible] | [illegible] | [illegible] | [illegible] | [illegible] | [illegible] | [illegible] | [illegible] | [illegible] | [illegible] | [illegible] | Leitrim. |
| [illegible] | [illegible] | [illegible] | [illegible] | [illegible] | [illegible] | [illegible] | [illegible] | [illegible] | [illegible] | [illegible] | [illegible] | Mayo. |
| [illegible] | [illegible] | [illegible] | [illegible] | [illegible] | [illegible] | [illegible] | [illegible] | [illegible] | [illegible] | [illegible] | [illegible] | Roscommon. |
| [illegible] | [illegible] | [illegible] | [illegible] | [illegible] | [illegible] | [illegible] | [illegible] | [illegible] | [illegible] | [illegible] | [illegible] | Sligo. |
| [illegible] | [illegible] | [illegible] | [illegible] | [illegible] | [illegible] | [illegible] | [illegible] | [illegible] | [illegible] | [illegible] | [illegible] | Total of Connaught. |
| [illegible] | [illegible] | [illegible] | [illegible] | [illegible] | [illegible] | [illegible] | [illegible] | [illegible] | [illegible] | [illegible] | [illegible] | Total of Ireland. |

TABLE 19.—Showing the Number of AGRICULTURAL MACHINES in Ireland in 1896, having for their object the diminution of Manual Labour, the power employed in working them, and the Total Number in the Years 1865, 1875, 1881, 1886 and 1890, respectively.

| Names of Machines. | 1896. Power Employed. Water. | Steam. | Horse. | Manual. | Total Number. | Total in 1865. | Total in 1875. | Total in 1881. | Total in 1886. | Total in 1890. |
|---|---|---|---|---|---|---|---|---|---|---|
| Bone Crushing Machines, | . | . | [illegible] | . | [illegible] | [illegible] | [illegible] | [illegible] | [illegible] | [illegible] |
| Churning Machines, | [illegible] | [illegible] | [illegible] | [illegible] | [illegible] | [illegible] | [illegible] | [illegible] | [illegible] | [illegible] |
| Furze Cutters, | . | . | [illegible] | [illegible] | [illegible] | [illegible] | [illegible] | [illegible] | [illegible] | [illegible] |
| [illegible], | . | . | [illegible] | [illegible] | [illegible] | [illegible] | [illegible] | [illegible] | [illegible] | [illegible] |
| Harrow [illegible], | – | – | . | . | . | [illegible] | [illegible] | [illegible] | [illegible] | . |
| Hay, Chaff, and Straw Cutters, | [illegible] | [illegible] | [illegible] | [illegible] | [illegible] | [illegible] | [illegible] | [illegible] | [illegible] | [illegible] |
| Hay Collectors and Rakes, | – | . | [illegible] | . | [illegible] | [illegible] | [illegible] | [illegible] | [illegible] | [illegible] |
| Hay-making Machines, | . | – | [illegible] | . | [illegible] | [illegible] | [illegible] | [illegible] | [illegible] | [illegible] |
| [illegible] | . | . | [illegible] | . | [illegible] | [illegible] | – | [illegible] | [illegible] | [illegible] |
| Land Rollers, | . | . | [illegible] | – | [illegible] | [illegible] | [illegible] | [illegible] | [illegible] | [illegible] |
| Manure Distributors, | . | . | [illegible] | – | [illegible] | [illegible] | [illegible] | [illegible] | [illegible] | – |
| Mowing Machines, | . | . | [illegible] | . | [illegible] | [illegible] | [illegible] | [illegible] | [illegible] | [illegible] |
| Mowing and Reaping Machines (combined), | . | . | [illegible] | . | [illegible] | [illegible] | [illegible] | | | |
| [illegible], | [illegible] | [illegible] | [illegible] | [illegible] | [illegible] | [illegible] | [illegible] | [illegible] | [illegible] | [illegible] |
| Oil Cake Breakers, | [illegible] | [illegible] | [illegible] | [illegible] | [illegible] | [illegible] | [illegible] | [illegible] | [illegible] | [illegible] |
| Plough [illegible], | – | [illegible] | . | . | [illegible] | [illegible] | [illegible] | [illegible] | [illegible] | . |
| Potato Diggers, | . | . | [illegible] | . | [illegible] | [illegible] | [illegible] | [illegible] | [illegible] | [illegible] |
| Reaping Machines, | | [illegible] | [illegible] | . | [illegible] | [illegible] | [illegible] | [illegible] | [illegible] | [illegible] |
| Root Pulpers, | . | . | . | [illegible] | [illegible] | . | [illegible] | [illegible] | [illegible] | [illegible] |
| [illegible], | [illegible] | [illegible] | [illegible] | [illegible] | [illegible] | [illegible] | [illegible] | [illegible] | [illegible] | [illegible] |
| [illegible], | . | | [illegible] | [illegible] | [illegible] | [illegible] | [illegible] | [illegible] | [illegible] | [illegible] |
| Threshing Machines, | [illegible] | [illegible] | [illegible] | [illegible] | [illegible] | [illegible] | [illegible] | [illegible] | [illegible] | [illegible] |
| Turnip, Corn, &c., Sowing Machines, | . | [illegible] | [illegible] | [illegible] | [illegible] | [illegible] | [illegible] | [illegible] | [illegible] | [illegible] |
| Turnip Slicers and Root Cutters, | [illegible] | [illegible] | [illegible] | [illegible] | [illegible] | [illegible] | [illegible] | [illegible] | [illegible] | [illegible] |
| Turnip Thinners and [illegible], | – | . | [illegible] | – | [illegible] | [illegible] | [illegible] | [illegible] | [illegible] | [illegible] |
| Winnowing Machines, | [illegible] | [illegible] | [illegible] | [illegible] | [illegible] | [illegible] | [illegible] | [illegible] | [illegible] | [illegible] |
| Total, | [illegible] | [illegible] | [illegible] | [illegible] | [illegible] | [illegible] | [illegible] | [illegible] | [illegible] | [illegible] |

In addition to the above-named machines, 1,350 others were enumerated in the Returns for 1896, including 236 threshing and churning machines, 226 corn drills, 216 reaping and binding, 112 corn, oat, and furze bruisers, 83 self-binders, 64 binders, 28 hay lifters, 16 mowing and raking machines, 16 threshing and winnowing machines, 17 clod crushers, 15 haycock shifters, 15 mowing and self-binding machines, 15 turnip slicers and pulpers, 14 cultivators, 18 turnip drills, 12 cabbage cutters, 11 threshing and mowing, and the following worked by electricity—1 threshing, reaping, and churning machine, 1 threshing machine, 1 hay cutter, 1 oats cutter.

# OBSERVATIONS

OF THE

## DISTRICT INSPECTORS OF THE ROYAL IRISH CONSTABULARY AND OF THE SERGEANTS OF THE METROPOLITAN POLICE,

WHO ACTED AS SUPERINTENDENTS OF THE AGRICULTURAL STATISTICS;

IN REPLY TO A CIRCULAR DATED 10TH OCTOBER, 1894, ON THE PROBABLE CAUSE TO WHICH THE GOOD OR BAD YIELD OF THE VARIOUS CROPS IN EACH OF THEIR DISTRICTS MAY BE ATTRIBUTED.

---

### PROVINCE OF LEINSTER.

PROVINCE OF LEINSTER.

CARLOW COUNTY. *Bagenalstown D.*—29th Oct.—The crops generally have been very fair. The potato crop is unusually large. Barley and oats were a good crop, but suffered somewhat from heavy rain just before they were cut. *Carlow D.*—1st Nov.—The yield of the crops here this year was very unequal and varied to a remarkable manner in districts quite close to each other. On the whole oats were fairly good, but damaged by excessive rain. Barley suffered much in quality from the same cause. Roots were fair on the whole, but in places failed from early drought. Early hay was good in quality, but light in yield. Late hay, on the other hand, was abundant, but damaged by rain. Potatoes were everywhere good both in quality and quantity, and there is very little disease.

DUBLIN COUNTY. *Balbriggan D.*—1st Nov.—The past season has been on the whole favourable for agriculture, the early hay crop and the turnip crop proper being alone much below the average, owing to the dryness of the spring and early summer months. There has not been any extensive damage to crops from insects or fungi. In the district around Lusk the potato crop has suffered from fungi somewhat, the estimated damage being about 10 per cent. *Clontarf D.*—5th Nov.—The yield of grain crops in this district has been very good as regards quantity, but owing to the constant rainfall in July and August the quality has been very much deteriorated. The early hay crop was very light, but was of a very good description, as the weather was very favourable for saving it. There was a very good second crop, which was also well saved, the weather in September having proved fine. Green crops promise to be a very fair crop, having got the rain in July and August. Potato crop is very good as regards quantity and quality. There is no injury, so far as I can learn, from insects or fungi to the crops, as the farmers generally burn all weeds after the removal of the crops from the ground. *Chancery Lane D.*—31st Oct.—The several crops were good owing to the richness of the land, except that the turnip crop and hay was not so good as expected on account of the dry weather in the commencement of the season. *Kingstown D.*—1st Nov.—All crops are up to the usual average. The weather was slightly against farmers owing to the drought in June last. Mangolds and turnips had in many cases to be sown a second time. Again, the wet weather in August left the harvest late, otherwise it is believed to be a good season. There are no complaints of insects, fungi, or weeds in this district during the season. *Dundrum D.*—30th Oct.—The crops have been good all through this district. The fine autumn gave the various crops a good opportunity for ripening and being saved. *Lucan D.*—6th Nov.—The yield generally of the crops was above the average both in quantity and quality, and there is a good deal to be attributed to the very fine weather in September. There was no special injury to crops from insects or fungi. The reports from all quarters concerning the potato crop are highly favourable.

KILDARE COUNTY. *Athy D.*—1st Nov.—The drought in May and June was unfavourable to hay and turnips, but most favourable to potatoes. The potato crop is quite above the average. First crop hay was very light owing to the drought, but the later meadows were not so bad. Oats and other grain crops are fair, and the weather for harvesting was for the most part favourable. Straw is very light owing to drought in the months of May and June. The wet weather in July and August brought on the root crops, which are very fair. I cannot ascertain that any material damage was done by insects, fungi, or weeds.—*Kildare D.*—1st Nov.—I have no reports of injury being done by insects or fungi. Potatoes have been good; grain crop light, but something better than at first expected; the wet weather was much against it. Turnips and mangolds on the whole fair. First cut hay bad, owing to wet; that cut later on much better. *Naas D.*—5th Nov.—The low rates of produce are owing to the very wet weather prevalent in July and August. In some few cases, where the land is in large farms (e.g., Celbridge) the crops have been very good, potatoes especially, which are elsewhere inferior. In places the first crop of oats being broken down by rain, a second crop was only sown, and, as at Timahoe, the farmers allowed the first crop to waste so as to secure the second, hence the bad yield. *Robertstown D.*—6th Nov.—The crops are up to the average this year. Corn has yielded fairly well as the season favoured it. Root crops are also good, and there are no complaints of injury by insects, fungi, &c. Weeds only exist on neglected farms, and where, of course, only poor crops were grown.

KILKENNY COUNTY. *Callan D.*—6th Nov.—The good yield of the potato crop may be ascribed to the warm season, and the poor yield of hay may be attributed to the same cause. The various other crops have produced scarcely anything above or below the average yield. No injury has been done by insects or fungi. *Castlecomer D.*—1st Nov.—There was a considerable amount of second growth in oats and barley due to the heavy rains in July and August, yet the yield is above the average. Potatoes are a good crop, unusually so, in places; in heavy lands there was a large proportion of diseased tubers. Mangel and turnips are a light crop; failing altogether in some places. Where sown late, however, the yield is good. Hay on old meadows was very heavy, but first crop hay was light and not nearly up to the average. This is also owing to the long drought followed by heavy rains. Cabbage did well on damp and boggy land, but was not so good on light land. *Johnstown D.*—22nd Oct.—The harvest has been a very good one, except first crop hay, which was rather a light crop, potatoes especially very good. Seasonable weather had had much to say to this, and also use of good seeds and treatment of the land. No special injury to crops by insects, &c., to report. *Kilkenny D.*—6th Nov.—The potato crop is somewhat beyond the average produce, owing to the dry weather in the early part of the season. Straw is somewhat short, and old meadows rather below the average, owing to the long continued dry weather in the early season. The grain of the

PROVINCE OF LEINSTER.

different sorts of crops suffered [illegible] in consequence of the heavy rains in August, but on the whole there is a fair average produce. Turnips and mangolds suffered from insects in the early part of the season owing to the drought, but made rapid progress when the rain came and are a fairly good crop. There have been no cases discovered of injury to crops from fungi, nor from insects except what has been mentioned regarding turnips and mangolds. *Kilkenny D.*—30th Oct.—There has been no injury done to the crops by fungi or insects. All the crops have been fairly good. *Thomastown D.*—6th Nov.—The potato crop was an excellent one owing to the fine dry weather in May and June. Oats and barley are not so good a crop as usual owing to the wet weather in August and September. The early crop of hay was light owing to the continued dry weather, but the after grass or second crop was very fair. No injury was done to the crops by insects or fungi.

KING'S COUNTY.—*Banagher D.*—15th Nov.—All attribute the good potato crop this year to the favourable season and the absence of blight. One sergeant (a very intelligent man) gives an additional reason, viz., that owing to the severe frost in early spring the growth of tubers was retarded, and these retained full strength when sown. Barley and oats are fully 30 per cent. below average of previous years, which is attributed to prolonged drought in early summer. Same remark applies to turnips and hay which are below the average. *Edenderry D.*—7th Nov.—Generally speaking the increase or decrease is of such small consequence that special remarks as to the cause regarding any particular crop seem unnecessary. The turnip crop is, perhaps, the exception, as owing to the very dry summer which prevented the growth of the seed a second sowing was in many cases necessary. Insects, fungi, or weeds have done no special injury this season. *Parsonstown D.*—31st Oct.—No complaint has been made of any special injury to crops by insects or fungi. The poor yield in first-crop hay is attributable to the continued drought that prevailed in the months of May and June. Oats, barley, and turnips also suffered from the same cause. Potatoes were a very plentiful crop owing to the dry weather and no blight appearing. *Shinrone D.*—7th Nov.—The yield of the crops has been affected only by the somewhat abnormal weather that has prevailed throughout the year, and I cannot ascertain that any special injury has been caused to the crops by insects or fungi. *Tullamore D.*—1st Nov.—The cereals are under the average on account of the long drought in the early part of the season. The barley crop, however, has been fairly good. Potatoes are a good crop—very abundant—but an increasing proportion is getting black as the season advances. Hay is a light crop, owing to the early drought. The turnip crop is under the average for the same reason. There has been no special injury from insects or fungi. On the whole the harvest has been fairly good in this district.

LONGFORD COUNTY.—*Ballymahon D.*—30th Oct.—The potato crop of all kinds is generally good, and scarcely any disease noticeable in them, and this is attributed to the dry season. Hay, oats, turnips and mangel wurzel have suffered from the dry weather in the early part of the season, and are not up to the yield of other years. There was no special injury done to any crops in this district by insects, weeds, or fungi. *Granard D.*—13th Nov.—The potato crop was considerably above the average owing to the drought in the early summer and the absence of "blight." The drought prevented the growth of weeds. In the case of oats, on the other hand, the yield was somewhat below the average owing to the drought, and the oats beginning to lay out before the rains in July and August. Turnips were greatly checked after sowing by insects, and in many cases had to be again sown, but the crop was very fair. This is the only case of injury to crops from insects or fungi that is recorded. *Longford D.*—29th Oct.—The potato crop is in general very considerably better this year than last, except those grown in moor land, which were injured by May frost. The good yield is attributed to the excellent spring and summer weather, and the absence of "blight" and late in the season. Turnips and mangolds are a generally bad crop owing to the very dry weather at time of their being planted. Oats, rye, and hay.—The bad yield of these crops is attributed to the very dry season. However, oats is considered above the average in deep soil.

LOUTH COUNTY.—*Ardee D.*—1st Nov.—Oats, very light crop, attributed to drought in May, June, and July. Barley a fair average crop, better able to stand drought than oats. Potatoes, an abundant crop, some blight in August. Hay, first crop, very light, owing to drought; second crop, very good, owing to fall of rain at end of July and during August. Turnips, a light crop, owing to drought after sowing, the seed taking too much late in sprouting overground. No special injury done to crops by insects, weeds, or fungi. *Collon D.*—1st Nov.—The crops were all good, owing probably to the fine weather in the early part of the season. There was no special injury to crops from insects or fungi during the season. *Drogheda D.*—22nd Oct.—The hay crop has been short, owing to the very dry months of early summer. Turnips, mangolds, and carrots were favoured by the wet weather in August and September. Same remarks apply to the potato crop, but the large yield has been curtailed in value by the quantity of diseased potatoes. Oats has been abundant, as the season was very favourable; same applies to all cereal crops. No crops have suffered from fungi or insects to any extent. *Dundalk D.*—5th Nov.—This year's harvest has not been up to the average. The long-continued drought in the spring, which was followed by excessive rains during July and August, was most detrimental to the growth of crops. Were it not that the weather in September and for a great portion of October was so exceptionally fine, the crops would have been irretrievably damaged. I have not heard of any special injury to crops from insects or fungi.

MEATH COUNTY. *Athboy D.*—2nd Nov.—The crops generally throughout this district are quite up to the average. The injury done to some of the crops by the frost and drought in June was obliterated by the growth which took place late in the summer. This was particularly noticeable in the heavy crops of late and second crop hay and also in the turnips. The potato crop is light and a good deal of disease is showing itself. This remark does not refer to the Oldcastle portion of the district (bordering on the co. Cavan), where the "spray" treatment appears to have improved the crop and averted the disease. As the treatment with "Bordeaux mixture" is not expensive, it is greatly to be wondered at that it is not more extensively used in this county. There has been no special injury to crops by insects or fungi. *Dunshaughlin D.*—25th Oct.—With reference to the apparently low average in some of the electoral divisions in this district, the cause arises from the land of the land being too long under tillage. This is especially the cause of the low average in the case of potatoes, which, although a fairly good crop at the beginning of the season, became black in this old tillage land after the heavy rainfalls we have had recently. I have not heard of any injury resulting to the crops from the presence of insects or fungi during last season. *Kells D.*—29th Oct.—The extraordinarily good crop of potatoes may be attributed to the very warm and dry early part of summer and to the rain which came in July and August. The bad yield of oats is owing to the early months of summer being very dry, and when the oats were beginning to mature wet weather set in and prevented them from filling properly. Scarcely any disease in potato crop in this neighbourhood. *Fenagh D.*—6th Nov.—The crops generally suffered from the continued drought in May and June. Owing to this cause the hay crop was much lighter than usual and turnip crop became almost a partial failure. The corn crop was generally short owing to same cause, but the yield of grain was not affected and is therefore good. The dry summer was favourable to the potato crop, which offers to be an abundant one, notwithstanding the injurious effect of the August rains. There was no specific injury to crops from insects or fungi. *[illegible] D.*—2nd Nov.—Hay was a light crop, not up to the average, owing to drought in the early summer, while continued wet weather late in the season interfered much with the making up of aftergrass. The oat crop, too, was inferior and straw short owing to continued dry weather. For the same reason the turnip crop is not up to the average. The early sowing missed owing to presence of fly. Potatoes are a heavy crop, but there are numerous complaints of disease on account of heavy rains late in the season. No special information forthcoming as to fungi or insects. *[illegible] D.*—12th Nov.—Wheat was an average crop but is not much sown. Oats are a fair crop but stunted by drought in early part of season. Barley is very little sown; it was an average crop. Bere and rye fair but little sown. Beans and peas fairly good: scarcely worth mentioning, they are so little sown. Potatoes are a good crop; some injury was inflicted by heavy rain in August and September. Turnips are below the average in consequence of the drought in early part of season. Mangel wurzel and beet root are not much sown; they were an average crop. Cabbage was a fairly good crop. Vetches and rape fair, but very little sown. Carrots, parsnips, and other green crops sown in small quantities; they were a fair crop. Flax not sown. New meadows were light in consequence of the drought. Old meadows were fairly good, having been improved considerably by the rain in July and August. Pasture grass was bad in early part of season, but afterwards improved and became plentiful but rather coarse at [illegible]. I cannot find that there has been any special injury to crops from insects or fungi during the past season.

Queen's County. *Abbeyleix D.*—[illegible] Oct.—The partial failure of the turnip crop is, I believe, to be attributed to continuous drought after sowing, necessitating in many cases two and three sowings in the same field. The year was exceptionally good for potatoes, caused by the heat of the summer and the [illegible] weather experienced while maturing. I have heard no complaints of any injury from noxious insects or fungi. *[illegible] D.*—25th Oct.—The crops this season are well up to the average—the potato crop, especially, being a good one. No special injury to crops has been caused by insects or fungi. *[illegible] D.*—1st Nov.—The potato crop has been decidedly above the average, probably owing to the dry spring and the absence of late frosts. Hay, except the earliest crops, is not well saved or very good. Oats and barley are not up to the average in quantity or quality, and the straw is short. Turnips and mangolds have not done well, though the crop is better than was anticipated. Speaking generally, the drought in the spring and early summer, with the wet weather which succeeded in July and August, militated greatly against the crops, but the extreme warmth and fineness in September turned the scale again and enabled farmers to reap a not altogether unfavourable harvest. There was no special damage done by insects, weeds, or fungi. *Mountrath D.*—23rd Oct.—All the crops in this district are an average yield, hay in general is light, owing to dry season. The potato crop was never known to be so good. None of the crops are injured by insects or fungi.

Westmeath County. *[illegible] D.*—27th Nov.—The good yield of crops, potatoes and oats especially, was attributed to the fine season following the late spring rains; these crops in particular exceeded the expectations of the farmers. The hay crop was light in the early season, but improved well later on. Regarding special injury to crops by insects, none suffered any save the turnips, one-half of which were destroyed by the "*Fly*"; if this is [illegible] prevented it would be an invaluable boon to agriculturists every year. Weeds injurious to farm crops—some more so than one called by an Irish name "[illegible]" is in the oat crop—as the seed of this weed mixes with the grain, thereby reducing its marketable value very much. *Castlepollard D.*—28th Oct.—There is nothing that requires special mention as to crops in this district. The season has been a favourable one, and crops have done well. I have heard of no complaints about bad crops, nor have I heard of any injury being done by insects or fungi. The season has been a dry one. *Delvin D.*—1st Nov.—All the crops in this district for the present season have been up to a fair average. The light crops of hay in the earlier months have been compensated for by heavy growth of aftergrass, which has been turned into good hay in many cases. Potatoes ought to be very good, and are an abundant crop. Turnips and mangolds, which threatened to turn out a complete failure, have turned out a fine yield from second or even third sowings. No harm appears to have been done by insects or fungi in past season. The book on those subjects is most interesting and useful. *Kilbeggan D.*—1st Nov.—The exceptionally good yield of potatoes is owing to the fine season and the absence of frost in May, and of blight till very late in the season. The crop of oats, barley and rye, is not so good, in all probability owing to the very dry weather in June and July. Turnips and mangolds are fair, but would have been better if there had been more rain in June and July. Carrots are not grown in large quantities in this district, but what there is of them is fine. The early meadows were very poor owing to the want of rain, but the late meadows made up for this, and the crop of hay is considered very fair. *[illegible] D.*—[illegible] Oct.—The yield of all crops, contrary to general expectation, is good, and is due to the beneficial rainfall succeeding dry and warm weather in early summer, again succeeded by favourable weather in late summer and early autumn. The first crop hay was deficient, because the dry weather lasted too long so far as it was concerned. *Mullingar D.*—8th Nov.—The potato crop in this district is far above the average owing to the dry and favourable season. Hay is light, as the dry weather was unfavourable to it. Mangolds are a fair crop, but the weather was not altogether favourable to them. Turnips are far under average owing to dry weather. There does not seem to have been any injury to the crops from insects or fungi.

Wexford County. *Enniscorthy D.*—28th Oct.—The wet weather at harvest time damaged many of the crops, otherwise they would have been better. There was no sign of disease or special injury to any crops. *Gorey D.*—25th Oct.—The corn crop has turned out fairly well, though in a few portions in districts the farmers complain about the small yield in oats. Still, on the whole, it has been up to the average, and what it has lacked in quantity is well made up in quality. All the farmers agree that there has been a very large yield in the potato crop. The weather appears to have suited it admirably. No reports as to the ravages of insects or fungi have reached me. Any discontent that prevails is on account of the price of farm produce being so low. *New Ross D.*—1st Nov.—The small yield in the hay crop was caused by the very dry weather in months of April and May, while all grain crops were injured to a very great extent by the continuous wet weather in July and August. There has been no special que-

Province of Leinster.

PROVINCE OF LEINSTER.

plaint regarding insects, fungi, or any special class of weeds. [illegible] D.—31st Oct.—Wheat, oats, barley, beans.—The partial failure of these crops is mainly attributed to the long-continued drought in the early part of the season. Potatoes.—The good yield of this crop is said to have been produced by the fine dry weather of spring and early summer; and also in consequence of the blight not having made its appearance so early this year as it had in previous years. Turnips, mangel wurzel, carrots, cabbage.—A poor crop, owing to the dry season after the seed was sown. Hay.—A very light crop, on account of the dry early summer. No complaints as regards injury to crops by insects or fungi during the past season. Wexford D.—15th Nov.—There has been very little variation in the yield of crops compared with recent years. There is an increase in the potato crop, which I consider is due to the favourable weather experienced for early planting in the spring, but the very wet weather of July and August has considerably injured the quality of the tubers. There has been no special injury to crops from insects or fungi in this district.

WICKLOW COUNTY. Arklow D.—1st Nov.—The yield of the various crops in my district appears to be about the average, except potatoes, which are considerably above the average, the good yield being attributed to the favourable weather in early summer, which matured the crop sufficiently to enable it to escape disease when wet weather was prevalent in late July and in August. The yield of turnips is bad, the first sowing having failed in most cases in consequence of the long drought in early summer, at which time also the insect, commonly called "the fly," did much damage to this crop. [illegible] D.—8th Nov.—The good yield of crops this harvest is due to fall of rain, coming at end of June, just in the nick of time. Every sort of crop at that time was very backward, and, indeed, gloomy anticipations were forebodeed, but the copious rain set all right, crops quickly revived, and apprehensions were soon removed, with the result of generally average crops, and the subsequent harvest weather was all that could be desired. No injury from insects or fungi. Dunlavin D.—25th Oct.—The only crop necessitating special mention is the potato crop. It is exceptionally good, due probably to the fine weather of early summer, following the spring rains. Other crops are well up to the average, as the year is a good one. Wicklow D.—1st Nov.—The decrease in the yield of hay is caused by the great drought of the months of April, May, and June. The late hay was well up to the average in yield. The lightness of the yield of oats and barley is attributable to the dryness of the season. For the same reason the straw was very short, and yielded not half as much as average years. Very little wheat sown in this district. The yield was up to the average. The increase in the produce of potatoes is caused by the almost continual rains of the months of July and August. Blight did not make its appearance till the tubers were well matured. Turnips and mangolds are a light crop in consequence of late sowing. The seeds put in in the usual time failed through drought. Wire-worm did some damage to the oats, and with this exception no damage appears to have been caused by insects or fungi.

## PROVINCE OF MUNSTER.

PROVINCE OF MUNSTER.

CLARE COUNTY. Ballyvaughan D.—25th Oct.—The exceptionally good potato crop is attributed to two causes—first, the dry, warm weather that has prevailed almost since they were planted, and second, the excellent seed potatoes supplied by the Guardians. Wheat, oats, and barley, though not so productive in straw as in other years, are, on the whole, a fair crop, the grain being very good. Hay is especially deficient in quantity, but excellent in quality, owing to the excessive drought, which was peculiarly injurious to the light soil in this craggy country. Turnips, mangel wurzel, and cabbage are a fair crop, as, though they suffered from the drought of summer, they improved under the moisture of August and September. There was no special injury to crops from insects or fungi, the unusually dry weather counteracting their effects. Corofin D.—25th Oct.—The only crops sown in this district are oats, rye, potatoes, turnips, mangel wurzel, cabbage, and hay, and the probable cause of the good or bad yield is as follows, viz.:—Oats, good, owing to the early part of the season being dry. Rye, good, same cause as above. Potatoes, very good, owing to the dry season and nonappearance of blight until the crop was nearly matured. Turnips, fair, early part of season too dry for them. Mangel wurzel, good, owing to the dry season and the moist land in which sown. Cabbage, good on pasty or low soils. Hay, middling, owing to the early part of the season being too dry. No special injury has been caused by insects, fungi, or weeds. Ennis D.—1st Nov.—The only green crops grown here are potatoes, turnips, and mangolds. I am not aware that much injury is done to these crops by insects or fungi, but certainly much injury must be done, particularly to the potato crop, by weeds, which in some cases strangle the crop. Ennistymon D.—1st Nov.—The only cause where the crops are not up to the average in this district this year is owing to the poorness of the land. Generally, the crops are good, and beyond the average. I regret to say that the farmers in the district pay very little attention to the extermination of weeds—the wonder to me is how they have such good crops from their negligence of this matter. The crops have not suffered this year from insects or fungi. Killadysert D.—25th Oct.—Corn grown on dry, or upland, made a very poor return, and the straw was very short; this was principally owing to the drought which followed the seed-sowing season; in low-lands the yield was considerably better; rye, for that reason, was good. Potatoes are excellent, and have made a far better return than in previous years, which was principally owing to the favourable weather for this crop. Turnips are not up to the average, owing to the very dry weather at the seed-sowing season, which prevented a considerable amount of the seed from taking root. The same remarks apply to the mangold crop. No special injury was caused by insects or fungi. Weeds, the farmers call "[illegible]," "[illegible]," and "[illegible] grass," have been much complained of, and they say that it is only by considerable labour they can be cleared away wherever they appear. Killaloe D.—1st Nov.—I am of opinion that the rates of produce are higher this year than last year in almost every crop, except hay, which, I believe, was a heavier crop last year. As regards the potato crop, the produce this year exceeds anything we had for some years past. Wheat is very little sown here. Oats is a heavier crop than last year. I attribute the good yield to the very good dry summer weather which we had. I have heard no complaints about any injury to crops from insects or fungi. Kilrush D.—4th Nov.—The potato crop has been abundant this year, owing to the good seed supplied generally by the Board of Guardians, and the favourable season. Other green crops have also been good. Meadow is light, but the hay well saved. No injury from insects or fungi. Sixmilebridge D.—25th Oct.—All the crops show a fair average yield. The potato crop has not been so good for several years past. There was no special injury to crops by insects

Province of Munster.

&c. *Tulla D.*—11th *Nov.*—The average yield of the various crops in this district is looked on as satisfactory. The potato crop has been excellent, owing to the fine season, and the plants escaping disease. The crop of hay is below the average in consequence of the dry weather which prevailed in the early summer. In one part of the district turnips were attacked by a disease known as the "finger and toe" disease, and though this seems to have been confined to a few farms, the loss is estimated at from 60 to 80 tons. In another part of the district turnips suffered severely from the "turnip fly," which is said to have attacked the turnips early in May. Its appearance is attributed to the warm dry weather experienced. No efforts were made to destroy the insects.

CORK COUNTY, E.R. *Ballincollig D.*—1st *Nov.*—There was a good yield of the various crops in this district, but the oats and barley were damaged by the wet weather which prevailed at the time of harvesting same, and the grain was soft and not of as good a colour as it might have been. The root crops which did not promise so well in the early part of the season were greatly improved by the rains in August and turned out a fair crop also. Potatoes are a very good crop this year about here. *Charleville D.*—31st *Oct.*—Wheat, a fair crop but little grown; slightly injured by heavy rains in month of August. Oats, this is a very good crop, which is attributed to the rather favourable weather in early portion of the season, the grain appears sound and healthy, on the whole, though in a limited area of district, a small portion got injured by the heavy rains of August. Barley, this crop is not grown in district. Bere and rye, very little grown. Same remarks apply to this crop as to wheat. Peas and beans, none grown in district. Potatoes (Champions), this is the favourite kind grown in district, the yield was excellent owing to a rather favourable season, and the absence of "blight" until the crop was nearly matured, but recent heavy rains appear to have had a bad effect, as portion of crop is becoming diseased. Turnips, this crop was rather stunted by the dry weather in June and July in portions of district where the soil was of a calcareous nature, and got injured by the "Fly," but the rains of August afterwards improved it a good deal, and the yield on the whole is very fair. Mangel wurzel, a good average crop. Same remarks as to turnips. Cabbage, this is a very good crop, but not much grown in district. Hay, this was a fair crop, but not well saved, owing to the wet weather in latter part of July and month of August, and is rather of an inferior quality on the whole. There was no special injury done to crops from insects or fungi as they were on the whole well attended to. *Cork, North D.*—30th *Oct.*—The crops grown in this district include potatoes, mangolds, turnips, oats, hay, and cabbage. Potato crop was a good one owing to the season turning in favourably. Mangolds, a good crop for similar reasons. Turnips, rather a poor crop in consequence of the very dry weather, the seeds having failed for want of moisture, but the crop is much improved for the past month. Oats and barley were a good crop, the straw was short in consequence of the dryness of the season. Hay, rather poor owing also to the dry weather. Cabbage, a very good crop. No special injury was done to crops by insects, &c. *Cork, South D.*—1st *Nov.*—The crops are good with the exception of the hay crop which was a light one owing to the dry weather in May and June. Mangolds and turnips turned out a good crop. Wheat and oats suffered a good deal from the wet weather of July and August but yielded a fair return. No injury has been caused by insects, fungi or weeds to the crops in this district. *Fermoy D.*—29th *Oct.*—Wheat, not sown. Potatoes, a very good sound crop, about twenty-five per cent. over last year's crop. Oats, hay, turnips, a light crop owing no doubt to the early drought. Oats, ten per cent., turnips, twenty per cent., and hay, twenty-five per cent., under last year's average. Mangolds, an excellent crop. None of the crops have been injured by insects, fungi, or weeds. *Kanturk D.*—25th *Oct.*—The return of produce all round are a good average. The potato crop is, I think, the most plentiful, and may be attributed to the warm weather just when the crop most required it. Turnips are not up to the average of recent years, owing to the long drought which set in after sowing. In many instances the seed had to be put in secondly, and in some places, thirdly. Hay in consequence of the rather wet weather in August is not so well saved as formerly, but it is not by any means scarce. There is nothing particular to note as regards other crops. *Kinsale D.*—1st *Nov.*—The yield in the various crops in the several electoral divisions in this district is rather better than in former years, especially the potato crop, which is very abundant, and is attributable to the favourable season, and absence from blight. I have made inquiries, and am informed that no special injury has been done to crops in this district during the past season by insects, fungi, or weeds. *Mallow D.*—25th *Oct.*—The potato crop has been generally a very good one. There has been a good yield from all the varieties of seed, but I hear many complaints that the "Champions," though apparently abundant in tubers, are to a great extent rotten in the centre. There is a feeling among farmers that the "Champion," as a seed potato, no longer suits the country, and some people tell me that in Scotland the same result has been experienced. Oats suffered some injury in the early dry weather, and from the heavy fall of rain just at the time when it was fit to cut, but, on the whole, it is a good crop. Turnips are a fair crop, although some injury was sustained from the fly in the early dry weather, so much so that some farmers found it necessary to make two and even three fresh sowings. Fungi did not show much in turnips. Farmers say that they are most prevalent in fields where the same crop has been repeated. Mangolds are a good sound crop, and show no signs of special injury. *Mitchelstown D.*—30th *Oct.*—The crops in this district generally are fairly good, and in quantity well up to the average. The first crop barley, extensively grown, suffered very much from the almost continuous rain late in July and throughout August. It was greatly discoloured and was unfit for malting, and not much more than half the ordinary price per barrel was got for it. The second crop barley has been a good crop, and sold pretty well. Oats is a very fair crop, and up to the average in quantity. The rain did not injure it much. Wheat is hardly grown. The potatoes are excellent and abundant. There was very little disease. Champions still are the standard crop. Turnips in many cases had to be sown twice. They are a fair crop, and mangolds are sound, large and plentiful. Hay has been a light crop in many places, and suffered from the rain. Straw is plentiful. All garden produce has been well up to the average. There was plenty of grass from the middle of July. The fine September saved the harvest in this district. *Skibbereen D.*—29th *Oct.*—With the exception of potatoes, turnips, and hay, the crops grown in this district are all up to the average. There is an appreciable increase in the potato crop, due chiefly to the dry season, and the absence of blight until late in the year. Hay is not so good as in former years owing to the drought in May. The late crop suffered much when being saved. The turnip crop also suffered from the dry weather, and in many instances had to be resown, and was therefore late, and will not yield as well as in previous years. I find that the crops have not suffered from insects or fungi during the past season. *Newmarket D.*—2nd *Nov.*—The harvest has been good generally. Early in the season the hay crop suffered considerably from the inclement weather. The late crop was well saved. Potato crop has been the best for many years, and the oat crop equally good, the price of which is less than in other years. No crops injured by any insects. *Queenstown D.*—30th *Nov.*—

[illegible]

the following are the causes to which the good or bad yield of crops may be attributed. Cereal crops.—The yield of wheat, oats, and barley, promised to be good up to harvest time, but then in consequence of wet weather the quality became very much deteriorated, thereby losing in value. Green crops.—Turnips were bad in consequence of the months of May and June being too dry, and fly attacking the crop, causing farmers to resow in some instances three times. Mangolds were very good, being earlier and stood the dry weather, the fly did not attack the crop. Hay crop.—Hay on new meadows was a good crop owing to the rains, but old meadows were bad in consequence of the rain later in the season. There was no special injury to crops from insects, fungi, or mildew, except in the case of the turnips which suffered from flies as before stated, and only on lands which were insufficiently manured or badly cultivated, have the crops suffered from weeds. *Youghal D.*—13th Nov.—The potato crop this year shows a great improvement owing to the absence of disease, and fine weather in the early part of the season. Other crops, except hay, are probably slightly under the average owing to the wet harvest. The yield would have been quite up to or over the average if the weather had been favourable for saving the crops. New meadow hay is very light owing to the dry season when it was cut. Old meadow heavy, but badly saved. Some farmers report that there is slight damage done to the turnip crop by fungi and fly, but not to any considerable extent.

Cork County, W.R. *Bandon D.*—1st Nov.—The various crops are good, and of a fairly good average, which is attributed to the continued mildness of the season. The potato crop in particular is very good. There was no special injury done to crops from fungi or insects. *Bantry D.*—30th Oct.—I have no information as to the probable cause of the generally good yield of the crops this year. No special injury appears to have been done by insects or fungi, and there has been a marked absence of potato blight. *Castletown Bere D.*—24th Oct.—The crops, generally, in this district are fairly good this year. The oat crop was slightly damaged by the August rains. However, oats is not an extensive crop in this district and therefore the farmers are not much affected by a partial failure in it. Neither fungi nor insects have injured the crops as far as I can learn. *Clonakilty D.*—1st Nov.—Wheat, oats, and barley are below the average, owing to the excessive rains during the month of August. Potatoes, a very good crop, 60 per cent. above the average, owing to favourable season, and dressing with sulphate of copper, which has been very extensively used in this district. Mangolds, a good crop owing to favourable season. Turnips below the average owing to continued wet weather, developed foliage instead of roots. Hay, first early crop good, owing to favourable weather. The second or late crop bad owing to continued wet weather. These are the principal crops grown in this district. *Dunmanway D.*—2nd Nov.—The crops this season are all good, especially the potato crop, which has a yield nearly three times as great as in past years. Supposed to be caused by the dryness of the season. The turnip crop is somewhat late as the seed sown at first failed in a good many cases and fresh seed had to be sown instead. This was caused by the great drought. *Macroom D.*—30th Oct.—The crops are generally good. The potato crop in particular is a very fine one, owing to the season being so favourable, and absence of blight. The hay crop in some parts of the district is rather light owing to the drought in May and June, this also applies to the mangold and turnip crops which failed in many places, so that the seed had to be resown. There is a complete absence of injury to crops from insects or fungi. *Mitchelstown D.*—28th Oct.—Oats, hay, and root crops suffered less or more in the beginning of the year from the continuous dry weather, and oats and hay later from the wet weather which followed. The potato is a good crop and is above the average, a dry season suits this crop in this district. All the other crops are fair, scarcely up to the average of other years. The hay crop is less or more damaged. There was no injury done by insects, fungi, or weeds. *Skibbereen D.*—1st Nov.—The yield of the various crops in the district generally has been over the average of past years. The increase has been attributed to the favourable season, the weather having been suitable to this part of the country. It was expected that the straw would be short, but the rain came at a good time, before the growth had stopped, and the crop on the whole has been very fair. It is generally admitted that the spraying was of benefit to the potato crop. It was resorted to by a comparatively large number of the farmers in the district, and no serious effects of blight have been observed. Some slight damage was done to the turnip crop by fly, and the drought in the early part of the month was unfavourable to the growth of root crops. *Skull D.*—1st Nov.—Grain crops not so good in quality or quantity as in previous years, and may be attributed to the very dry spring and wet autumn. Potatoes of all kinds have been exceptionally good and free from disease, this is due to the almost total absence of blight and to the very extensive use of spraying machines. Root crops are not so good as in former years; they appear to have suffered from insects during the summer. Hay is not quite up to the average of other years, the early meadows were light in consequence of the dry spring. There was no injury to crops from insects or fungi save that done by the farmer to root crops during the summer, especially to turnips.

Kerry County. *Cahersiveen D.*—30th Oct.—The crops, generally, are good. The good weather in the early part of the year materially assisted the potato crop, the greater portion of which is manured with sea-weed and sand. There has been no injury caused to any class of crop by insects, &c. Farmers of this district pay very little attention to weeding; in fact the greater portion of them do not weed their potatoes at all. If they did weed, I believe a greater yield would be obtained annually. *Castleisland D.*—4th Nov.—The good yield of the various crops is owing to the very favourable weather during the growth of those crops. The season, on the whole, was very mild; rain and heat came alternately, and at the proper time, and to that I attribute the good yield. There was no special injury to crops from insects or fungi this year. *Dingle D.*—28th Oct.—The potato crop, owing to the blight not appearing until an advanced stage of the season, and even then in a mild form, is the best experienced for years. The other root crops, owing to the rainfall at the end of the summer, are a very fair average. The oat crop is a good one, but straw is short, owing to the drought in the early summer. The hay crop is also light for the same reason. Scarcely any other crops are sown. *Kenmare D.*—1st Nov.—The bad yield of crops is attributed to the wet climate and the farmers not changing their seeds frequently, also not keeping their tillage land properly clean of weeds. There was no special injury to crops in this district from insects or fungi during season. *Killarney D.*—1st Nov.—All crops grown have been up to a good standard this year, especially potatoes. The latter crop has scarcely ever been excelled, but as a good deal of them are still in the ground, they may suffer from frost. The weather was favourable on the whole. The wet weather in July just took up in time to save the corn crops in this county. *Killorglin D.*—3rd Nov.—The crops, as a whole, were remarkably good. The potato crop was very heavy, and there was no disease. The imported seed did very well, and the season was favourable. The oat and hay crops were good. The early crops of hay were rather light; those cut later were heavier, and the quality very fair. The oat crop was very

Statement of Enumerators.

heavy, the straw being very heavy, and the seed good. There was no injury done to crops by disease, or by insects or fungi, the potato crop especially being almost entirely free from blight. *Listowel D.*—2nd Nov.—The various crops are good, but particularly the potato crop. The only cause to be assigned for this is owing to the very dry and warm weather during the season. The growth, in the early part of spring, was much retarded by the frost, which was severe in this locality, but this was more than counterbalanced by the heat which afterwards set in. I cannot discover that any special injury has been done to the crops in this district this season by insects or fungi. *Tralee D.*—4th Nov.—The yield of the various crops has been good. Potato crop very good, which may be attributed to the favourable weather and the absence of blight until the crop had nearly reached maturity. Yield of grain crops good, owing to the fine season we have had. Root crops are all generally good, owing to same cause. No injury to the crops has been done by either insects or fungi during the past season.

*Limerick County.* *Abbeyfeale D.*—12th Nov.—There is no information of interest to be obtained regarding the crops in this locality. The yield, generally, has been good, especially that of the potato crop, which is considerably above the average. The cause to which the good yield may be attributed is mainly due to the long term of dry weather we have had during the summer and autumn months. No injury to crops, from either insects or fungi, was perceptible during past season. *Adare D.*—5th Nov.—The rates of produce have been up to the usual standard, except in the case of hay and oats. The deficiency in these was due to the very dry May and June. The potato crop was exceedingly good. There has not been such a yield since 1868. Weeds were not numerous, and no appreciable injury was done by insects or fungi. *Bruff D.*—4th Nov.—There is not much tillage. The land is good, and it is chiefly under pasture and meadow. This year potatoes were a good crop. The yield was abundant, but a pretty considerable share suffered from disease. The oats crop was rather light, as were early meadows. This is attributed to the dry weather in May, June and July. However, I believe the corn turned out better than was expected, an improvement having set in when there was a fall of rain after July. To this rainfall may be attributed the very fair yield of hay in old meadows. There is very little wheat in this district. Turnips and mangolds are a fair crop, but they also suffered by the long drought in early part of season. There was no special injury to crops from insects or fungi. *Kilfinnane D.*—2nd Nov.—I attribute the good crops all through this district to the great heat we had in June, and moisture in July and August. The hay crop was rather light, owing to the drought in June. The potato blight did so little worth mentioning. All through it has been a bountiful year. *Kilmallock D.*—1st Nov.—No injury to crops from insects or fungi occurred. There was no special cause affecting the crops beyond the state of the weather. Being dry in early part, and very wet in July and August, hay, root crops and corn were here affected similarly to other portions of the country. The fine weather in September and October, however, materially improved crops of every kind, and enabled harvesting to be successfully carried out. *Newcastle West D.*—28th Oct.—The yield of the several crops in this district has been good this year. The potato crop has been above the average of previous years, and this is attributable to the season being favourable. *Rathkeale D.*—4th Nov.—The potato crop is the only one in which there is any perceptible increase in yield over last year. The cause is attributable to very dry and warm weather from the middle of August to the end of September. Hay, turnips and mangolds are deficient in yield, attributable as regards hay to dry, harsh, and frosty weather during the months of April and May, and, as regards turnips and mangolds, to failures in the seed, owing to drought in June and July, also ravages of the fly on the young turnip plants. All the other crops appear up to the average. There has been no special injury done to crops from insects or fungi. *Rathkeale D.*—24th Oct.—Wheat—This crop produced a fair average yield. Oats—Considered a fairly good yield, but the straw is rather short, owing to the dryness in the early part of the season. Barley—Considered a good yield. Potatoes—This crop was very good, and produced a good average yield. The crop was fully grown before the blight set in. Turnips and mangel wurzel—These crops are considered only a fair average yield, owing to the drought in the months of May and June. Cabbage—A fairly good yield. Hay—This crop is considered only a fair average yield, owing to the dry season.

*Tipperary County, N.R.* *Borrisokane D.*—1st Nov.—The early hay crop as well as the turnip and mangold crops were injured seriously by the drought in May and June. The same cause rendered the straw of oats and barley very short, and it is rather scarce this year. The very dry weather in September improved the corn crops and rendered the potato crop one of the best we have had for many years. I have heard no complaints regarding any injury done by insects or fungi. *Nenagh D.*—5th Nov.—The oat, turnip, and mangold crops are somewhat deficient owing to the very dry period in May and June; also the hay crop, for a like reason. The potato crop on the other hand is exceptionally good, as the cause referred to had a contrary effect on it. I cannot discover that any injury has been caused to the crops from insects or fungi. *Newport D.*—30th Oct.—The various crops have given a fairly good yield, and the farmers from whom the information was obtained have declared that they have no cause of complaint. *Roscrea D.*—1st Nov.—The good yield of corn crops is attributed to the dry season. The soil being naturally cold, a warm season produces a better yield. The same applies to the potato crop, the "blight" not having appeared till the crop was ripe. Turnips were an unexpectedly good crop, due to some showers having set in just at the right time. Mangolds throve well in the dry season. Wheat had a heavy produce owing to drought. Barley was the best crop for years, the dry season suiting it. The drought was unfavourable to cabbage, early corn turnips, hay, carrots, and grasses under meadow, but owing to rainfalls in August, the ill effects of the early drought were not so great as was at one time anticipated. There has been no special injury to crops in this district owing to insects, fungi, etc. *Templemore D.*—28th Oct.—The crops have been a fair average all round. There is therefore nothing special to report on, except the potato crop, which is above the average, due to the fine weather in the early part of the year, which suited this heavy land. *Thurles D.*—30th Oct.—The yield of all crops has been good this year. This is owing to the generally favourable season we have had. The mountainous portion of district is damp, and the dry season suited it admirably, besides there was very good weather during the harvest and most crops were efficiently saved. There has not been any special injury to any of the crops by insects, fungi, or weeds.

*Tipperary County, S.R.* *Cahir D.*—8th Nov.—The yield of all the crops has been very good, especially root crops. This is owing to the weather being favourable. At first the weather was extremely dry, but rain came in sufficient time. There has been no special injury to crops from insects or fungi, or weeds injurious to crops. *Carrick-on-Suir D.*—1st Nov.—The crops were injuriously affected by a long continued drought in the early summer months. It cannot, however, be considered a bad season, as, speaking generally, the crops are good. No injury from insects or fungi is reported. *Cappawhite D.*—24th Oct.—The yield of the various crops is, on the whole, very good.

Province of Munster.

The potato crop is an excellent one, and free from disease or blackness. The turnip and mangel wurzel is a very good crop in quality and yield, as also is the oat crop and wheat crop (but the latter is very little grown); this is attributable to a favourable season and absence of blight. Hay—A plentiful crop, but bad quality, owing to the wet weather in months of July and August. No injury has been caused to crops from insects or fungi. *Cashel D.*—20th Oct.—All the crops are very good this year. Potatoes excellent, oats good, but in some places straw is a little short. Hay plentiful, but somewhat light compared with last year. I am informed no special injury has been caused by insects or fungi. Turnips and mangolds very good. Prices low for oats and potatoes. *Clonmel D.*—[illegible] Nov.—Cereals were in general a good crop. Hay light in consequence of a dry spring. Potatoes good and very little diseased. Root crops good. *Killenaule D.*—1st Nov.—The favourable state of the crops this year in this district is attributable to the good weather which came at a suitable season. Little injury from fungi was observed in district owing also to the favourable weather. *Tipperary D.*—1st Nov.—On the whole, the harvest this year is a fair average one. The hay crop was good, and on the whole well saved. Oats and potatoes good, especially the latter. Wheat and barley very little grown, but what there is is good. All root crops are good, and so far as I can learn no damage has been done to them.

Waterford County. *Cappoquin D.*—[illegible] Nov.—The crops all round are good this year, especially the potato crop, which has yielded a splendid return owing to the sprayers at the proper time and the absence of the blight till late in the season. *Dungarvan D.*—[illegible] Oct.—The good yield in the potato crop is attributed to the dry weather (which is always favourable to this crop) up to the middle of July. The small yield in the grain crops is attributed to the continuous wet weather from the middle of July to the end of August, much of the grain having been shed on the ground. Hay, turnips, mangolds and cabbage would have yielded much better but for the very dry weather from the beginning of May to the middle of July. Pasture crop meadows were specially affected by the drought. The foregoing are the only crops grown to any extent, and they have not, so far as I can gather, been injured by insects, fungi, or weeds. *Portlaw D.*—[illegible] Nov.—The crops are, I think, fairly up to the average. [illegible] crop hay was short in consequence of the dry spring. *Waterford D.*—16th Nov.—The different crops have reached a fairly good average, and compare favourably with the crops of past years, the only exception being the hay crop, which is much below the average owing to dry weather experienced in May and June. Turnips, mangel wurzel and other green crops, which at one time appeared almost a failure, improved so much as the season advanced, that in the end the yield is up to the average of former years. Insects did little, if any, damage this season to green crops, owing to the fact that most of them appeared above ground until the rains in June, which completely destroyed that pest, and no trace of fungi was observed.

---

## PROVINCE OF ULSTER.

Province of Ulster.

Antrim County. *Antrim D.*—1st Nov.—The only crop which was generally light throughout this district was flax. This was due to the long continued drought in the spring. Turnips suffered to some [illegible] from the same cause. There has been no special injury from insects or fungi during the season. *Ballymena D.*—1[illegible]th Nov.—The crops in this district of every description have been fully up to the average both as regards quantity and quality, with the exception of flax. Owing to climatic changes, which were disadvantageous, there is a short and inferior crop. No injuries done by weeds, fungi, or other causes over which the farmers had any control. *Ballymoney D.*—[illegible] Oct.—The excellent yield of potatoes all over the district has, in my opinion, been caused by the dry weather at the latter part of the summer which prevented the "blight" spreading. The yield of turnips for the same reason is bad. The flax crop also yields badly, the early part of the season being too wet. None of the other crops require special remark. *Belfast, East D.*—[illegible] Oct.—The early potatoes suffered much from frost, but later ones have turned out a signal success owing to the sunshine and heat during latter part of summer, which appears to have materially suited the climate for potato growing. The hay produce is a partial failure owing to want of rain in season. Turnips and cabbage are a good crop, and as will be seen there are no grain crops in this division. There has been no special injury done to crops this year by fungi, insects, or weeds. *Belfast, North D.*—1st Nov.—In consequence of the prolonged drought in the months of April, May, and June, the hay and turnip crops are below the average. The oats, potatoes, and cabbage are above the average, as the rain in July came in time to favour their growth. I am unable to obtain any information relative to insects, fungi, or weeds injurious to crops, as tillage operations are necessarily very limited. *Belfast, N. W. D.*—6th Nov.—Only a small portion of this district is under tillage. All crops have yielded a fair average except the hay crop, which was lighter than usual owing to the drought in the early summer. The potato crop is fairly good. No injuries from insects or fungi have been observed. *Belfast, South D.*—[illegible] Oct.—Owing to the long continued drought in the early summer the crops in general suffered. The rain in June and July were of great benefit, and helped to bring the crops generally up to the average yield. No special injury appears to have been caused by insects or fungi; superphosphate and gas lime is used to prevent such injury. The agricultural portion of the district is very small. *Belfast, West D.*—[illegible] Oct.—There have been only a few acres of meadow or arable land in this district. What meadow crop there was was light owing to the long drought in May and June. The potato crop was a good average one; the tubers were healthy, and owing to the absence of frosts in May and the dryness of the summer the year was favourable for this crop. Cabbages were a light crop owing to the dryness of the weather and absence of rain in May and June. *Larne D.*—8th Nov.—All the crops were fairly good, with the exception perhaps of flax, which seemed to have suffered materially from the dryness in the early part of the season. There was no injury caused to crops this year from insects, fungi, &c. *Lisburn D.*—[illegible] October.—The potato crop is somewhat better than last year, owing to the dry summer. Oats, hay, and turnips are not so good as in previous years, as want of moisture in early part of year damaged them considerably. The other green crops are much the same as in previous years, and seem to be fairly good. There was no special injury done to crops in the district from insects or fungi during the past season.

Armagh County.—*Armagh D.*—[illegible] Nov.—The turnip, mangold, and flax crops are poor this year owing to the very dry weather in the early part of the season. The flax suffered too from the heavy rains later on. Hay is also a light crop owing to the early dry weather, although there was a plentiful supply of meadowing hay. Potatoes are a very fine crop and have given almost double the average yield, however there are complaints that a good proportion of them are black. Wherever spraying has been tried it has proved of the greatest efficiency in checking and preventing blight. As far as I can discover no special injury to crops has been caused by insects or fungi. *Lurgan D.*—[illegible] Oct.—The rates of produce are in general below the average. Wheat and other grain crops suffered from drought in May and June. Upland hay suffered from same cause. There is a *fair* crop of meadow hay. Potatoes would have been a good crop only for the rain in July and August; the same applies to turnips and flax. No special injury has been done to crops by insects or fungi. *Newry D.*—[illegible] Oct.—The yield of corn, hay, flax, and turnips is light owing to the dry months of May and June. Oats is also rather a light crop owing to the same cause. Potatoes is a very good crop—the best for years—owing to the dry season. Late meadow hay is also a fair crop owing to the rain in month of July. Other green crops seem to have a fair yield. No special injury to crops this year from insects, fungi, or weeds. *Portadown D.*—[illegible] Oct.—All the crops are above the average yield except second grass or first crop hay, which on the whole is fairly good. In many instances a second crop of this hay has been cut and saved. No special injury has been caused from insects or fungi. This may be attributed to the dry summer, and the good yield of the various crops is attributable to the favorable weather. Wherever the spraying operation has been performed on the potato crop the most satisfactory results have followed.

Cavan County. *Bailieborough D.* 2nd Nov.—The oats are a fair yield but straw very short owing to the dry weather. Potatoes an excellent crop, above the average. Turnips, mangel wurzel, and cabbage are a very light crop owing to the dry weather. Hay crop is also very light owing to dry weather. Flax is very bad, but not much sown in this district. The crops in this district have not suffered any special injury from insects or fungi during the present season. *Cootehill D.*—[illegible] Oct.—The crops in this district have turned out much better than was expected. Oats are a fair crop but below average owing to the continued drought last summer. Wheat but little grown and of fair quality. Potatoes are a very good crop except on boggy low-lying land. Where sprayers were used most satisfactory results followed. Turnips, mangold, and cabbage are not up to the average owing to drought. Flax short and yield not good and also poor quality, being affected by drought. Hay—New grass light owing to dry weather; about half a crop. Old meadows not early were light and badly saved. A large portion of old meadows were not cut till September and are well saved, the weather being fair. There appears to be a good supply of hay in this part of the country. *Kilnaleck D.*—[illegible] Nov.—The only crops grown are potatoes, corn, and hay, with a few turnips. The former crop is above the average in spite of severe frost in May. I attribute this to the fine dry weather in September, which delayed the blight. The corn and hay crops are rather below the average owing to the drought in the early summer, but the corn was very well "headed"—i.e., the oats are well filled. The turnip crop is good, although some portions failed entirely owing to dry weather following the time they were sown. No appreciable injury to crops is attributable to insects, fungi, &c. *Swanlinbar D.*—4th Nov.—The potato crop is a good one this year in consequence of the dry spring and summer, and the absence of the blight until late in the season. In bog or low lands the frost did much injury to the crop in the summer. The oat crop is not a good one owing to the dry weather and the straw is short; for the same reason the turnip crop is not a good one. The hay crop in low lands is an average crop, but in upland it is a bad crop owing to the dry weather. There are but few other crops cultivated in this district. No injury appears to have been done to crops by insects, &c. *Virginia D.*—27th Oct.—The yield of the several crops has been good. Potatoes are an excellent crop and free from disease. Oats fairly good, but the yield is not so good as expected owing to the dry weather in early part of the year. Hay has been a good crop and well saved. Flax is hardly up to an average crop owing to the dry weather.

Donegal County. *Ardara D.*—[illegible] Oct.—The good crop of potatoes is owing to the dry fine summer which was also favourable to the grain crops. This dry summer was rather unfavourable to the turnip crop. However, the latter did better in the more damp soil of Ardara district than in dry upland. A dry warm summer is always the best for this part of Donegal, as the spongy soil retains sufficient moisture without the aid of rain for the nourishment of the plant. The crops suffer most from weeds, and little from insects or fungi. The great majority of the small farmers do not realise the injury caused to their crops by weeds. *Ballyshannon D.*—7th Nov.—The crops have been good this year. Early meadow was light owing to drought in spring and early summer. Late meadow was a good crop, due to heavy rains of July and August, and was well saved in the fine weather in September. Potatoes an abundant and sound crop. Turnips have after all done fairly well, though the drought in spring necessitated resowings, but the rains of July and August helped them wonderfully. Flax, a good crop. I have no knowledge of any injury to crops by insects or fungi. *Buncrana D.*—2nd Nov.—The average crop appears to be good. There is no trace of insects or fungi destroying the crops. The potato crop is very good. The weather has also been very good for saving the crops, and the farmers are fairly well satisfied. *Dunfanaghy D.*—[illegible] Nov.—The principal crops are potatoes, oats, and meadow, and all these were good this year. Hay and oats well up to the average, and potatoes above the average. Of the latter I have not seen so good a crop for many years, and there is no disease. I consider the weather, on the whole, was favourable for crops. All other crops show an equally good yield. *Dungloe D.*—1st Nov.—As regards the potato crop, the yield in the sub-districts of Dungloe, Annagry, Burtonport, and Lettermacaward, is very good, which may be attributed to the dryness of the season. In month of June the potato crop was damaged by frost, in the sub-districts of Rosbeg, Doherty Bridge, [illegible], and Gweedore, and consequently the yield is merely fair in those places. The yield of the other crops is fair. There has not been any special injury caused to crops in district by insects or fungi. *Letterkenny D.*—[illegible] Oct.—The yield of the several crops is good—in fact above the average—except the turnip crop, which, owing to the drought, in May and June, was not so good as in former years. The good yield of the crops, is caused, in my opinion, by the warm weather in June; and September being a good warm month for ripening and saving the several crops raised in this district. No injury has been caused by insects or fungi. *Moville D.*—1st Nov.—There has been a good general harvest in this district. Potatoes, owing to dry weather, are an excellent crop. Oats are good, though the straw is rather short, owing to drought. Turnips are a fair crop, though late. The early sowings missed through drought. Hay was a light crop, owing to drought. What there was was well saved. *Raphoe D.*—3rd Nov.—I have no special observations to make regarding the various crops, with the exception of the turnip crop, which was in many places throughout this district injured by insects in early part of the season during the drought. *Stranorlar D.*—[illegible] Nov.—The crops are, on the whole, of a fairly good average, except the turnip, which can hardly be said to be up to

M

PROVINCE OF ULSTER.

the average. The long drought in the early part of the season injured this crop (the turnip) very much, and in many cases the seed had to be resown from the cause above stated. The potato is more than an average crop, although of late symptoms of disease in the form of a dry-rot are appearing, which are attributed to the wet weather. No special injury has been caused by fungi, &c.

DOWN COUNTY. *Banbridge D.*—4th Nov.—The late spring, followed by the long spell of dry weather, and then another spell of wet, accounts for the yield not being better this year. Potatoes are most disappointing, a splendid yield was anticipated, but the October digging showed a very large amount of disease. Those potatoes which were "sprayed" showed little or no disease, and, in addition, the yield was much greater than of the potatoes which were not "sprayed." No injury to crops by insects or fungi. *Downpatrick D.*—1st Nov.—The flax crop was not a good one, the drought in May and June proving very detrimental. Owing to the same cause the hay crop is lighter than last year. Potatoes are a remarkably good crop, the recent dry weather and the absence of blight are responsible for this. Turnips, &c. (second sowing), a good crop owing to the wet July. Wheat and oats not very good, though this remark does not apply generally. No fungi or insects have caused any special injury. *[illegible] D.*—15th Nov.—The crops are very good, and owing to the month of September being so dry, crops generally were saved to much advantage. No complaints are made, and from inquiry it does not appear that crops have suffered from insects, fungi, &c., during the past season. *Kilkeel D.*—5th Nov.—The crops which have yielded badly are flax, hay, and turnips in particular. The failure of the flax crop is attributed to the cold wet spring followed by a very hot summer. The failure of the hay crop is due to the early dry weather; and the turnip crop (which had to be resown in some instances) to the very dry weather at sowing-time. Potatoes, cabbage, carrots, &c., are up to the average. Oats a fair yield. No injury has been done to crops from insects, fungi, &c., so far as I can learn.

FERMANAGH COUNTY. *Derrygonnelly D.*—6th Nov.—The crops are very fair. Potatoes have been exceptionally good this year owing to the fair weather. Hay is a very light crop owing to want of rain in early part of year. There have been no crops injured in this district by insects, fungi, or weeds. *Enniskillen D.*—31st Oct.—The yield of potatoes exceeded the general expectation of the farmers, also the hay crop. There was no apparent injury to the crops from insects or fungi, which is accounted for by the dry weather. *Kesh D.*—7th Nov.—The various crops have been very satisfactory, chiefly owing to the favourable year for agricultural purposes. Insects or fungi had no injurious effect. *Lisnaskea D.*—30th Oct.—The crops so far as I have learned are quite up to the average, and the heavy rains in August came at the right time for nearly all crops; so that with the exception of the early hay crop, which was light, every crop has matured wonderfully clean. There is an exceptionally good potato crop.

LONDONDERRY COUNTY. *Coleraine D.*—30th Oct.—The principal corn crop grown is oats, and on the whole it has been a very good crop, fully up to average of other years, both as to yield of grain and straw. Some barley is grown, and it has also been a good crop. The potato crop is the best I have known in my time. The returns in Form O do not give, in my opinion, a fair report of the crop. I have seen the crop being dug out in many places, and on certain the return was at least 240 cwt. to the Irish acre. Turnips are a fair crop, but not so good as last year, as some of the late sowing have not grown very large, and the crop missed altogether in patches in fields. Mangolds are a good crop, but were not very largely sown. It has been an excellent year for cabbage. There are all the corn and root crops sown, except a few patches of carrots, and a little rye, but nothing worth speaking of. The early meadows did not yield well owing to the dry weather, but the quality of the hay is very good; a good deal of late cut hay was damaged by rain, but none very seriously. The flax crop, which is a leading one in this district, yielded well, but there are complaints that the quality is inferior; these complaints are grounded on the fact that the price is lower than last year, rather than on the real inferiority of the flax, though I think it is not of so good a quality as last year's crop. During latter part of the season, pasture was very good, and I notice that cattle generally appear in very good condition. *Limavady D.*—28th Oct.—The very fair general average yield of crops is, in my opinion, attributable to the favourable weather which prevailed during the past season. The only striking exception was the turnip crop, which, owing to the drought in the early season, failed badly; the later sowings of this crop did fairly well. There was no special injury done to crops from insects or fungi, and therefore I have no suggestions to offer. *Londonderry D.*—1st Nov.—All crops, with the exception of turnips, show a good yield this season; in the case of turnips the bad yield is attributed to the drought in May and June. Potatoes are good, owing, it is believed, to the dry season and absence of disease, which has done very little damage to the crop so far. In some parts of this district corn is not nearly up to the average, in low districts, however, the crop is fairly good; the straw is much shorter than usual, and this is attributed to the long continued drought. Hay in some parts of the district is not quite up to the average, and this is also a result of the drought. I cannot ascertain that any damage has been done to any crops in this district by insects or fungi. *Magherafelt D.*—31st Nov.—All the crops are up to the average, except the flax crop, which has failed, owing to the dry spring and summer. The potato crop is good, as the season was favourable.

MONAGHAN COUNTY. *Carrickmacross D.*—1st Nov.—Owing to the want of rain in months of May and June, the hay crop was light. The straw was short generally, but a fair yield of oats. The potato crop was good, notwithstanding the few nights' frost in June. No special injury to crops in this district from insects or fungi. *Clones D.*—7th Nov.—As the crops all round are a fair average, I have few remarks to offer. Some of the potatoes on low lands were injured greatly by late frost. Those on high land escaped. On the whole they are an exceptionally good crop, and blight is almost unknown. The long drought injured early hay, oats, and flax. *Monaghan D.*—5th Nov.—The potato crop is above the average of other years, and is attributable to the favourable season, and the blight not setting in so early as in other years. A few farmers sprayed their crop with "[illegible]," which preserved it from blight and increased the yield one quarter more than where it was not used. Oats, meadows, flax, and turnips, are a very light crop, and much under the average of other years, which is attributed to the want of rain in May and June. In many instances the turnip crop failed, and the second sowing, which was of a later kind, was but a light crop. Cabbage and other green crops improved a good deal in the harvest owing to rain, and on the whole are considered a fair crop. I have not received any reports of injury to crops from insects or fungi during the season.

PROVINCE OF ULSTER.

TYRONE COUNTY. *Aughnacloy D.*—1st Nov.—Owing to the very dry weather early in the season the turnip and [illegible] crops are not an average crop. The same applies to flax and meadow. No special injury to crops by insects or fungi. The potato crop is very abundant in consequence of the dry season, and absence of blight until late in September. *Cookstown D.*—2nd Nov.—The real cause of the good potato crop arises from two causes, (1) the early months being dry, (2) the farmers sprayed them once or twice. Flax, [illegible] grass, and turnips are light owing to the dry weather in May and June. No particular species of insects or fungi have been injurious to crops in the district this year. The farmers are pretty familiar with the injurious effects of weeds and have cleaned their land fairly well of them. *Dungannon D.*—[illegible] Oct.—All the crops are well up to the average. The potato crop is exceptionally good, both as regards produce and quality. This may be attributed to the favourable weather, and to the fact that the spraying of the plants has become a [illegible] practice in this neighbourhood. First crop hay was light and it is many cases badly saved. The weather was very dry in May and June, while it rained heavily in July when crop was being saved. The quality of the flax is not good and it is rather scarce. *Newtownstewart D.*—2nd Nov.—The good yield in the potato crop—particularly in high ground—is attributable to the favourable weather. In low-lying land the crop was much injured by frost in June last. The dry weather has caused a poor oats crop and the straw is short. The turnip crop has been a bad yield, when first sown the dry weather and the "fly" destroyed it—and in most cases a second and third sowing had to be made. The hay crop is poor owing to the very dry weather. Flax a middling crop owing to dry season. The "blight" only made a slight appearance this season amongst the potato crop. The oats in some instances have been slightly blackened with "smut." No injury done by "grub" or "worm." *Omagh D.*—[illegible] Nov.—There is a very fair crop of potatoes this year and is attributed to a dry autumn season; the yield would be far better only for the frost in June last, which very much injured the low lands. Turnips not so good as other years, neither is upland hay, but old meadows proved very successful, owing to the wet in July and August and the dry end of season, which was the means of saving a good surplus of old meadow hay. On the whole there is a very fair average produce for all crops. *Strabane D.*—6th Nov.—The harvest has been very good. Scarcely any damage has appeared amongst the potatoes and the yield is above the average. I consider this attributable to the favourable dry season. Turnips are a fair crop, but in several farms, a second sowing had to be made on account of the drought in the early summer. Hay and straw are light in most places, but the hay was very well saved. The flax harvest is a little below the average, owing to the dry season. No special injury has been done to the crops by insects or fungi.

PROVINCE OF CONNAUGHT.

GALWAY COUNTY. *Athenry D.*—[illegible] Nov.—The bad yield of hay, oats, and turnips was caused by the very dry season, which favoured on the other hand the potato crop. There has been no injury to crops by insects, &c. *Ballinasloe D.*—[illegible] Oct.—The crops (save hay and oats, which were injuriously affected by the dryness of the spring and early summer months) in this district, especially the potato crop, gave a very good yield this year, owing to the fine harvest weather and absence of disease, which, with a few exceptions, increased the produce in all crops, notably the potato crop, the yield of which far exceeds that of a good many previous years. It had reached its full growth before the blight set in. No special injury reported to have been caused by insects or fungi—as grubs and insects were scarce, owing to the severity of last winter weather, and there was a marked absence of weeds owing to the dryness of the spring and early summer season which, however, left hay (first crop), and oats both a light crop for want of moisture. Old meadows, though not so good as last year, produced a fair average yield as rain set in before they had done growing, and the fact that they were let grow on as long as possible before being cut. Grass is now a good crop, especially aftergrass, and should the winter not set in severe early, should suffice for feeding purposes almost until Christmas. *Clifden D.*—1st Nov.—It may be stated generally that all crops were considerably retarded by the drought in the early part of the year—in May and June. Turnips were attacked by a maggot which first made its appearance about 10th July. It has been examined and found to be the grub of the turnip or cabbage fly. It exists for three weeks, and after that time ceases to be able to do damage as it turns into a fly or beetle. It did serious damage by cutting the plant across about an inch below the surface of the clay. It continued the damage to the turnips up till about 1st August. The same insect (I think) has been attacking the potatoes, by cutting the stem across, which killed the plants. *Clonbur D.*—30th Oct.—The only crops which are cultivated to any extent are potatoes and oats. The former is a most excellent crop, and no complaints are heard as to damage from insects or otherwise. Oats is rather short owing to dry weather in April. *Dunmore D.*—1st Nov.—On the whole there is a fair average produce of all the crops, especially the potato, which is abundant. The oats crop is not quite so good as formerly, and the straw is short. I have not heard that any injury has been caused to any crop by either insects or fungi. *Galway D.*—4th Nov.—The good yield of the various crops may be attributed to the favourable season. The crops have not suffered any special injury from insects or fungi during the past season. *Gort D.*—31st Oct.—The lighter than usual yield of cereals may be attributed to the unfavourable condition of the weather owing to the long drought which prevailed during the latter part of the spring and the greater portion of the summer season. The hay crop suffered slightly as also did pasture lands from the same cause. The periodical rains which came opportunely during the latter part of summer account for the generally good yield of potatoes, turnips and other root crops. The crops in general were not affected by insects or fungi, from both of which they were entirely free this year. *Loughrea D.*—[illegible] Nov.—The crops have been a good deal above the average this year, with the exception of the corn crop, which was rather short, but the grain was fair. The dry summer was the cause of the oats crop being scanty. There was no special injury to crops from insects or fungi during the past season. *Moylough D.*—1st Nov.—The potato crop is a plentiful and good one, caused I believe from having been sown early and the weather favourable to their growth. The oat crop has yielded a rather poor return in consequence of the continued drought after being sown. Root crops, notwithstanding poor appearance of them early in the season, will owing to the rains towards the end of summer, be almost up to the average of former years. Hay is also a poor crop, owing to absence of rain in the early part of the year. *Oughterard D.*—[illegible] Oct.—The potato crop is good, owing to the absence of excessive rain. The hay crop is poor, owing to the same cause. *Portumna D.*—[illegible] Oct.—The yield of the several crops was good, which is, I would say, attributable to the very favourable weather that prevailed in the autumn for harvesting operations. No special injury to crops took place in this district.

[illegible]

during the past season from insects or fungi. *Roundstone D.*—[illegible] *Nov.*—The yield of the potato crop grown in this district is on the whole good. The early part of the year being dry, and the rain which fell in August, together with the absence of blight, assisted materially in bringing about a good yield. The yield from oats, barley, and rye, though not much grown, is fairly good; this result was brought about by the fall of rain late in summer. The crop is grown late in this district. Turnips and mangel wurzel produced a fair yield though little grown, owing to the rain in latter part of year. Hay gave a better return than was anticipated in early part of year, in consequence of the service to meadow land by the rain which fell late in the season. Cabbage proved a good yield, the year on the whole being favourable to that crop. No special injury has been caused by "insects or fungi." *Spiddal D.*—20th *Oct.*—The potato crop is in this district this year much above the average. There is practically no other crop attempted. The success of the potato crop is attributed entirely to the weather, which favoured it exceedingly, as during the early months of drought it was not at a stage to be injured, and the rain came at the time when its want would have been greatly felt. Insects and fungi do not cause much annoyance in this locality. Weeds on the contrary are specially encouraged through all crops. They are pulled in June and July, when green food is scarce, and serve as food for cattle. *Tuam D.*—6th *Nov.*—The good yield of the various crops in this district may be attributed to the favourable season. *Woodford D.*—4th *Nov.*—The yield of the crops (in [illegible]) may be looked upon as average. The potato crop is exceptionally satisfactory both as regards quantity and the quality of the tubers. Where blight did appear it was too late to cause injury. Hay is a fair crop, but straw light owing to the early drought acting on a light poor soil. The grain however is fair. Wheat not grown here. There does not appear to be any injury due to fungus. In some cases however green crops appeared to have suffered from the "green fly."

LEITRIM COUNTY.—*Ballinamore D.*—11th *Dec.*—The produce of the several crops is above the average yield of other seasons, which is attributed to the dry weather in early part of season. As far as I can observe, little or no damage worthy of notice was caused by insects or fungi in this district. *Carrick-on-Shannon D.*—1st *Nov.*—The potato crop is very good, except in [illegible] or lowlands, where the late frost in month of June destroyed them. Hay is a poor crop, owing to continued drought when rain was required, and subsequently continued rains when fine weather was required for saving. All the other crops yield a fair average. *Drumshanbo D.*—2nd *Nov.*—The crops are generally good, and above the average this year. Potatoes are abundant. This crop suffered some injury from frost in June, but in other places where not affected the yield is nearly double the average. This is attributed to the favourable weather, also to the fact that good seed was used—Scotch Champions, supplied by the Local Government Board. The hay, oats, and turnip crops, also pastures were injuriously affected by the dry weather in the early part of the season, but the showery weather in August and the very fine weather in September brought them up to or perhaps above the average. *Manorhamilton D.*—13th *Nov.*—Of the crops grown, the potato is the principal, and of this there has been a good yield this season, owing to the absence of the blight, thus allowing the crop to fully mature. The other crops having given the usual average yield, no special remarks are necessary concerning them. No crop has suffered any special injury from insects or fungi. *Mohill D.*—2nd *Nov.*—Crops are generally fair. Potatoes are good in the uplands, where they were not injured by the frosts, and were also protected by spraying materials (copper-sulphate). The frost has damaged them very considerably in the moor and lowland. Oats are good; but short in straw, owing to dry season. Owing to the same cause hay is poor, except such as was gathered late, which was good owing to the rain following the drought. Turnip fly appeared, but only in small quantities, and no other damage was done by insects or fungi.

MAYO COUNTY.—*Ballaghaderreen D.*—25th *Oct.*—I consider the good yield of the various crops, especially the potato crop, is to be attributed to the good weather which we had the greater part of the season. *Ballina D.*—4th *Nov.*—The exceptionally dry, hot weather in May and June had certainly retarded the growth of grass of all kinds, also of turnips and oats. This accounts for the low average of hay and straw. Turnips, though late, have done well, and potatoes are a high average. The importation of new seed has done much to increase the yield of potatoes, which are of excellent quality, as well as abundant. There is no marked injury from weeds, except where indifferent cultivation and poor manure have contributed to their growth. The "spraying" of potato crop has not been carried out to such an extent as would enable us to pronounce a valuable opinion as to its efficacy. With such a good potato crop, and fair prices for cattle, there is no reason to expect any acute poverty or distress during the coming winter. *Ballinrobe D.*—14th *Nov.*—There is a nearly average yield in all crops except potatoes, which are above the average, and this is due to the favourable dry weather at the commencement of the season, and a supply of rain at the right time, followed by generally dry weather. There is no special injury done to crops by insects or fungi during the past season. *Belmullet D.*—18th *Nov.*—There was a good fair average yield this season of all crops. *Castlebar D.*—2nd *Nov.*—There is a much larger yield of potatoes this year than in former times, owing to the early part of the season being so dry. This same cause led to early meadows being very light, the straw of the oat crop to be short (though the grain is good), and also, in some places, turnips to be rather a light crop. All other crops are much the same as other years. I have not heard of any special injury to crops by insects or fungi. *Claremorris D.*—28th *Oct.*—The potato crop was a good deal above the average, owing to the dry weather. Hay, straw and turnips are below the average, owing to the same cause. All other crops are up to the average. There was no injury to any of the crops by insects or fungi. *Newport D.*—7th *Nov.*—The potato crop is considerably good this year, which is attributed to the dry and warm weather in the months of May and June. For the same reason the hay is a little below the average, as this crop requires moisture during these months. Every other crop grown will be a fair average crop owing to the favourable weather. There was no injury done to any crops by insects or fungi. *Swinford D.*—28th *Oct.*—The increase in the potato crop this year has been due to the favourable season, and freedom from blight. There have been no complaints so far as regards damage to crops by insects, fungi, or weeds, and the season has been fairly good for the farmers. *Westport D.*—29th *Nov.*—The season having been favourable, the yield of every crop is somewhat over the average, hay alone excepted. The methods of farming remain unchanged. The crops are infested with weeds, which, of course, harbour insects and fungi, while the land is exhausted by weeds which, after weeding, are wasted by being burnt instead of being rotted for manure. Further, very little effort is made to preserve manure. A little systematic exertion on the part of the cultivators in saving manure repays the trouble well, but the inland small farmers cannot conceive means of increasing the manure heap or the advantage of deepening the soil by tillage.

ROSCOMMON COUNTY.—*Athlone D.*—[illegible] Oct.—The drought in June and July caused the oats and early hay to be a light crop. It also affected the turnip crop as the seeds did not [illegible] at all until the rain came. The dry weather suited the potato crop, and prolonged their growth; they will be a plentiful crop. I have not heard of any special injury to crops in this district from insects or fungi. *Boyle D.*—[illegible] Nov.—As a rule the good yield on these [illegible] was on the good land, and the bad yield on small and [illegible] farms. The latter, too, have the disadvantage of being very weedy. The small farmers in this district seem to have a total disregard for weeds, and make no attempt to clean and improve the land. It would be beneficial to this country if farmers were compelled by law to keep down weeds. It was [illegible], in some places, to see the state the potato crop was left in this respect. As regards the hay crop, there was but a light crop with very little "[illegible]" in the early part of the season, and a consequently bad yield in crops cut early, owing to the early dry season. The later rains, however, made a good [illegible] growth, and the yield of later crops was much improved; but much of this was badly saved, owing to rain, and so far as I can see we have not such good hay as last year. *Castlerea D.*—[illegible] Nov.—On the whole the crops are good. Potatoes are excellent as a rule. The only crops not up to average are the early hay crop, which was light owing to drought of early summer (the later hay crop was heavy) and the turnip crop, which failed in some places, owing to the ravages of the fly in months of May and June. Fungi do not seem to have been particularly injurious this year. *Roscommon D.*—1st Nov.—The potato crop is the best on record. June frosts injured them in [illegible], but they recovered, and the result is as stated. Very green hay was saved, but aftergrass was also nearly a record crop. Oat straw is good and plentiful, oats are thin and [illegible]. The cause in these was the great heat and drought early in the season, and [illegible] rain later on. Turnips show much leaf and small bulb, the result of green rain and no heat later on. In [illegible] some damage [illegible] [illegible], but it was very partial, and did very little general injury. *Strokestown D.*—31st Oct.—The wheat, oats, rye, and hay in this district are a fair average, owing to the latter part of the season having been so good. The straw in the three former cases is somewhat short, owing to the extreme dryness of the early summer. Turnips, mangolds, and cabbages are also fair for the same reason. The potato crop is exceptionally good, owing to the dry season and the consequent absence of blight to any appreciable extent. In bog lands the potato crop is not so good owing to early frosts. None of these crops have been affected by flies or fungi of any sort.

PROVINCE OF CONNAUGHT.

SLIGO COUNTY.—*Ballymote D.*—2nd Nov.—The fairly good yield of crops is attributed to the fine spring, moist summer, and fine harvest weather. There has been no injury of any consequence to crops from insects or fungi during the past season. *Collooney D.*—[illegible] Nov.—The potato crop is, generally, very good as regards quality and quantity, and is far superior to last year's crop, chiefly due to favourable weather, selection of good seed, as well as more care in the preparation, &c., of the crop while growing. Turnips, mangolds, cabbage, and other green crops are good throughout the district, due to the good season and freedom of the soil from destructive worms, &c. The farmers, generally, appear to have devoted more care and attention to the crops than usual, hence the satisfactory results of a very good yield this year. The oat crop, although fairly good, is scarcely up to its usual average, owing to the dry season. The grain is sound, but the straw is short, and taking the whole district into consideration the farmers are fairly satisfied. With regard to meadows in this district the return is fairly good also. Although the crop is somewhat light, yet from the fact of being cut and saved in good weather the quality is excellent. I am glad to be in a position to inform you that no injury has been done to crops in this district by insects or fungi during the past season; and taking all the surrounding circumstances into consideration it is safe to state that the average yield of all crops in this district this season, are as good as we have had for a number of years past. *Easky D.*—1st Nov.—There were no crops injured by insects or fungi during the past season so far as I could ascertain. *Sligo D.*—[illegible] Nov.—Generally the potato is above the average this year, attributable to the favourable weather. Latterly a rot has shown itself in many places, believed to be due to the rain in August. Other crops are fair as compared with other years except hay and oats which are somewhat below the average. *Tubbercurry D.*—1st Nov.—Crops of all classes are fairly good. Potatoes are very good owing to the dry season and occasional showers. Some farmers used the spraying machines with good and satisfactory results. No remarkable injury was done to crops by insects or fungi.

# APPENDIX—SILOS

The following statements have been received from persons who have made Ensilage in Ireland in 188[illegible]

PROVINCE OF

| [illegible] | [illegible] | [illegible] | [illegible] | Materials of [illegible] | | | [illegible] | [illegible] | [illegible] |
|---|---|---|---|---|---|---|---|---|---|
| | | | | Walls. | Floor. | Roof. | | | |
| **CARLOW COUNTY.** | | | | | | | | | |
| [illegible] | – | 1 | – | – | – | – | – | – | [illegible] |
| **DUBLIN COUNTY.** | | | | | | | | | |
| [illegible] | 1 | – | [illegible] | Concrete, | [illegible] | Wood. | [illegible] | [illegible] | No. |
| [illegible] | – | 1 | – | – | – | – | – | – | [illegible] |
| **KILDARE COUNTY.** | | | | | | | | | |
| [illegible] | 1 | – | [illegible] | [illegible] | [illegible] | [illegible] | No. | [illegible] | Not this year. |
| [illegible] | – | 1 | – | – | – | – | – | – | [illegible] |
| **KILKENNY COUNTY.** | | | | | | | | | |
| [illegible] | – | 1 | – | – | – | – | – | – | [illegible] |
| [illegible] | – | 1 | – | – | – | – | – | – | [illegible] |
| [illegible] | – | 1 | | – | – | – | – | – | [illegible] |
| [illegible] | – | 1 | – | – | – | – | – | – | [illegible] |

# AND ENSILAGE.

The names and addresses have been inserted in those cases where permission has been given to include them.

## LEINSTER.

PROVINCE OF

| [illegible] | [illegible] | [illegible] | [illegible] | [illegible] | | | [illegible] | [illegible] | [illegible] |
|---|---|---|---|---|---|---|---|---|---|
| | | | | [illegible] | [illegible] | [illegible] | | | |
| KING'S COUNTY. | | | | | | | | | |
| [illegible] | - | 1 | — | [illegible] | | — | — | — | [illegible] |
| [illegible] | | 1 | — | — | — | | — | — | [illegible] |
| [illegible] | - | 1 | | — | — | — | — | — | [illegible] |
| [illegible] | - | - | — | — | — | — | | — | — |
| [illegible] | | 1 | — | — | — | | — | — | [illegible] |
| [illegible] | - | | — | — | | | — | — | |
| [illegible] | - | 1 | — | — | — | — | — | — | [illegible] |
| [illegible] | - | 1 | — | — | — | — | — | — | [illegible] |
| [illegible] | 1 | - | [illegible] | [illegible] | [illegible] | [illegible] | [illegible] | [illegible] | [illegible] |
| [illegible] | - | 1 | — | — | — | — | | — | [illegible] |
| [illegible] | - | 1 | — | — | — | — | — | — | [illegible] |
| [illegible] | - | 1 | — | — | — | — | — | — | [illegible] |
| [illegible] | 1 | - | [illegible] | [illegible] | [illegible] | [illegible] | [illegible] | [illegible] | [illegible] |

LEINSTER—*continued.*

| [illegible] | [illegible] | Temperature. | | [illegible] | [illegible] | Remarks. |
|---|---|---|---|---|---|---|
| | | [illegible] | [illegible] | | | |
| — | — | — | — | — | — | |
| [illegible] | [illegible] | — | — | [illegible] | [illegible] | [illegible] |
| — | — | — | — | — | — | [illegible] |
| — | — | — | — | — | — | [illegible] |
| [illegible] | [illegible] | [illegible] | | [illegible] | [illegible] | [illegible] |
| — | — | — | — | | | [illegible] |
| [illegible] | [illegible] | [illegible] | [illegible] | [illegible] | [illegible] | [illegible] |
| [illegible] | — | — | — | [illegible] | [illegible] | [illegible] |
| [illegible] | [illegible] | [illegible] | | [illegible] | [illegible] | |
| [illegible] | [illegible] | [illegible] | | [illegible] | [illegible] | [illegible] |
| [illegible] | [illegible] | [illegible] | | [illegible] | [illegible] | — |
| [illegible] | [illegible] | [illegible] | | [illegible] | | [illegible] |
| — | [illegible] | — | — | — | — | [illegible] |

PROVINCE OF

| [illegible] | [illegible] | [illegible] | [illegible] | Materials of Silos. | | | [illegible] | [illegible] | [illegible] |
|---|---|---|---|---|---|---|---|---|---|
| | | | | Walls. | Floors. | Roof. | | | |
| [illegible] COUNTY. [illegible] | - | 1 | — | — | — | — | — | — | [illegible] |
| [illegible] | - | 1 | — | — | — | — | — | — | [illegible] |
| [illegible] | - | 1 | — | — | — | — | — | — | [illegible] |
| LOUTH COUNTY. [illegible] | - | 1 | — | — | — | — | — | — | [illegible] |
| [illegible] | 1 | - | [illegible] | [illegible] | [illegible] | [illegible] | [illegible] | [illegible] | W |
| [illegible] COUNTY. [illegible] | 1 | 2 | [illegible] | [illegible] | [illegible] | [illegible] | [illegible] | [illegible] | [illegible] |
| [illegible] | - | 1 | — | — | — | — | — | — | [illegible] |
| [illegible] | - | 1 | — | — | — | — | — | — | [illegible] |

LEINSTER—*continued.*

| [illegible] | [illegible] | [illegible] | | [illegible] | [illegible] | Remarks. |
|---|---|---|---|---|---|---|
| | | [illegible] | [illegible] | | | |
| [illegible] | [illegible] | [illegible] | [illegible] | [illegible] | [illegible] | [illegible] |
| [illegible] | [illegible] | [illegible] | — | [illegible] | [illegible] | [illegible] |
| — | [illegible] | — | — | — | [illegible] | — |
| [illegible] | [illegible] | [illegible] | [illegible] | [illegible] | [illegible] | [illegible] |
| [illegible] | [illegible] | — | — | [illegible] | [illegible] | [illegible] |
| [illegible] | [illegible] | [illegible] | [illegible] | [illegible] | [illegible] | [illegible] |
| — | [illegible] | — | — | — | — | [illegible] |
| [illegible] | [illegible] | [illegible] | [illegible] | [illegible] | [illegible] | [illegible] |

PROVINCE OF

| [illegible] | No. of [illegible] | No. of [illegible] | [illegible] | Materials of Silo: Walls | Floor | Roof | [illegible] | [illegible] | [illegible] |
|---|---|---|---|---|---|---|---|---|---|
| [illegible] COUNTY—continued. | | | | | | | | | |
| [illegible] | . | 1 | — | — | — | — | — | — | [illegible] |
| [illegible] | . | 1 | — | — | — | — | — | — | [illegible] |
| [illegible] | . | 1 | | — | — | — | — | — | [illegible] |
| [illegible] | — | 1 | — | — | — | — | — | — | [illegible] |
| [illegible] | 1 | — | [illegible] | [illegible] | [illegible] | [illegible] | [illegible] | [illegible] | [illegible] |
| [illegible] | . | 1 | — | — | — | — | — | — | [illegible] |
| [illegible] | 1 | — | [illegible] | [illegible] | [illegible] | [illegible] | [illegible] | [illegible] | — |
| [illegible] | 2 | — | [illegible] | [illegible] | [illegible] Do. | [illegible] Do. | [illegible] | [illegible] | [illegible] |
| [illegible] | . | 1 | — | — | — | — | — | — | [illegible] |
| [illegible] | . | 1 | — | — | — | — | — | — | [illegible] |
| [illegible] COUNTY. | | | | | | | | | |
| [illegible] | 1 | — | [illegible] | [illegible] | [illegible] | [illegible] | [illegible] | [illegible] | — |
| [illegible] | . | 1 | — | — | — | — | — | — | [illegible] |
| [illegible] | 1 | — | [illegible] | [illegible] | [illegible] | [illegible] | [illegible] | [illegible] | [illegible] |
| W[illegible] COUNTY. | | | | | | | | | |
| [illegible] | . | 1 | — | — | — | — | — | — | [illegible] |

LEINSTER—continued.

| [illegible] | [illegible] | Temperature. | | [illegible] | [illegible] | Remarks. |
|---|---|---|---|---|---|---|
| | | [illegible] | [illegible] | | | |
| [illegible] | [illegible] | [illegible] | [illegible] | [illegible] | [illegible] | — |
| [illegible] | [illegible] | Not taken. | | [illegible] | [illegible] | [illegible] |
| — | [illegible] | [illegible] | [illegible] | [illegible] | [illegible] | [illegible] |
| [illegible] | [illegible] | Not taken. | | [illegible] | [illegible] | [illegible] |
| [illegible] | [illegible] | — | — | [illegible] | Cattle. | |
| [illegible] | [illegible] | — | — | [illegible] | [illegible] | [illegible] |
| [illegible] | [illegible] | [illegible] | | — | [illegible] | [illegible] |
| — | [illegible] | — | — | — | [illegible] | — |
| [illegible] | [illegible] | Not taken. | | [illegible] | [illegible] | — |
| [illegible] | [illegible] | Not taken. | | [illegible] | [illegible] | [illegible] |
| [illegible] | [illegible] | Not taken. | | [illegible] | [illegible] | [illegible] |
| [illegible] | [illegible] | — | — | [illegible] | [illegible] | — |
| [illegible] | [illegible] | — | — | [illegible] | [illegible] | [illegible] |
| — | [illegible] | Not taken. | | [illegible] | [illegible] | [illegible] |

PROVINCE OF

| [illegible] | [illegible] | [illegible] | [illegible] | [illegible] | | | [illegible] | [illegible] | [illegible] |
|---|---|---|---|---|---|---|---|---|---|
| | | | | [illegible] | [illegible] | [illegible] | | | |
| [illegible] COUNTY—continued. | | | | | | | | | |
| [illegible] | [illegible] | [illegible] | — | — | — | — | — | — | [illegible] |
| [illegible] | [illegible] | [illegible] | — | — | — | — | — | — | [illegible] |
| [illegible] | [illegible] | [illegible] | — | — | — | — | — | | [illegible] |
| [illegible] | [illegible] | [illegible] | — | — | — | — | — | — | [illegible] |
| [illegible] | [illegible] | [illegible] | — | [illegible] | — | — | — | — | [illegible] |
| [illegible] | [illegible] | [illegible] | — | — | — | — | — | — | [illegible] |
| [illegible] | [illegible] | [illegible] | — | — | — | — | — | — | [illegible] |

LEINSTER—continued.

| [illegible] | [illegible] | Temperature. | | [illegible] | [illegible] | Remarks. |
|---|---|---|---|---|---|---|
| | | [illegible] | [illegible] | | | |
| [illegible] | [illegible] | [illegible] | [illegible] | [illegible] | [illegible] | [illegible] |
| [illegible] | [illegible] | [illegible] | [illegible] | [illegible] | [illegible] | [illegible] |
| [illegible] | [illegible] | [illegible] | [illegible] | [illegible] | [illegible] | [illegible] |
| [illegible] | [illegible] | [illegible] | [illegible] | [illegible] | [illegible] | [illegible] |
| [illegible] | [illegible] | [illegible] | [illegible] | [illegible] | [illegible] | [illegible] |
| [illegible] | [illegible] | [illegible] | [illegible] | [illegible] | [illegible] | [illegible] |
| [illegible] | [illegible] | [illegible] | [illegible] | [illegible] | [illegible] | [illegible] |

PROVINCE OF [illegible]

| [illegible] | [illegible] | [illegible] | [illegible] | [illegible] | | | [illegible] | [illegible] | [illegible] |
|---|---|---|---|---|---|---|---|---|---|
| | | | | [illegible] | [illegible] | [illegible] | | | |
| **[illegible] COUNTY—continued** | | | | | | | | | |
| [illegible] | [illegible] | [illegible] | — | — | — | — | — | — | [illegible] |
| **WEXFORD COUNTY.** | | | | | | | | | |
| [illegible] | [illegible] | [illegible] | [illegible] | Old walls, | Earth, | Slates, | [illegible] | Level with surface. | — |
| | | | [illegible] | Do. | Concrete, | Do. | Do. | Do. | |
| [illegible] | [illegible] | [illegible] | — | — | — | — | — | — | [illegible] |
| **WICKLOW COUNTY.** | | | | | | | | | |
| — | [illegible] | — | [illegible] | Stone and mortar. | Concrete, | Galvanised corrugated iron. | Drained, | Partly below [illegible] | No. |
| [illegible] | [illegible] | [illegible] | — | — | — | — | — | — | [illegible] |
| [illegible] | [illegible] | [illegible] | — | — | — | — | — | — | [illegible] |
| [illegible] | [illegible] | — | [illegible] | [illegible] | [illegible] | [illegible] | [illegible] | [illegible] | [illegible] |
| | | | [illegible] | Do. | Do. | Do. | [illegible] | [illegible] | |

PROVINCE OF [illegible]

| | | | | | | | | | |
|---|---|---|---|---|---|---|---|---|---|
| **CLARE COUNTY.** | | | | | | | | | |
| [illegible] | [illegible] | [illegible] | — | — | — | — | — | — | [illegible] |
| [illegible] | [illegible] | [illegible] | — | — | — | — | — | — | [illegible] |
| [illegible] | [illegible] | — | — | [illegible] | [illegible] | [illegible] | [illegible] | [illegible] | [illegible] |

LEINSTER—continued.

| [illegible] | [illegible] | Temperature. | | [illegible] | [illegible] | Remarks. |
|---|---|---|---|---|---|---|
| | | [illegible] | [illegible] | | | |
| [illegible] | [illegible] | [illegible] | [illegible] | [illegible] | [illegible] | [illegible] |
| [illegible] | [illegible] | [illegible] | [illegible] | [illegible] | — | [illegible] |
| [illegible] | [illegible] | [illegible] | — | [illegible] | [illegible] | [illegible] |
| [illegible] | [illegible] | [illegible] | [illegible] | [illegible] | [illegible] | [illegible] |
| [illegible] | [illegible] | [illegible] | [illegible] | [illegible] | [illegible] | — |
| [illegible] | [illegible] | [illegible] | [illegible] | [illegible] | [illegible] | [illegible] |
| [illegible] | [illegible] | [illegible] | [illegible] | [illegible] | [illegible] | [illegible] |

MUNSTER.

| | | | | | | |
|---|---|---|---|---|---|---|
| [illegible] | [illegible] | [illegible] | [illegible] | [illegible] | [illegible] | [illegible] |
| [illegible] | [illegible] | [illegible] | [illegible] | [illegible] | [illegible] | [illegible] |
| [illegible] | [illegible] | [illegible] | [illegible] | — | [illegible] | [illegible] |

PROVINCE OF

| Name and Residence. | No. of Silos. | No. of Stacks. | Dimensions [illegible] | Materials of Silo: Walls. | Floor. | Roof. | Whether drained or not. | [illegible] | [illegible] |
| --- | --- | --- | --- | --- | --- | --- | --- | --- | --- |
| CORK COUNTY. | | | | | | | | | |
| [illegible] | 1 | 1 | [illegible] | [illegible] | [illegible] | [illegible] | Do. | [illegible] | [illegible] |
| | | | [illegible] | Do. | Do. | Do. | Do. | Do. | |
| KERRY COUNTY. | | | | | | | | | |
| [illegible] | 1 | – | [illegible] | [illegible] | [illegible] | [illegible] | No. | [illegible] | No. |
| [illegible] | 1 | – | [illegible] | [illegible] | [illegible] | [illegible] | Yes. | [illegible] | No. |
| LIMERICK COUNTY. | | | | | | | | | |
| [illegible] | – | 1 | – | – | – | – | – | – | [illegible] |
| [illegible] | – | 1 | – | – | – | – | – | – | [illegible] |
| [illegible] | 1 | – | [illegible] | [illegible] | [illegible] | [illegible] | [illegible] | [illegible] | – |
| [illegible] | – | 1 | – | – | – | – | – | – | [illegible] |
| [illegible] | – | 1 | – | – | – | – | – | – | [illegible] |
| [illegible] | – | 1 | – | – | – | – | – | – | [illegible] |
| [illegible] | – | 1 | – | – | – | – | – | – | [illegible] |

MUNSTER—continued.

| Number of days [illegible] | Materials put in [illegible] | Temperature. | | Quantity of Ensilage [illegible] | To what description of Stock [illegible] | Remarks. |
|---|---|---|---|---|---|---|
| | | [illegible] | [illegible] | | | |
| [illegible] | [illegible] | [illegible] | | [illegible] | [illegible] | [illegible] |
| — | [illegible] | [illegible] | | [illegible] | [illegible] | — |
| [illegible] days. | [illegible] | | Not [illegible] | Not measured. | [illegible] | [illegible] |
| [illegible] | Ordinary [illegible] | | — | — | [illegible] | — |
| — | [illegible] | About [illegible] | About [illegible] | [illegible] | [illegible] | [illegible] |
| [illegible] | [illegible] | [illegible] | | — | [illegible] | — |
| [illegible] | [illegible] | [illegible] | | [illegible] | [illegible] | [illegible] |
| [illegible] days. | [illegible] | [illegible] | | [illegible] | [illegible] | [illegible] |
| [illegible] | [illegible] | [illegible] | | [illegible] | [illegible] | [illegible] |
| [illegible] days. | [illegible] | About [illegible] | About [illegible] | [illegible] | [illegible] | [illegible] |

PROVINCE OF

| [illegible] | [illegible] | [illegible] | [illegible] | Materials of Silo. | | | [illegible] | [illegible] | [illegible] |
|---|---|---|---|---|---|---|---|---|---|
| | | | | Walls. | Floor. | Roof. | | | |
| LIMERICK COUNTY—con. | | | | | | | | | |
| [illegible] | – | 1 | | – | | – | – | – | [illegible] |
| [illegible] | – | 1 | – | | – | | – | – | [illegible] |
| COUNTY TIPPERARY. | | | | | | | | | |
| [illegible] | 1 | [illegible] | [illegible] | [illegible] | [illegible] | [illegible] | [illegible] | [illegible] | [illegible] |
| | | | [illegible] | Do. | Do. | Do. | Do. | Do. | |
| [illegible] | – | 1 | – | – | – | – | – | – | [illegible] |
| [illegible] | 1 | [illegible] | [illegible] | [illegible] | [illegible] | [illegible] | [illegible] | [illegible] | [illegible] |
| [illegible] | – | 1 | – | – | | | – | – | [illegible] |
| [illegible] | 1 | 1 | [illegible] | [illegible] | [illegible] | [illegible] | [illegible] | [illegible] | [illegible] |
| [illegible] | – | 1 | | – | – | – | – | – | [illegible] |
| WATERFORD COUNTY. | | | | | | | | | |
| [illegible] | 1 | [illegible] | [illegible] | [illegible] | [illegible] | [illegible] | [illegible] | [illegible] | – |
| [illegible] | [illegible] | [illegible] | [illegible] | [illegible] | [illegible] | [illegible] | [illegible] | [illegible] | [illegible] |
| | | | [illegible] | Do. | Do. | Do. | Do. | Do. | |

MUNSTER—*continued.*

| [illegible] | [illegible] | Temperature. | | [illegible] | [illegible] | Remarks. |
|---|---|---|---|---|---|---|
| | | [illegible] | [illegible] | | | |
| [illegible] | [illegible] | [illegible] | [illegible] | [illegible] | [illegible] | [illegible] |
| [illegible] | [illegible] | [illegible] | [illegible] | [illegible] | [illegible] | [illegible] |
| — | [illegible] | — | — | [illegible] | [illegible] | [illegible] |
| — | — | — | — | — | — | [illegible] |
| [illegible] | [illegible] | [illegible] | [illegible] | [illegible] | [illegible] | [illegible] |
| [illegible] | [illegible] | — | — | [illegible] | [illegible] | [illegible] |
| [illegible] | [illegible] | [illegible] | | — | [illegible] | [illegible] |
| [illegible] | [illegible] | [illegible] | | [illegible] | [illegible] | [illegible] |
| — | [illegible] | [illegible] | [illegible] | — | [illegible] | [illegible] |
| [illegible] | [illegible] | | [illegible] | — | [illegible] | [illegible] |

PROVINCE OF

| [illegible] | [illegible] | [illegible] | [illegible] | Materials of Silos | | | [illegible] | [illegible] | [illegible] |
|---|---|---|---|---|---|---|---|---|---|
| | | | | Walls. | Floor. | Roof. | | | |
| ANTRIM COUNTY. | | | | | | | | | |
| [illegible] | [illegible] | [illegible] | [illegible] | [illegible] | [illegible] | [illegible] | [illegible] | Above. | No. |
| [illegible] | [illegible] | [illegible] | [illegible] | [illegible] | [illegible] | [illegible] | [illegible] | Above. | — |
| [illegible] | [illegible] | [illegible] | [illegible] | [illegible] | [illegible] | [illegible] | — | All above. | |
| [illegible] | [illegible] | [illegible] | — | | — | [illegible] | — | | [illegible] |
| [illegible] | [illegible] | [illegible] | [illegible] | [illegible] | [illegible] | [illegible] | [illegible] | [illegible] | [illegible] |
| CAVAN COUNTY. | | | | | | | | | |
| [illegible] | [illegible] | [illegible] | — | — | — | — | — | — | [illegible] |
| [illegible] | [illegible] | [illegible] | [illegible] | [illegible] | [illegible] | [illegible] | [illegible] | [illegible] | [illegible] |
| [illegible] | [illegible] | [illegible] | — | — | — | — | — | — | [illegible] |
| DONEGAL COUNTY. | | | | | | | | | |
| [illegible] | [illegible] | [illegible] | — | — | — | — | — | — | [illegible] |
| [illegible] | [illegible] | [illegible] | — | — | — | — | — | — | [illegible] |
| [illegible] | [illegible] | [illegible] | [illegible] | [illegible] | [illegible] | [illegible] | [illegible] | [illegible] | No. |
| DOWN COUNTY. | | | | | | | | | |
| [illegible] | [illegible] | [illegible] | [illegible] | [illegible] | [illegible] | [illegible] | [illegible] | [illegible] | No. |
| [illegible] | [illegible] | [illegible] | — | — | — | — | — | — | [illegible] |

CLOVER.

| [illegible] | [illegible] | Temperature. | | [illegible] | [illegible] | Remarks. |
|---|---|---|---|---|---|---|
| | | Greatest Heat. | [illegible] | | | |
| [illegible] | Meadow grass. | Not taken. | | About [illegible] | [illegible] | [illegible] |
| [illegible] | Grass. | [illegible] | | [illegible] | [illegible] | [illegible] |
| — | — | — | — | [illegible] | — | [illegible] |
| [illegible] | [illegible] | — | [illegible] | About [illegible] | [illegible] | — |
| [illegible] | Meadow grass [illegible] | [illegible] | Not taken. | About [illegible] | [illegible] | [illegible] |
| [illegible] | Grass. | [illegible] | | [illegible] | [illegible] | [illegible] |
| [illegible] | [illegible] | Not taken. | | [illegible] | [illegible] | [illegible] |
| About [illegible] | [illegible] | [illegible] | [illegible] | [illegible] | [illegible] | [illegible] |
| [illegible] | — | | — | — | [illegible] | [illegible] |
| [illegible] | [illegible] | Not taken. | | — | [illegible] | — |
| — | [illegible] | Not taken. | | [illegible] | [illegible] | [illegible] |
| [illegible] | [illegible] | [illegible] | [illegible] | [illegible] | [illegible] | [illegible] |
| [illegible] | [illegible] | [illegible] | — | [illegible] | — | — |

PROVINCE OF

| [illegible] | [illegible] | [illegible] | [illegible] | [illegible] of Silo. | | | [illegible] | [illegible] | [illegible] |
|---|---|---|---|---|---|---|---|---|---|
| | | | | Walls. | Floors. | Roof. | | | |
| [illegible] | [illegible] | [illegible] | [illegible] | [illegible] | [illegible] | [illegible] | [illegible] | [illegible] | [illegible] |

ULSTER—*continued.*

| [illegible] | [illegible] | Temperature. | | [illegible] | [illegible] | Remarks. |
|---|---|---|---|---|---|---|
| | | [illegible] | [illegible] | | | |
| — | [illegible] | — | — | — | [illegible] | [illegible] |
| [illegible] | [illegible] | — | — | [illegible] | [illegible] | [illegible] |
| [illegible] | [illegible] | [illegible] | | [illegible] | [illegible] | [illegible] |
| [illegible] | [illegible] | [illegible] | | [illegible] | [illegible] | [illegible] |
| [illegible] | [illegible] | [illegible] | [illegible] | [illegible] | [illegible] | [illegible] |
| [illegible] | [illegible] | [illegible] | [illegible] | [illegible] | [illegible] | [illegible] |
| — | — | — | — | — | — | [illegible] |
| — | [illegible] | [illegible] | | [illegible] | [illegible] | [illegible] |
| [illegible] | [illegible] | — | — | [illegible] | [illegible] | [illegible] |
| [illegible] | [illegible] | — | — | [illegible] | [illegible] | [illegible] |
| — | [illegible] | [illegible] | | [illegible] | [illegible] | [illegible] |
| [illegible] | [illegible] | [illegible] | | [illegible] | [illegible] | [illegible] |

PROVINCE OF [illegible]

| [illegible] | No. of Silos. | No. of Stacks. | [illegible] | Materials of Silo. | | | [illegible] | [illegible] | [illegible] |
|---|---|---|---|---|---|---|---|---|---|
| | | | | Walls. | Floor. | Roof. | | | |
| [illegible] COUNTY—continued. | | | | | | | | | |
| [illegible] | 1 | – | [illegible] | [illegible] | [illegible] | [illegible] | [illegible] | [illegible] | [illegible] |
| [illegible] | – | 1 | | | — | | | | [illegible] |

PROVINCE OF [illegible]

| | | | | | | | | | |
|---|---|---|---|---|---|---|---|---|---|
| GALWAY COUNTY. | | | | | | | | | |
| [illegible] | 1 | – | [illegible] | [illegible] | [illegible] | [illegible] | [illegible] | [illegible] | [illegible] |
| [illegible] | 1 | 1 | [illegible] | [illegible] | [illegible] | [illegible] | [illegible] | [illegible] | [illegible] |
| [illegible] | 1 | – | [illegible] | [illegible] | [illegible] | [illegible] | [illegible] | [illegible] | [illegible] |
| [illegible] | – | 1 | — | — | — | — | — | — | [illegible] |
| [illegible] | – | 1 | — | — | — | — | — | — | [illegible] |
| [illegible] | 1 | – | [illegible] | [illegible] | [illegible] | [illegible] | [illegible] | [illegible] | — |
| [illegible] COUNTY. | | | | | | | | | |
| [illegible] | – | 1 | — | — | — | — | — | — | [illegible] |
| [illegible] | 1 | – | [illegible] | [illegible] | [illegible] | [illegible] | [illegible] | [illegible] | [illegible] |
| [illegible] | 1 | – | [illegible] | [illegible] | [illegible] | [illegible] | [illegible] | [illegible] | [illegible] |
| [illegible] | 2 | – | [illegible] | [illegible] | [illegible] | [illegible] | [illegible] | [illegible] | [illegible] |
| | | | [illegible] | [illegible] | [illegible] | [illegible] | [illegible] | [illegible] | |

ULSTER—continued.

| [illegible] | [illegible] | Temperature. | | [illegible] | [illegible] | Remarks. |
|---|---|---|---|---|---|---|
| | | Greatest Heat. | [illegible] | | | |
| — | — | — | — | — | — | [illegible] |
| [illegible] | — | [illegible] | | | [illegible] | [illegible] |

CONNAUGHT.

| | | | | | | |
|---|---|---|---|---|---|---|
| [illegible] | [illegible] | [illegible] | | — | [illegible] | [illegible] |
| [illegible] | Grass | [illegible] | | [illegible] | [illegible] | [illegible] |
| [illegible] | Meadow grass | [illegible] | | [illegible] | [illegible] | [illegible] |
| [illegible] | Grass | [illegible] | | [illegible] | [illegible] | [illegible] |
| [illegible] | [illegible] | — | — | [illegible] | [illegible] | [illegible] |
| [illegible] | [illegible] | Not taken. | | [illegible] | [illegible] | [illegible] |
| [illegible] | Grass | [illegible] | | [illegible] | [illegible] | [illegible] |
| [illegible] | Meadow grass | [illegible] | | [illegible] | [illegible] | [illegible] |
| [illegible] | [illegible] | Not taken. | | — | [illegible] | [illegible] |
| [illegible] | [illegible] | [illegible] | | [illegible] | [illegible] | [illegible] |

PROVINCE OF

| [illegible] | [illegible] | [illegible] | [illegible] | [illegible] | | | [illegible] | [illegible] | [illegible] |
|---|---|---|---|---|---|---|---|---|---|
| | | | | Walls. | Floors. | Roof. | | | |
| MAYO COUNTY. | | | | | | | | | |
| [illegible] | 1 | – | [illegible] | Common | Common | Iron | England | [illegible] | [illegible] |
| | | | | Do. | Sandstone, (granite) | Do. | Do. | | |
| [illegible] | 1 | – | [illegible] | Common | Cement | [illegible] | [illegible] | [illegible] | Do. |
| [illegible] | – | 1 | – | – | – | – | – | – | [illegible] |
| [illegible] | – | 1 | – | – | – | – | – | – | [illegible] |
| ROSCOMMON COUNTY. | | | | | | | | | |
| [illegible] | – | 1 | – | – | – | – | – | – | [illegible] |
| [illegible] | 1 | 1 | [illegible] | Stone | – | – | – | – | [illegible] |
| [illegible] | 1 | 1 | – | – | – | – | – | – | – |
| SLIGO COUNTY. | | | | | | | | | |
| [illegible] | – | 1 | – | – | – | – | – | – | [illegible] |
| [illegible] | – | 1 | – | – | – | – | – | – | [illegible] |
| [illegible] | – | 1 | – | – | – | – | – | – | [illegible] |

CONNAUGHT—continued.

| [illegible] | [illegible] | [illegible] | | [illegible] | [illegible] | [illegible] |
|---|---|---|---|---|---|---|
| | | [illegible] | [illegible] | | | |
| [illegible] | [illegible] | [illegible] | [illegible] | [illegible] | [illegible] | [illegible] |
| [illegible] | [illegible] | [illegible] | | [illegible] | [illegible] | [illegible] |
| [illegible] | [illegible] | [illegible] | | [illegible] | [illegible] | [illegible] |
| — | [illegible] | — | — | [illegible] | [illegible] | — |
| [illegible] | [illegible] | [illegible] | | [illegible] | [illegible] | [illegible] |
| [illegible] | [illegible] | [illegible] | | [illegible] | [illegible] | — |
| — | — | — | — | — | — | [illegible] |
| [illegible] | [illegible] | [illegible] | [illegible] | [illegible] | [illegible] | — |
| [illegible] | [illegible] | [illegible] | [illegible] | [illegible] | [illegible] | [illegible] |
| [illegible] | [illegible] | [illegible] | [illegible] | [illegible] | [illegible] | [illegible] |

## THE WEATHER.

Abstract of Meteorological Observations registered at the Ordnance Survey Office (Height above the Sea 155·3 Feet), Phœnix Park, Dublin, during the year 1893:—

The barometer stood highest in 1893, on the 2nd May, at 9 A.M., wind W., when it was [illegible] inches; it was lowest at 9 P.M. on 10th November, when it was 28·507 inches, wind S. The highest temperature of the air during the year was 77·6 degrees of Fahrenheit on 25th June, and the lowest 7·9 degrees on 7th February. The greatest quantity of rain which fell in a day (24 hours) was 1·680 inches on 25th July, with wind N.E. The point from which the wind chiefly prevailed was the W.; it blew from that direction on 113 days, at 9 A.M. The strongest wind was from the S.S.E. on the 22nd December, when the pressure was 8·75 lbs. per square foot.

| 1893 | Barometer | Temperature |
| --- | --- | --- |
| [illegible] | [illegible] | [illegible] |
| Total | [illegible] | [illegible] |
| Mean | [illegible] | [illegible] |

| 1893 | Rain | Clouds | Wind |
| --- | --- | --- | --- |
| [illegible] | [illegible] | [illegible] | [illegible] |
| Total | [illegible] | [illegible] | [illegible] |
| Mean | [illegible] | [illegible] | [illegible] |

# METEOROLOGICAL OBSERVATIONS

## FOR EACH MONTH OF THE YEAR 1895.

By J. W. MOORE, Esq., M.D., F.R.C.P.I., F.R. Met. Soc.

(Extracted from the *Dublin Journal of Medical Science*.)

JANUARY.—A very severe month, with much snow and frost alternating with frequent thaws. The wind was very variable in direction, but came generally from polar quarters—from W. to S.E. through the northerly points of the compass. The coldest January since 1881, and as regards rainfall a record month. The precipitation was chiefly in the form of snow or sleet and hail. It amounted to 5·711 inches, or considerably more than double the average rainfall for January, and 1·389 inches in excess of the rainfall for this month in 1877, which had been the record January rainfall up to the present year. The snowstorm of the 12th was in Dublin a perfect blizzard.

In Dublin the arithmetical mean temperature (35·6°) was much below the average (41·6°); the mean dry bulb readings at 9 a.m. and 9 p.m. were 34·6°. In the thirty years ending with 1894, January was coldest in 1881 (M. T. = 33·2°), and warmest in 1873 (M. T. = 46·6°). In 1867 the M. T. was 35·7°, and in 1868 it was 37·8°. In 1871 and in 1886 the M. T. was 37·9°; in 1879 (the "cold year") it was 35·3°. In 1888 the M. T. was 42·1°; in 1889, 47·6°; in 1890, 44·3°; in 1891, 40·3°; in 1892, 38·6°; in 1893, 40·5°, and in 1894, 41·0°. As a general rule, January in Dublin is not colder, but a shade warmer, than December. This is owing to the full development in January of a winter area of low pressure over the Atlantic, to the northwestward of the British Isles, and to a resulting prevalence of S.W. winds in their vicinity. January, 1895, proved an extreme exception to this rule, the M. T. being 8·5° below that of December, 1894 (43·9°).

The mean height of the barometer was 29·760 inches, or 0·114 inch below the corrected average value, for January—namely, 29·874 inches. The mercury rose to 30·630 inches at 7 p.m. of the 30th, and fell to 28·733 inches at 1.30 a.m. of the 14th. The observed range of atmospheric pressure was, therefore, as much as 1·897 inches—that is, a little less than one inch and nine-tenths.

The mean temperature deduced from daily readings of the dry bulb thermometer at 9 a.m. and 9 p.m. was 34·6°, or 8·4° below the value for December, 1894. Using the formula, *Mean Temp. = Min. + (max.—min. × ·32)*, the M. T. becomes 33·6°, compared with a twenty-five years' average of 41·6°. The arithmetical mean of the maximal and minimal readings was 35·6°, compared with a twenty-five years' average of 41·8°. On the 22nd the thermometer in the screen rose to 44·8°—wind, W.; on the 9th the temperature fell to 16·3°—wind, W. The minimum on the grass was 10·0°, also on the 9th.

The rainfall was 5·711 inches, distributed over 25 days. The average rainfall for January in the twenty-five years, 1865-89, inclusive, was 2·[illegible] inches, and the average number of rainy days was 17·8. The rainfall, therefore, and the rainy days were both much above the average. In 1877 the rainfall in January was very large—4·322 inches on 24 days; in 1869, also, 4·[illegible] inches fell—on, however, only 19 days. On the other hand, in 1876, only ·406 inch was measured on but 9 days; and in 1880 the rainfall was only ·458 inch on but 8 days. In January, 1888, 2·244 inches of rain was measured on 20 days; in 1887 ("the dry year"), 1·418 inches fell on 16 days; in 1888, 1·347 inches on 9 days; in 1889, 2·313 inches on 16 days; in 1890, [illegible] inches on 22 days; in 1891, only ·678 inch on 14 days; in 1892, 1·[illegible] inches on 13 days; in 1893, 2·[illegible] inches on 19 days, and in 1894, 3·[illegible] inches on 23 days.

Lunar halos were seen on the 5th and 6th. The atmosphere was foggy on the 6th, 9th, 16th, 19th, and 28th. High winds were noted on 10 days, reaching the force of a gale on 4 days—the 6th, 11th, 12th, and 24th. Hail fell on the 2nd, 6th, 7th, 9th, 10th, 13th, 21st, 24th, 25th, and 31st, and snow or sleet on the 3rd, 5th, 6th, 7th, 8th, 10th, 12th, 13th, 25th, 27th, 29th, 30th, and 31st. Temperature never exceeded 45° in the screen; while it fell to or below 32° in the screen on 19 nights, compared with 7 nights in 1894, 6 nights in 1893, 13 nights in 1892, 7 nights in 1891, 1 night in 1890, and 3 nights in 1889. The minima on the grass were 32°, or less, on 29 nights, compared with 17 nights in 1894, 16 nights in 1893, 22 nights in 1892, 21 nights in 1891, 15 nights in 1890, and 16 nights in 1889.

The record for the period ended Saturday the 5th, is one of very cold, changeable weather, fresh to strong westerly to northerly winds, alternate cloud and sunshine, rain or snow and frost. Tuesday, the 1st, was fair and frosty, but a thaw set in at night and a good deal of cold rain fell on Wednesday. In the evening squalls of heavy rain and hail passed over Dublin, and the wind (which had backed to W. or W.S.W.) began again to veer towards N. By Thursday morning a depression of some intensity had formed over the Straits of Dover and the N.E. of France. This caused cold showers, and strong northerly winds in the British Isles. In Dublin the weather on this day was very bright and dry, but heavy showers were seen to pass southwards out at sea, and thunder, lightning and hail occurred in the Scilly Islands at night. Sharp frost set in on Friday, but the approach of a new depression from N.W. brought sleet and rain on Saturday, the phenomenon of a "glazed frost" being observed in Dublin throughout the forenoon. The height of the barometer in Dublin ranged between 29·705 inches at 9 p.m. of Wednesday (wind, W.N.W.) and 30·313 inches at 9 p.m. of Friday (wind, N.W.) On Wednesday the screened thermometers rose to 48·0°; on Saturday, they fell to 28·0°. The minimum on the grass on the latter day was 21·0°. Rain fell on three days to the total amount of ·316 inch, ·213 inch being measured on Wednesday. The prevailing wind was N.W. Hail fell on Wednesday; sleet, or snow, on Thursday and Saturday.

Weather of exceptional severity held throughout Western Europe all through the week ended Saturday the 12th. Until Wednesday, the barometer was highest off the W. and N.W. of Ireland, low over Great Britain and Central Europe, lowest over Italy and the Mediterranean. Severe polar winds prevailed, and there were frequent falls of snow and hail. On Tuesday snow fell in large quantities in and about Dublin at a temperature of [illegible]°—the depth of snow on the level was [illegible] inches. The sky became cloudy at night, checking radiation; but afterwards the clouds dispersed and temperature fell with great rapidity to [illegible]° in the screen and [illegible]° on the snow. Hard frost prevailed throughout Wednesday, cirro-cumulus clouds coming from E.S.E. and S.E., while a light westerly land breeze and much fog held all day. Atmospheric pressure now gave way in the W., so that a decided southerly air-current spread over Ireland, with a rising thermometer, thaw, and falls of rain, sleet, and hail. At this time, the frost "stiffened" in England and remained intense in Scotland. On Friday, at 8 a.m., the thermometer read 11° at Aberdeen, 14° at York, 16° at Loughborough, 1[illegible]° at Shields, and 1[illegible]° at Oxford. In Dublin there was a steady thaw on this day, with a piercingly cold S.S.E. wind, which momentarily freshened, until at night it blew a fresh to strong gale. After midnight the most violent snowstorm experienced since January 18, 1881, began and raged until late on Saturday afternoon. It was renewed on Saturday night, so that no such snowfall has occurred in Dublin since 1855—the "Crimean winter." In Dublin the mean atmospheric pressure was [illegible] inches, the barometer rising to [illegible] inches at 9 p.m. on Monday (wind, N.N.E.), and falling to [illegible] inches at 9 p.m. of Saturday (wind, S.E.). The corrected mean temperature was [illegible]°. The mean dry bulb reading at 9 a.m. and 9 p.m. was 3[illegible]°. On Sunday the screened thermometers rose to [illegible]°, on Wednesday they fell to 1[illegible]°. The rainfall (which consisted chiefly of snow and hail) amounted to [illegible] inches, on six days, [illegible] inch being credited to Friday and 1·[illegible] inches to Saturday. The prevailing winds were N.N.E. and S.S.E.

The record of the week ended Saturday, the 19th, is again one of cold, wintery, and generally unsettled weather. The cold was certainly not so severe as that felt in the previous week, but in Dublin especially it was intensified by a prolonged thaw during the early days of the period—in fact, masses of snow lay here and there even on Saturday, a week after the "blizzard" of the 12th. On Sunday and Monday the centre of the large and deep depression, which had caused the south-easterly gale and snowstorm, lay almost stationary over the Co. Kerry and the adjacent parts of the Atlantic. The wind remained in the S.E., except in Brittany and off the entrance to the English Channel, where it was south-westerly. Rain fell at most stations in variable amounts. In Dublin the precipitation was considerable, in consequence probably of a local chill caused by the melting snow. The depression moved eastwards on Tuesday and then passed up St. George's Channel, crossing Wales and the North of England, and finally joining another depression off the North of Scotland on Thursday morning. From the time of its appearance on Friday, January 11, until it passed away on Friday, the 18th, this depression caused a rainfall of no less than [illegible] inches in the City of Dublin—this is nearly double the average January rainfall in Dublin—[illegible] inches. Friday was fine and frosty, but at night the weather again became rainy, and Saturday was wet and gloomy in the afternoon. In Dublin the mean atmospheric pressure was only [illegible] inches—the barometer remaining below 29 inches for as many as [illegible] hours—from 10 p.m. of Saturday, the 12th, until midnight of Wednesday, the 16th. The absolute minimum at this station was [illegible] inches at 7.30 a.m. of Monday (wind, S.E.). The maximum pressure was [illegible] inches at 9 p.m. of Friday (wind, calm). The corrected mean temperature was [illegible]°. The mean dry bulb reading at 9 a.m. and 9 p.m. was [illegible]°. On Tuesday and again on Saturday temperature rose to [illegible]° in the screen; on Friday it fell to [illegible]° in the screen, and to [illegible]° on the grass. The rainfall was 1·[illegible] inches on six days, [illegible] inch being registered on Wednesday. Snow and hail fell on Sunday.

The weather during the week ended Saturday, the 26th, continued wintery and inclement as in past weeks. Polar winds prevailed, and blew strongly, as barometric gradients were at times very steep. Considerable quantities of cold rain, hail, and snow fell generally, and thunder and lightning, followed by a snowstorm, were reported from London on Wednesday afternoon. At the beginning of the week a depression lay near the mouth of the English Channel, and from this position it travelled south-eastwards across France, gradually filling up and finally dispersing. This disturbance brought copious falls of rain to England and the French shores of the Channel. Temperature also rose very decidedly but transitorily over the South of England—to 5[illegible]° in London and [illegible]° at Prawle Point on Sunday. In Scotland on that day the thermometer failed to read 4[illegible]°, and in Ireland the highest reading was 44° in Dublin and at Roche's Point, Cork. From Tuesday onward the barometer remained very low in the North of Europe, and more or less serious secondary depressions passed in a south-easterly direction down the North Sea or across the British Islands. At 8 a.m. of Thursday the barometer read only [illegible] inches at Wick, but [illegible] inches at Valentia (Kerry). On Friday, a rush of intensely cold, dry polar air passed southwards over the United Kingdom, and dry powdery snow fell. On the morning of this day the thermometer read −1[illegible]° F. at Haparanda, on the Gulf of Bothnia. In Dublin, the mean atmospheric pressure was [illegible] inches, the barometer ranging from [illegible] inches at 9 p.m. of Monday (wind, N.N.E.) to [illegible] inches at 1[illegible] p.m. of Thursday (wind, W.N.W.). The corrected mean temperature was [illegible]°. The mean dry bulb temperature at 9 a.m. and 9 p.m. was [illegible]°. On Tuesday, the screened thermometers rose to [illegible]°—the maximum of this cold month; on Saturday they fell to [illegible]°. The rainfall was [illegible] inch, on six days, [illegible] inch being measured on Wednesday. Hail fell on Monday, Thursday, and Friday; snow on Friday. The prevalent winds were N.E. and N.W.

Frequent changes from frost to thaw, and an almost uninterrupted prevalence of winds from polar quarters made the last days of the month very trying. The striking features of the period were the intensity of the cold in all parts of Western Europe from time to time and the sudden and unusual alterations of atmospheric pressure which occurred. On Sunday and Monday a chain of shallow barometric depressions stretched from the Arctic Circle across Norway down the North Sea and across France to the Mediterranean. Fresh northerly winds blew in Scotland and Ireland, which lay to the west of the trough of low pressure, and snow and hail fell at intervals. On Sunday evening lightning was seen in Dublin, at Prawle Point, Devon, and in Jersey. On Monday night a shallow V-shaped depression advanced over Ireland from the Atlantic, causing a thaw and rain on Tuesday. This low-pressure system was filled up, as an anticyclone of unusual intensity formed over the South of Scandinavia, where the barometer rose to 31·0 inches at 8 a.m. of Wednesday. The barometer remaining low in the Mediterranean basin, fresh easterly gales and bitter cold prevailed until the close of the month. Throughout the period large quantities of snow or sleet and hail fell in nearly all districts. In Dublin atmospheric pressure ranged between 29·309 inches at 9 a.m. of Sunday (wind, W.N.W.) and 30·590 inches at 7 p.m. of Wednesday (wind, E.). On Monday the screened thermometers fell to 12·5°; on Tuesday they rose to 41·9°. The prevalent winds were N.W., E., and N.E. The rainfall (chiefly in the form of snow, sleet, and hail) was ·161 inch on three days—·080 inch being measured on Thursday, the 31st.

In Dublin the rainfall up to January 31, 1895, amounted to 3·711 inches on 24 days, compared with a twenty-five years' average (1866–1890) of 2·239 inches on 17·3 days.

At Knockdolian, Greystones, Co. Wicklow, 6·190 inches of rain fell on 19 days. The heaviest falls in 24 hours were 1·040 inches on the 12th, and ·810 inch on the 10th.

At Cloneevin, Killiney, Co. Dublin, the rainfall was 3·930 inches on 24 days, 1·070 inches being measured on the 12th. This was the highest rainfall recorded at this station in January during the past 11 years. The average fall for the preceding 10 years was 2·019 inches on 16·0 days. Snow fell on the 1st, 2nd, 6th, 7th, 12th, 13th, and 31st. In 1894, the rainfall was 2·390 inches on 23 days.

FEBRUARY.—The coldest February experienced for forty years—that is, since 1855—the "Crimean winter." The mean temperature was 8·5° below the average, 10·7° below that of February, 1894, and 1·6° below that of January, 1895. There was an overwhelming prevalence of strong easterly and south-easterly winds. The rainfall was very scanty, and consisted principally of snow and hail. Absolute drought held from the 7th to the 20th, inclusive. On several occasions the thermometer fell below zero in the screen in various parts of the United Kingdom, the lowest recorded reading of all being—17° at Braemar on the 11th.

In Dublin the mean temperature (30·3°) was 8·6° below the average (42·8°); the mean dry bulb readings at 9 a.m. and 9 p.m. were 33·0°. In the thirty years ending with 1894, February was coldest in 1873 (M. T. = 37·9°), and warmest in 1869 (M. T. = 45·7°). In 1886 the M. T. was 39·7°. In the year 1879 (the "cold year") it was 40·1°. In 1855 it was as low as 33·0°; in 1889 it was 40·3°; in 1890, 41·5°; in 1891, 44·7°; in 1892, 41·2°; in 1893, 43·7°; and in 1894, 44·5°.

The mean height of the barometer was 30·113 inches, or 0·246 inch above the average value for February—namely, 29·863 inches. The mercury rose to 30·548 inches at 9 p.m. of the 18th, and fell to 29·576 inches at 9 p.m. of the 6th. The observed range of atmospheric pressure was, therefore, 0·972 inch—that is, a little less than an inch.

The mean temperature deduced from daily readings of the dry bulb thermometer at 9 a.m. and 9 p.m. was 33·6°, or 10·1° below the value for February, 1894, and 1·0° below that for January, 1895. Using the formula, *Mean Temp.* = *Min.* + (*max.* − *min.* × ·50), the M. T. is 34·2°, compared with a twenty-five years' average of 42·5°. On the 28th the thermometer in the screen rose to 46·6°—wind, W.S.W.; on the 7th the temperature fell to 19·0°—wind, calm. The minimum on the grass (snow) was 10·4° also on the 7th.

The rainfall was only ·625 inch, distributed over 9 days. The average rainfall for February in the twenty-five years, 1865–89, inclusive, was 2·160 inches, and the average number of rainy days was 17·2. The rainfall, therefore, and also the rainy days, were much below the average. In 1883 the rainfall in February was large—3·752 inches on 17 days; in 1879, also, 3·706 inches fell on 19 days. On the other hand, in 1873, only ·922 inch was measured on but 8 days; in 1890, only ·503 inch fell on but 7 days; and in 1887 only ·841 inch fell on 11 days. The rainfall in 1891 was much the smallest recorded in February for very many years. The record is probably unparalleled—·023 inch on 2 days. The nearest approach to this drought was in September, 1865, when only ·051 inch of rain was measured on but 3 days. In 1892, the rainfall was 1·719 inches, on 19 days; in 1893, 2·669 inches fell on 23 days, and in 1894, 1·903 inches on 16 days.

Snow or sleet fell on 7 days—the 1st, 2nd, 4th, 5th, 7th, 9th, and 10th, while hail was observed on 6 days—the 1st, 2nd, 5th, 6th, 7th, and 28th.

The atmosphere was foggy on 6 days—namely, the 7th, 11th, 18th, 19th, 21st and 22nd. The amount of cloud—55·0 per cent.—was considerably in defect of the average—65 per cent. High winds were noted on 15 days, reaching the force of a gale on 7 occasions—namely, the 1st, 3rd, 4th, 9th, 10th, 14th and 15th.

The temperature reached or exceeded 40° in the screen on 6 days, but it never reached 50°, and only twice exceeded 45°. On the other hand, it fell to or below 32° in the screen on as many as 16 nights, compared with only 8 nights in 1894, 5 nights in both 1893 and 1892, and 9 nights in 1891. The minima on the grass were 32°, or less, on every night, compared with 10 nights in 1894, 13 nights in 1893, 16 nights in 1892, and 17 nights in 1891. The thermometer failed to rise to or above 40° in the screen during the daytime on 20 days.

On Friday, the 1st, the frost relaxed in Norway, Scotland, the North of England and Ireland, while it "stiffened" in Germany, France, and the South of England. Snow, or sleet, and hail fell abundantly on this and the following day in nearly all districts.

The cold weather, which had set in on December 27, 1894, and had continued with varying intensity ever since, reached a climax in the week ending Saturday, the 9th, and frost of almost unparalleled severity was felt in nearly all parts of the British Islands in the latter part of the period. To this result the distribution of atmospheric pressure over Western Europe and the presence of large quantities of snow upon the ground alike contributed. An anticyclone, near the centre of which the barometer rose to 31 inches on Wednesday, lay over Scandinavia and the extreme North of Russia throughout. On the other hand, atmospheric pressure was unusually low over the Peninsula and the Atlantic between Portugal and the Azores. At 8 a.m. of Sunday the barometer read only 29·93 inches at Ponta Delgada in the Azores. Consequently, strong easterly or north-easterly winds prevailed all along the western seaboard of Europe. On Wednesday an irregular low-pressure area was formed over Scotland and Ireland, where it caused severe snowstorms followed by intense frost—at night the screened thermometer fell to 0° (zero) at Edgeworthstown, Co. Longford, to -2° at Brookeborough, Co. Fermanagh, and to -4° at Tullamore, King's Co. At 8 a.m. of Friday the reading at Loughborough, Leicestershire, was -6°. In London, it was +15° at the same time. On Saturday the cold became less severe, but no sign of a permanent thaw appeared, and the week closed with some of the great rivers of the British Islands frozen across or blocked with ice floes. In Dublin the mean height of the barometer was 29·240 inches, pressure ranging between 30·187 inches at 9 p.m. of Monday (wind, E.), and 29·378 inches at 9 p.m. of Wednesday (wind, N.N.E.) The mean temperature was only 21·6°. The mean dry bulb temperature at 9 a.m. and 9 p.m. was 21·5°. On Monday the screened thermometers rose to 29·9°. On Thursday they fell to 19·0°, the minimum on the snow being 18·6°. Rainfall amounted to ·230 inch on two days—it was exclusively in the form of snow and hail, ·210 inch being measured on Wednesday. The prevalent winds were E. and S.E.

During the week ended Saturday, the 16th, very severe weather was again felt in Scandinavia, Germany, France, and the British Isles. In the Peninsula, and at times in Italy also, more genial conditions prevailed. On Sunday and again on Thursday an Atlantic depression was found off the S.W. of Ireland; but in neither instance did the disturbance make any headway in forcing a passage northeastwards. The first system travelled southeastwards to France and disappeared. The second behaved in a very similar way. The former system caused a heavy snowstorm on Sunday in the south of Ireland, leading to a delay of 22 hours in the despatch of the American mails from Queenstown, the mail train having been blocked for that space of time by enormous snowdrifts on the Great Southern and Western Railway between Limerick Junction and Mallow. In Dublin the sky was overcast throughout Sunday, lofty cirro-stratus coming in an upper current from N.W., while the wind was strong from S.E. Only a few flakes of snow, however, fell in or near the city; but at Roche's Point, Co. Cork, melted snow and rain yielded 1·10 inches of water in the rain-gauge for the two days. The second depression produced a partial thaw on Wednesday and Thursday—the thermometer rising to 40° at Valentia Island—but on Thursday afternoon frost returned. The wind rose to a fresh gale from E. on Friday evening. Saturday was cloudless, with bright sunshine and a gradual thaw in the daytime, but frost at night. In Dublin the mean height of the barometer was 30·072 inches, the range of pressure being from 29·823 inches at 9 p.m. of Sunday (wind, S.E.), to 30·466 inches at 9 p.m. of Saturday (wind, E.S.E.). The mean temperature was 32·4°. The mean dry bulb temperature at 9 a.m. and 9 p.m. was 31·0°. On Wednesday and also on Saturday the screened thermometers rose to 39·8°. On Tuesday they fell to 21·1°. The minimum on the snow on Tuesday was 17·0°. The prevailing winds were S.E. and E. There was no measurable rainfall.

The week ended Saturday, the 23rd, while still very cold, witnessed a gradual but decided advance of temperature and a general mitigation in the rigours of an exceptionally severe and protracted "cold snap." So far as the British Islands were concerned, an anticyclonic distribution of atmospheric pressure held almost to the close—on Saturday, however, a depression was evidently encroaching upon our Northern and North-western coasts. At 8 a.m. of Sunday, the isobar of 30·8 inches enclosed the east of Scotland and temperature was as low as 7° at Nairn. Keen easterly winds prevailed in Ireland. Next morning the thermometer read only 3° at Nairn, where it had been down to 2° in the night. The anticyclone now moved in a S.W. direction to Ireland, over which country it remained lying until Saturday. This change of position in the area of high pressure caused the keen, dry easterly winds to die out, their place being taken by moist N.W. winds, which brought with them more or less clouded skies, a higher temperature, haze and some damp fog. Very little precipitation, however, took place in any part of the British Isles. In Norway and Portugal, on the contrary, rain fell pretty freely, the measurement at Lisbon being particularly large—3·41 inches on the last five days of the week. In Dublin the mean height of the barometer was 30·410 inches, pressure ranging from 30·519 inches at 9 a.m. of Sunday (wind, E.S.E.), to 30·[illegible] inches at 9 p.m. of Saturday (wind, W. by N.). The mean temperature was 35·1°. The mean dry bulb temperature at 9 a.m. and 9 p.m. was 34·0°. On Saturday the thermometers in the screen rose to 43·9°. On Thursday they fell to 25·6°. On Thursday for the first time in February temperature rose above 40·0°. Rain fell on that day, but only to the amount of ·010 inch. On Sunday morning, the 24th, an additional rainfall of ·011 inch occurred, the total measurement for the week thus becoming ·021 inch on two days. The prevalent winds were at first E.S.E., afterwards W.N.W.

During the closing period (24th—28th, inclusive) there was again an advance in temperature, although not of a pronounced or permanent kind. Both in the North of Europe and in the extreme South, the distribution of atmospheric pressure was cyclonic. Between these areas and especially over Ireland the barometer stood relatively high and at times the isobars were of the anticyclonic type. This was the case from Monday until Thursday, when sharp night frosts occurred in Central England and also in Central Ireland—at Parsonstown the screened thermometer fell to 22° on Monday night. The day maxima were, however, higher than for many weeks past. On Thursday, for example, the thermometer rose to 50° at Valentia Island, 49° at Leith, Donaghadee, Parsonstown, and in Dublin (48·6°); 48° at Aberdeen, Loughborough, Roche's Point, and Scilly; and 47° in many other places. On Thursday the screened thermometers rose to 48·6°, on Tuesday they fell to 29·8°. The prevailing wind was N.W. Rain fell on three days to the total amount of ·[illegible] inch, ·049 inch being measured on Thursday.

In Dublin the rainfall up to February 28, 1895, amounted to 6·230 inches on 35 days, compared with 4·761 inches on 39 days in 1894, 6·906 inches on 41 days in 1893, 3·617 inches on 39 days in

1892, ·714 inch on 16 days in 1891, and a twenty-five years' (1865–1889) average of 4·350 inches on 24·3 days.

At Knockdolian, Greystones, Co. Wicklow, ·763 inch of rain fell in February on 5 days. The heaviest fall in 24 hours was ·353 inch on the 1st. The total fall to February 28th inclusive was 6·951 inches on 24 days.

The rainfall in February at Cloneevin, Killiney, Co. Dublin, amounted to only ·46 inch on 7 days. The average rainfall for February during 10 years (1885–94) at this station was 1·614 inches, on 13·4 days. The greatest rainfall in 24 hours was ·19 inch on the 5th. Absolute drought prevailed from the 7th to the 20th, both inclusive. Since January 1, the rainfall was 6·29 inches, on 31 days.

MARCH.—A changeable, dull, and rather rainy month. The cold weather, which had prevailed throughout January and February, lasted until Wednesday, the 13th, when the thermometer touched 50° in the shade in Dublin for the first time since December 23, 1894. A mild spell followed, continuing to the 24th, after which temperature fell away again and remained below average to the end of the month. This period of renewed cold was also one of heavy and persistent rainfall, 1·234 inches being measured in the week ended Saturday, the 30th.

In Dublin the arithmetical mean temperature (44·1°) was one degree above the average (43·1°); the mean dry bulb readings at 9 a.m. and 9 p.m. were 43·0°. In the thirty years ending with 1894, March was coldest in 1867 and 1883 (M. T. = 39·0°), and warmest in 1893 (M. T. = 46·1°), and in 1869 (M. T. = 47·3°). In 1870 the M. T. was 41·3°, in 1879 (the "cold year") it was 42·5°, in 1894 it was as high as 45·4°, but in 1893 it had been as low as 39·1°. In 1869 February was actually 3·3° warmer than March.

The mean height of the barometer was 29·633 inches, or 0·283 inch below the corrected average value for March—namely, 29·916 inches. The mercury rose to 30·313 inches at 9 a.m. of the 17th, and fell to 28·650 inches at 6·45 a.m. of the 25th. The observed range of atmospheric pressure was, therefore, 1·663 inches—that is, almost an inch and seven-tenths.

The mean temperature deduced from daily readings of the dry bulb thermometer at 9 a.m. and 9 p.m. was 43·0°, or 0·6° above the value for February, 1893. Using the formula, *Mean Temp.* = *Min.* + (*max.*—*min.* × ·465), the M.T. becomes 43·5°. The arithmetical mean of the maximal and minimal readings was 44·1°, compared with a twenty-five years' average of 43·1°. On the 19th the thermometer in the screen rose to 58·7°—wind, W.S.W.; on the 18th the temperature fell to 29·8°—wind, W. The minimum on the grass was 24·9° on the 4th.

The rainfall was 2·746 inches, distributed over 19 days. The average rainfall for March in the twenty-five years, 1865–89, inclusive, was 2·051 inches, and the average number of rainy days was 16·3. The rainfall, therefore, and also the rainy days, were considerably above the average. In 1867 the rainfall in March was very large—4·673 inches on 22 days; in 1888, 3·732 inches fell on 18 days; in 1883 also 3·633 inches fell on 21 days. On the other hand, in 1871, only ·436 inch was measured on 14 days, and in 1874 only ·843 inch fell on 12 days. In 1887 (the "dry year"), 1·485 inches of rain fell on 16 days; in 1889, 1·070 inches fell on, however, as many as 17 days; in 1890 the fall was 2·423 inches on 17 days, but in 1891 only ·830 inch fell on 14 days, and in 1892 only ·891 inch on but 9 days. The smallest March rainfall was ·285 inch on 8 days in 1893. In 1894, 1·287 inches fell on 14 days.

The atmosphere was more or less foggy in the city on 6 days—viz., the 5th, 11th, 18th, 16th, 18th, and 27th. High winds were noted on 16 days, reaching the force of a gale on three occasions—the 23rd, 24th, and 25th. Snow or sleet occurred on the 2nd, 3rd, 25th, and 29th, and hail fell on the 2nd, 3rd, 24th, 25th, 29th, and 31st. The temperature exceeded 50° in the screen on 13 days, compared with as many as 22 days in 1894, 16 days in 1893, only 7 days in 1892, 9 days in 1891, and 19 days in 1890, while it fell to 32° in the screen on 5 nights. In March, 1892, frost had occurred in the shade on as many as 16 nights; but no shade frost occurred in March, 1893. The minima on the grass were 32°, or less, on 10 nights, compared with 11 nights in 1894 and 1893, 23 nights in 1892, 20 nights in 1891, and 15 nights in 1890. The thermometer never rose to 60° in the screen, while it even failed to reach 40° (on the 3rd). In March, 1893, the thermometer did not rise to 40° in the screen on 9 days. A solar halo was seen on the 18th, and a lunar halo appeared on the 13th. Brilliant aurora borealis also occurred on the night of the 18th. Lightning was seen on the evening of the 24th.

The first two days of the month were changeable, with frequent showers. On Friday, the 1st, a large depression spread south-eastwards down the North Sea, causing falls of rain, hail, and sleet in most districts. Saturday was a raw, dull, wet day, and snow, sleet, and hail were again reported, the rainfall being ·168 inch.

Although it began with a snowstorm, the week ended Saturday the 9th was not unfavourable, and a further slight advance in temperature is to be recorded. Rain also fell more freely than in past weeks. At the beginning of the period the barometer was low to the eastward, high to the westward, and accordingly fresh winds from northerly points of the compass prevailed. Hence on there came a heavy snowstorm on Sunday morning, followed by a sharp frost in the afternoon and at night. On Tuesday the western area of high pressure moved south-eastwards from the West of Ireland to the Bay of Biscay, and a V-shaped depression came in from the Atlantic over Ireland and Scotland. In front of this system quantities of cirrus cloud in long streaks spread across the sky from N.N.W., almost against the surface wind, which became southerly. Rain fell in many places—freely in the S.W. of Ireland. On Thursday a larger and deeper depression advanced eastwards across the British Isles. It caused fresh S. and S.E. winds and considerable falls of rain. At 8 a.m. of Friday the barometer was down to 29·17 inches both at Belmullet and at Valentia Island. Heavy rain fell at both these stations. On Saturday, the wind backed to E. and N.E. in Ireland, as a subsidiary depression advanced to the English and St. George's Channels. In Dublin the mean atmospheric pressure was 29·657 inches, the barometer rising to 30·078 inches at 9 p.m. of Monday (wind, W.N.W.)

and falling to 29·308 inches at 9 p.m. of Saturday (wind, N.E.) The corrected mean temperature was 39·7°. The mean dry bulb reading at 9 a.m. and 9 p.m. was 39·8°. On Monday the screened thermometers fell to 29·4°; on Thursday they rose to 48·5°. The rainfall was ·418 inch on five days, ·138 inch being measured on Thursday and again on Friday. The prevailing winds were N.W. and S.E.

Cold and inclement as in past weeks at first, the weather of the week ended Saturday, the 16th, underwent a sudden and complete change on Wednesday, the 13th, and spring followed hard upon the retreating footsteps of the winter. On the day named the thermometer reached 50° in the screen in Dublin for the first time in 1895, or indeed since Christmas Day, 1894. The mean temperature of the first four days was 38·9°, that is 1·8° below the average; that of the three last days was 50·4°, or 7·4° above the average. The mean temperature for the whole week was 43·8°, or 0·9° above the average. On Sunday morning a well-marked area of low pressure lay over the extreme S.E. of Ireland. Cold, gloomy, wet weather prevailed, with a breeze from N.E. in Dublin, but from S. in London. The total eclipse of the moon in the early morning hours of Monday was rendered invisible by clouds in Dublin. It was, however, well observed at Greenwich and in the English Midlands. At this time a very deep depression was passing south-eastwards across Portugal and Spain, the barometer having fallen to 28·91 inches at Lisbon on Sunday evening. As this system advanced, pressure became more uniform in the British Islands, so that calm weather, with fog at times, was felt. On Wednesday, the barometer rose over France and England, and an anticyclone formed which threw a warm S.W. current upon the Irish and Scotch coasts. This afterwards spread over England, where the thermometer rose to a maximum of 57° from a minimum of 31° on Thursday. A very fine display of aurora borealis occurred on Wednesday evening and was seen from nearly all parts of the British Islands. In Dublin the mean height of the barometer was 29·973 inches, pressure ranging between 29·357 inches at 9 a.m. of Sunday (wind, N.E.), and 30·305 inches at 9 p.m. of Saturday (wind, W.S.W.) The corrected mean temperature was 43·8°. The mean dry bulb reading at 9 a.m. and 9 p.m. was 43·4°. On Wednesday the screened thermometers fell to 28·6°; on Saturday they rose to 54·7°. The prevalent winds were W. and S.W. Rain fell on Sunday only, to the amount of ·248 inch.

The weather of the week ended Saturday, the 23rd, was uneventful, save in one particular—namely, its remarkable mildness in contrast to the severity of so many previous weeks in succession. It was in character autumnal rather than spring-like, the air being very soft and damp, and the sky often cloudy or overcast, with frequent light rain. Sunday, however, was beautiful—sunny and mild as well as calm. On this day a broad band of high atmospheric pressure—30·60 inches and upwards—embraced England, Ireland, Germany, and the northern two-thirds of France. To the northward pressure diminished to 29·09 inches at Bodo, in Norway, in a depression which afterwards travelled eastwards to Russia. A series of areas of low pressure subsequently crossed the British Islands in an easterly direction, causing the mild, damp, changeable weather of which mention has been made above. The most important of these systems advanced over Ireland on Saturday, bringing with it warm, squally S.W. winds and a considerable rainfall. On Sunday and Monday the thermometer rose to 60° or 61° at several inland English stations. On Wednesday a maximum of 60° was recorded at Roche's Point, Cork Harbour; on Thursday the thermometer reached 61° in London, 63° at Prawle Point, Devon, and 63° at Oxford; on Friday maxima of 64° to 66° were reported from several English stations. In Dublin the mean height of the barometer was 30·112 inches, pressure ranging from 30·315 inches at 9 a.m. of Sunday (wind, W.) to 29·823 inches at 9 p.m. of Saturday (wind, S.W.) The corrected mean temperature was 49·6°, or 5·8° above that of the previous week. The mean dry bulb reading at 9 a.m. and 9 p.m. was 49·2. On Monday the screened thermometers fell to 35·7°, on Thursday they rose to 57·6°. Rain fell in measurable amount on three days, the total precipitation being ·110 inch, of which ·092 inch was received on Saturday. The prevailing winds were W. and W.S.W.

Extremely unsettled, wet, stormy, and generally inclement weather held throughout the week ended Saturday, the 30th. The distribution of atmospheric pressure over North-Western Europe was cyclonic in type, and on Sunday and again on Thursday the barometer fell to about 28½ inches in the centre of deep and extensive depressions. At 8 a.m. of Sunday the barometer read exactly 28·90 inches at Sumburgh Head, in the Shetlands, whereas it stood as high as 30·35 inches at Lisbon. A well-marked secondary depression lay over the S.E. of Ireland at the hour named. This system crossed England in the course of the day, causing very severe and destructive gales over Wales and the central and eastern English counties. The rainfall was slight within the storm area, but very heavy in the south of Ireland. Thunder occurred at Scilly and York, and lightning was seen at night throughout England and Ireland. The storm was apparently violent in Scandinavia and accompanied by falls of wet snow, for it destroyed telegraphic communication. Snow also fell heavily on the Dublin Mountains, and in the city there were sharp showers of cold rain, sleet, and hail. On Tuesday forenoon a small partial eclipse of the sun (·03 in Dublin, the sun's diameter being taken as 1·00) was very well seen. On Wednesday, the second great atmospheric disturbance of the week came in over the S.W. of Ireland, thence travelling towards E.N.E. across this country and the North of England to the North Sea. Under its influence the weather remained broken, rainy, and cold to the end of the week. In Dublin the mean height of the barometer was only 29·180 inches, pressure ranging from 28·658 inches at 4.45 a.m. of Thursday (wind, N.W.) to 29·586 inches at 9 p.m. of Saturday (wind, N.) The corrected mean temperature was 43·3°. The mean dry bulb temperature at 9 a.m. and 9 p.m. was 42·4°. On Sunday the screened thermometers rose to 53·5°; on Thursday they fell to 34·7°. Rain fell on every day, the total measurement being 1·234 inches, including ·469 inch on Wednesday. Hail fell on Sunday, Monday, and Friday; sleet on Monday and Thursday. The most prevalent wind was the N.W.

Sunday, the 31st, was a cold, changeable, showery day. Hail fell in the afternoon, and the N. wind blew freshly.

The rainfall in Dublin during the three months ending March 31st amounted to 6·064 inches on 53 days, compared with 6·026 inches on 63 days in 1894, 5·194 inches on 49 days in 1893, 4·403 inches on 48 days in 1892, only 1·450 inches on but 33 days in 1891, 7·470 inches on 45 days in 1890, 5·720 inches on 53 days in 1889, 0·037 inches on 61 days in 1888, and a twenty-five years' average of 6·211 inches on 51·0 days (1865–1889, inclusive).

At Knockdolian, Greystones, Co. Wicklow, 5·110 inches of rain fell on 20 days during March; and the total rainfall since January 1, 1895, equals 10·033 inches on 44 days. The corresponding figures for 1894 are 1·905 inches on 14 days, the total rainfall since January 1 having been 6·233 inches on 33 days.

The rainfall in March at Cloneevin, Killiney, Co. Dublin, was 3·29 inches on 18 days, compared with 1·11 inches on 11 days in 1894, ·23 inch on 9 days in 1893, ·90 inch on 10 days in 1892, and a ten years' average of 1·636 inches on 12·9 days. The maximum in the 10 years was 3·59 inches in 1889, the minimum was ·26 inch in 1893. At this station the total rainfall since January was 9·63 inches on 53 days, compared with a fall of 5·79 inches on 31 days in the first quarter of 1893, and 5·56 inches on 53 days in that of 1894.

APRIL.—Speaking generally, April, 1895, was a favourable and an "average" month. The wind was singularly variable, blowing from all points of the compass in nearly equal proportions. The distribution of atmospheric pressure was for the most part cyclonic, but at Eastertide a large anticyclone lay over the British Islands and the North Sea for several days. This high pressure caused nipping easterly wind, but fine, dry weather.

In Dublin the arithmetical mean temperature (48·1°) was 0·4° above the average (47·7°); the mean dry bulb readings at 9 a.m. and 9 p.m. were 47·6°. In the thirty years ending with 1894, April was coldest in 1879 (the cold year) (M. T. = 44·5°), and warmest in 1893 (M. T. = 51·4°). In 1886 the M. T. was 46·8°, in 1887 it was as low as 45·1°, in 1888 it was (as also in 1891) only 45·7°, in 1889, 46·1°; in 1890, 47·3°; in 1892, 46·8°; and in 1894, 49·9°. The month of April, 1893, was the warmest for at least 30 years.

The mean height of the barometer was 29·668 inches, or 0·018 inch above the average value for April—namely, 29·850 inches. The mercury rose to 30·470 inches at 9 p.m. of the 11th, having fallen to 29·287 inches at 4.15 p.m. of the 6th. The observed range of atmospheric pressure was, therefore, 1·183 inches—that is, a little less than an inch and two-tenths.

The mean temperature deduced from daily readings of the dry bulb thermometer at 9 a.m. and 9 p.m. was 47·6°, or 4·5° above the value for March, 1895. Using the formula, *Mean Temp. = Min.* + (*max.—min.* × ·476), the value is also 47·6°, or 0·4° above the average mean temperature for April, calculated in the same way, in the twenty-five years, 1865–89, inclusive (47·2°). The arithmetical mean of the maximal and minimal readings was 48·1°, compared with a twenty-five years' (1865–1889 inclusive) average of 47·7°. On the 21st the thermometer in the screen rose to 64·0°—wind, S.W.; on the 4th the temperature fell to 33·9°—wind, calm. The minimum on the grass was 27·8° on the 5th. There were 3 frosty nights on the grass.

The rainfall was 1·143 inches, distributed over 13 days. The average rainfall for April in the twenty-five years, 1865–89, inclusive, was 2·043 inches, and the average number of rainy days was 13·2. The rainfall, therefore, was considerably below the average, while the rainy days were also in defect. In 1877 the rainfall in April was very large—4·107 inches on 21 days; in 1882 also, 3·409 inches fell on 20 days, and in 1886, 3·183 inches on 20 days. On the other hand, in 1873, only ·498 inch was measured on 8 days; and in 1870, only ·539 inch fell, also on 8 days. The fall in 1890 was 1·475 inches on 16 days, in 1891, 1·553 inches on 14 days, in 1892, 1·114 inches on 13 days, and in 1893, 1·044 inches on 7 days.

No lunar or fogs were observed. High winds were noted on 6 days, but never reached the force of a gale in Dublin. Sleet and hail fell on the 1st, hail also on the 11th. The temperature exceeded 50 in the screen on every day except 6, compared with every day but 1 in 1894, every day in 1893, 24 days in 1892, and 16 days in 1891. As in April, 1894, it rose to or above 60° on only 8 days, but never fell to 32° in the screen. The minimum on the grass was 37°, or less, on five nights, compared with five nights in 1893, and only one night in 1894. The mean lowest temperature on the grass was 37·8°, compared with 40·0° in 1894, 38·7° in 1893, 33·6° in 1892, 34·1° in 1891 and 1890, 34·6° in 1889, 34·8° in 1888, and 31·5° in 1887. There was an aurora borealis on the evening of the 11th.

Until Friday, the 5th, polar winds prevailed and temperature ruled low, the nights being even frosty. On the day named a large atmospheric depression approached Ireland and Scotland from the Atlantic, and under its influence clouds increased, temperature rose, the wind backed towards S.W. and freshened, and rain fell from time to time. Early on Monday, the 1st, cold rain and sleet fell in Dublin, and there was a heavy hail shower at 11.30 a.m. The weather then remained fine and dry, but cold for the time of year, until Friday. During this period a deep depression passed across Scandinavia, where snow and frost returned their way. In Scotland also snow or sleet fell, and sharp night frosts occurred. At 8 a.m. of Friday a broad band of high barometer—30·3 inches and upward—stretched from the S. of Ireland across England to France and Switzerland, but pressure had begun to give way briskly in the N.W. On Saturday the barometer stood about an inch lower in Dublin than it had done on Thursday evening, and the centre of a deep depression lay over the N. of Scotland, where the barometer was down to 28·83 inches. In Dublin the barometer rose to 30·238 inches at 9 p.m. of Thursday (wind, calm), and fell to 29·287 inches at 4.15 p.m. of Saturday (wind, W.N.W.) On Thursday the screened minimum sank to 33·9°. On Saturday, the screened maximum rose to 58·7°. The prevailing wind was northerly up to Friday, then W.S.W. The rainfall was ·108 inch on three days, ·051 inch being measured on both Friday and Saturday.

Favourable weather characterised the week ended Saturday, the 13th. It is true that the conditions either of atmospheric pressure or of air temperature were not stable; nevertheless the weather was dry, and there were intervals of pleasant, warm sunshine, which gave a considerable impetus to vegetation. Speaking generally, the barometer stood low, and a cyclonic distribution of pressure prevailed at the beginning of the period, whereas a high barometer and anticyclonic conditions held at its close. On Sunday morning, two areas of low pressure, in which the barometer was down to 28·60 inches, lay over the northern half of Scandinavia, and several inequalities of pressure were observed at the British and Irish Stations. The weather was consequently cold and showery, with northerly winds. During the next three days depressions moved northwards or north-eastwards outside our N.W. coasts, causing fresh S.W. to W. winds and changeable weather. The S.W. wind brought genial warmth for a short while, and on Tuesday the thermometer rose above 60°—to 60·6—in the screen for the first time in Dublin since November 1, 1894, on which day the maximum had been 61·6°. On Thursday an area of high pressure came in from the Atlantic, and by evening the barometer rose to 30·50 inches and upwards in the S. of Ireland. Temperature fell fast at night, and ground frost was felt. Good Friday proved cloudy and cool, but Saturday became brilliant as the day advanced. In Dublin the mean height of the barometer was 29·984 inches, pressure having been only 29·573 inches at 9 a.m. of Sunday (wind, N.N.W.), but rising to 30·475 inches at 9 p.m. of Thursday (wind, N.W.) The corrected mean temperature was 48·3°. The mean dry bulb reading at 9 a.m. and 9 p.m. was 47·9°. On Tuesday the thermometer rose to 60·6°, on Friday it fell to 33·3° in the screen. The prevalent winds were S.W. and N.W. Very light showers fell on several days, but the resulting rainfall was only ·003 inch—a quantity which is not considered registrable.

Favourable, springlike weather prevailed during the week ended Saturday, the 20th. On Sunday and Monday, the British Isles were entirely under the influence of an anticyclone, the centre of which was off the east of Scotland at 8 a.m. of Sunday, when the barometer read 30·40 inches at Aberdeen, 30·18 inches at Valentia Island, and 30·09 inches in the Scilly Isles. Easterly winds, and cold, dry, generally bright weather prevailed. In Dublin the mean temperature of Easter Day was only 44·1°, or 3·8° below that of last Christmas Day, which was, however, unusually mild, the mean temperature being 47·9°. At the beginning of the week a depression lay over Spain and Portugal, where thunderstorms and heavy rain occurred. This disturbance moved northwards, reaching the Bay of Biscay on Tuesday and—in a modified form—the British Islands on Thursday. Thunderstorms accompanied the passage of its eastern side across France on Tuesday and England on Wednesday. As this disturbance travelled northwards the wind shifted to W. in its rear, and the air became much milder and more humid than of late, while genial showers fell in some districts. On Saturday a new depression, with steeper baric gradients, came in over Ireland from S.W., causing freshening southerly winds, clouds, and finally rain. In Dublin the mean atmospheric pressure was 30·020 inches, the barometer reading as high as 30·310 inches at 9 a.m. of Monday (wind, E.), but only 29·585 inches at 7 a.m. of Thursday (wind, W.S.W.). The corrected mean temperature was 48·8°. The mean dry bulb reading at 9 a.m. and 9 p.m. was 48·1°. On Monday the screened thermometers sank to 33·8°; on Friday they rose to 65·7°. Rain fell on two days to the amount of ·063 inch, ·043 inch being measured on Saturday. The wind was at first easterly, then westerly, and finally southerly.

During the week ended Saturday, the 27th, exceedingly changeable, showery or rainy, and finally cold, weather prevailed. Over the British Isles and in their immediate neighbourhood the distribution of atmospheric pressure remained cyclonic—after Wednesday it became very complex, a number of areas of low pressure being observed at the same time. As always happens when this is the case, there was a considerable mingling of easterly and south-westerly air-currents, causing very unstable temperature. Sunday was at first mild and pleasant, the thermometer rising in the shade to 66° in Dublin and in some English towns (to 63° at Cambridge). In the evening heavy showers fell. Monday turned out wet owing to the passage northwards outside the West of Ireland of a large Atlantic depression. Tuesday was fair to showery, thunder occurring in the North of Ireland. Wednesday was rainy and cold. On Thursday morning centres of low pressure were found over Caithness and the English Channel and to the southward of Ireland. Thunderstorms occurred in France and subsequently at Roche's Point, Cork Harbour. Friday proved squally, wet, and cold; but on Saturday the weather improved, becoming drier and brighter, while continuing cold. In Dublin the mean height of the barometer was 29·563 inches, the range being from 29·189 inches at 9 p.m. of Monday (wind, S.S.W.) to 29·891 inches at 9 p.m. of Saturday (wind, N.W.). The corrected mean temperature was 50·7°. The mean dry bulb temperature at 9 a.m. and 9 p.m. was 49·7°. On Sunday the screened thermometers rose to 64·0°; on Thursday they fell to 38·1°. The rainfall measured ·797 inch on six days, ·253 inch falling on Friday. The wind was variable in both force and direction—it was chiefly S.W. at first, afterwards N.N.W. On Saturday evening a conjunction of Venus and the crescent moon formed a beautiful sight in the western sky after sunset.

Sunday, the 28th, was cool and fair to cloudy at times. On Monday, the 29th, the weather was mild but changeable. On Tuesday, the 30th, it was cloudy to overcast and finally very wet.

The rainfall in Dublin during the four months ending April 30th amounted to 10·232 inches on 63 days, compared with 9·161 inches on 73 days in 1894, 6·268 inches on 64 days in 1893, 8·953 inches on 61 days in 1892, only 5·233 inches on 40 days in 1891, 9·045 inches on 59 days in 1890, 8·345 inches on 74 days in 1889, 6·000 inches on 56 days in 1888, and a twenty-five years' average of 8·464 inches on 65·2 days.

At Knockdolian, Greystones, Co. Wicklow, the rainfall amounted to 2·471 inches on 10 days. The heaviest falls in 24 hours were ·690 inch on the 22nd, ·530 inch on the 24th, and ·450 inch on the 30th. In 1894, the April rainfall at this station was 4·171 inches on 17 days; in 1893, it was 1·055 inches on 6 days. The total rainfall in 1895 up to April 30 was 12·879 inches on 54 days, compared with 13·856 inches on 70 days in 1894 and [illegible] inches on 54 days in 1893.

At Clonsevin, Killiney, Co. Dublin, 1·60 inches of rain fell on 14 days in April. The maximal fall in 24 hours was ·37 inch on the 22nd. The average rainfall in April of the ten preceding years was 1·716 inches on 13·2 days. Since January 1, 1895, 11·29 inches of rain fell at this station on 66 days, compared with 8·09 inches on 74 days in 1894, and 6·94 inches on 57 days in 1893.

MAY.—A beautiful month—bright and dry, without any severe nipping night frosts. Prevalent easterly sea breezes by day along the east coast of Ireland tempered the heat of an often unclouded sun. The amount of cloud was very low—only 37·8 per cent. At 9 a.m. it rose to 47·1 per cent., but at 9 p.m. it fell to 27·4 per cent. Rain fell in Dublin on only 8 days, and the total measurement was only about one-sixth of an inch, or slightly over one-twelfth of the average rainfall for May.

In Dublin the arithmetical mean temperature ([illegible]°) was decidedly above the average ([illegible]°); the mean dry bulb readings at 9 a.m. and 9 p.m. were [illegible]°. In the thirty years ending with 1894, May was coldest in 1869 (M. T. = [illegible]°); in 1885 (M. T. = [illegible]°); in 1879 (the "cold year") (M. T. = 48·6°); and in 1856 (M. T. = [illegible]°). It was warmest in 1833 (M. T. = [illegible]°), in 1868 (the "warm year") (M. T. = 55·6°); and in 1875 (M. T. = [illegible]°). In 1886 the M. T. was [illegible]°; in 1887, 51·5°; in 1888, 50·6°; in 1889, 51·6°; in 1890, [illegible]°; in 1891, only [illegible]°; and in 1893, 55·6°.

The mean height of the barometer was 30·111 inches, or 0·183 inch above the corrected average value for May—namely, 29·928 inches. The mercury rose to 30·611 inches at 9 a.m. of the 2nd, and fell to 29·630 inches at 11 p.m. of the 31st. The observed range of atmospheric pressure was, therefore, 1·170 inches.

The mean temperature deduced from daily readings of the dry bulb thermometer at 9 a.m. and 9 p.m. was [illegible]°, or [illegible]° above the value for April, 1895 ([illegible]°). Using the formula, *Mean Temp. = Min. + (max.—min. × ·47)*, the value was also [illegible]°, or [illegible]° above the average mean temperature for May, calculated in the same way, in the twenty-five years, 1865–89, inclusive ([illegible]°). The arithmetical mean of the maximal and minimal readings was [illegible]°, compared with a twenty-five years' average of 53·0°. On the 30th the thermometer in the screen rose to 71·[illegible]°—wind, E.; on the 31st the temperature fell to [illegible]°—wind, E.S.E. The minimum on the grass was 31·[illegible]°, also on the 31st.

The rainfall amounted to only ·177 inch, distributed over only 8 days, thus establishing a record for dryness. The average rainfall for May in the twenty-five years, 1865–89, inclusive, was 2·030 inches, and the average number of rainy days was 15·4. The rainfall and the rainy days, therefore, were much below the average. In 1886 the rainfall in May was very large—5·672 inches on 21 days; in 1880, also, 3·418 inches fell on 19 days. On the other hand, in 1871, only ·778 inch was measured on 8 days; in 1878, only ·798 inch fell on 6 days, in 1887, only ·[illegible] inch on 10 days; and in 1888, only ·675 inch on 11 days. In 1890, 2·[illegible] inches fell on 17 days. In 1891 May was the first month in which the rainfall exceeded the average. It amounted to 2·793 inches on 17 days. In 1892 the large amount of 4·177 inches fell on 19 days. In 1893 the fall was 1·[illegible] inches on 18 days; and in 1894, 2·[illegible] inches on 17 days.

Solar halos were seen on the 3rd and 4th, lunar halos on the 2nd, 3rd, and 9th, and an aurora on the 2nd. High winds were noted on only 3 days, attaining the force of a gale on the 31st only. Thunder was heard on the 1st and 24th. Hail and sleet fell on the 1st. The atmosphere was slightly foggy on the 2nd and 4th.

During the month the thermometer did not fall below 32° in the screen, but it indicated frost on the grass on the night of the 31st. The mean minimal temperature on the grass was 41·[illegible]°, compared with 37·[illegible]° in May, 1894; [illegible]° in 1893, [illegible]° in 1892, 37·7° in 1891, [illegible]° in 1890, [illegible]° in 1889, 37·[illegible]° in 1888, and 37·[illegible]° in 1887.

The period ended Saturday, the 4th, was changeable but for the most part favourable. The nights were generally very cold, but bright sunshine raised the temperature in the daytime so considerably that the daily range on some occasions amounted to between 27° and 30° at some inland stations—in London, on Thursday the 2nd, max. 63°, min. 35°, range 28°; at Parsonstown, on Friday, the 3rd, max. 61°, min. [illegible]°, range 25°. On Wednesday, the 1st, splendid clouds formed and thunder and hail showers occurred in the east of Ireland. In Dublin two peals of thunder were heard about 3 p.m., followed by a heavy shower of soft hail and sleet. The barometer at that time rose fast and an anticyclone with central readings above 30·60 inches became established over the British Islands. A good deal of cirriform cloud formed, in which solar halos by day and lunar halos by night were developed. The air was very "thin" and nipping on Thursday and Friday, but it became softer and more genial on Saturday. In Dublin the barometer rose to 30·614 inches at 9 a.m. of Thursday (wind, W.). On Saturday the thermometer rose to [illegible]° in the screen, having fallen to 33·[illegible]° on Friday. Rain fell on the 1st to the amount of ·[illegible] inch. Easterly winds were the most prevalent.

Exceptionally fine, dry, bright weather prevailed during the week ended Saturday, the 11th. Temperature, in particular, showed a decided advance and the evenings were for the most part summerlike. Until Wednesday North-Western Europe was covered by a large area of high atmospheric pressure (anticyclone), with slight or moderate gradients. On Monday and Tuesday the barometer stood as high as 30·70 inches, or slightly more, over Scandinavia. Light, variable winds prevailed, except on the Continent and in the S.E. and S. of England, where a fresh north-easterly breeze was blowing. The amount of cloud was small, so that much bright sunshine was recorded by day, while the nights were very sharp. As the week advanced, shallow depressions, of irregular and changing shape, advanced northwards across France and the Bay of Biscay from the Peninsula.

These disturbances caused heavy rains in the South of France and thundershowers later on in several parts of the British Isles and of the Continent. No general break-up of the weather, however, occurred, and on Friday the distribution of atmospheric pressure again became anticyclonic. The amount of bright sunshine was unusually large—in London, 69·3 hours; at Cambridge, 65·9 hours or 63 per cent. of its possible duration; in the Phoenix Park, Dublin, 66·1 hours; at Markree Castle, 67·8 hours; at Armagh, 60·6 hours; at Parsonstown, 58·6 hours, and at Valentia Island, 54·0 hours. In Dublin the mean height of the barometer was 30·165 inches, pressure falling from 30·417 inches at 9 p.m. of Sunday (wind, E.) to 29·900 inches at 7 p.m. of Wednesday (wind, also E.). The corrected mean temperature was 53·6°. The mean dry bulb reading at 9 a.m. and 9 p.m. was 53·7°. On Monday the screened thermometers sank to 40·9°; on Saturday they rose to 63·6°. The prevailing wind was easterly. There was no measurable rainfall. On Thursday the thermometer rose to 76° in the shade in London and at Cambridge.

During the week ended Saturday, the 18th, the weather was by no means as settled as in the previous week, but the prevailing character of dryness was maintained, especially in Ireland. At first temperature was high—the thermometer rising in London to 79° on Sunday, 75° on Monday, and 73° on Tuesday; but it afterwards fell away greatly, so that the last three days were really cold. This decided change was brought about by the substitution of an area of low atmospheric pressure for one of high pressure over the S. of Scandinavia, Denmark, and the Netherlands. In this region the barometer stood at 30·3 inches on Sunday morning, but only at 29·2 inches on Thursday morning. On Sunday a large, but shallow, depression lay over Ireland, where a grateful fall of soft, warm rain occurred in the course of the day. Monday was a warm day, the thermometer marking 67·7° in Dublin and 69° at Parsonstown. Tuesday was ushered in by a vapour fog, but this soon dispersed and fair, warm weather prevailed. At this time a depression was advancing from N.W. to the N. of Scotland, whence it passed south-eastwards to Denmark, growing much deeper as it travelled. Under the influence of this disturbance, the wind veered to N. and freshened, with a serious fall of temperature, an increase of cloud, and in Great Britain showers of cold rain, sleet, and hail. May—in a word—gave place to March. On Friday the air was particularly dry and searching. In Dublin the mean height of the barometer was 30·106 inches, pressure ranging from 30·373 inches at 9 a.m. of Tuesday (wind W.) to 29·820 inches at 7.30 a.m. of Saturday (wind W.N.W.). The corrected mean temperature was 51·0°. The mean dry bulb readings at 9 a.m. and 9 p.m. were 51·1°. On Monday the screened thermometers rose to 67·7°, on Saturday they fell to 39·6°. Rain fell on Sunday to the amount of ·049 inch. The prevalent winds were—first, W., afterwards N.

Exceptionally fine weather prevailed throughout the week ended Saturday, the 25th. In Dublin the period was rainless, but in many parts of Great Britain and Ireland thundershowers occurred in the latter half of the week. On Sunday morning a rather deep depression was found lying over Holland, Denmark, and Belgium—at 8 a.m. its centre was near the Hague. This system caused cold northerly winds in the British Isles and showers at many places in Scotland and England—in Ireland the weather was generally dry but cold. After Sunday, atmospheric pressure became comparatively uniform over Western Europe, but several shallow depressions developed here and there, causing local electrical disturbances in many places. On Wednesday evening a sharp thunderstorm broke over Paris, where the resulting rainfall was as much as ·67 inch. On Thursday a thunderstorm occurred in London and thundershowers fell in many parts of England. Similarly on Friday, electrical cumuli and cirro-cumuli came up from S. to the westward of Dublin, and in the afternoon heavy thundershowers occurred a few miles inland, the weather remaining fine and dry in the city and along the coast. Saturday was a bright, warm day, with a moderate to fresh westerly wind. In Dublin the mean height of the barometer was 29·894 inches, pressure falling to 29·744 inches at 1 p.m. of Tuesday (wind, S.E.) and rising to 30·107 inches at 2.15 p.m. of Saturday (wind, W.N.W.). The corrected mean temperature was 51·5°. The mean dry bulb reading at 9 a.m. and 9 p.m. was also 51·6°. On Tuesday morning the thermometer sank to 38·2° in the screen and to 31·9° on the grass in Dublin. The maximum was 64·7° on Thursday. On the first three days temperature failed to reach 60° in the shade. Easterly winds prevailed except on Saturday. There was no rainfall in the city—at Glen-na-Smoel Water-works ·73 inch of rain fell in Friday's thunderstorm.

Very fine, summerlike weather prevailed during the greater part of the period from the 26th to the 31st inclusive, but after a burst of heat on Thursday, the 29th, thunderstorms and rain occurred in Great Britain and rain with strong southerly winds in Ireland. Until Wednesday, atmospheric pressure ruled high in the British Islands, and the weather was anticyclonic in character—that is, fine, dry, and bright. Off the S.E. coast of England, much fog prevailed at this time, and temperature in consequence remained very low—on Monday the thermometer did not exceed 58° at the North Foreland, whereas it rose to 71° in London and at Cambridge, and to 73° at Loughborough and Oxford. In the centre and west of Ireland on this day much cloud prevailed and slight showers fell in places. On Wednesday a decided fall of the barometer set in and gradients for southerly winds became somewhat steep. With the coming of the S. wind temperature rose fast—the maxima on Thursday being 73° in Dublin, 77° at Parsonstown, 80° in Liverpool, 83° at York, 83° at Oxford and Loughborough, 85° in London, and 87° at Cambridge. Thunderstorms followed in nearly all parts of England, and at Cambridge rain and hail fell to the amount of 1·01 inches. On Friday, the 31st, the S. wind blew freshly in Dublin, and at 3.30 p.m. rain fell heavily for a short time, the wind afterwards freshening to a gale of brief duration. At 11 p.m. the barometer fell to 29·436 inches. In Dublin the barometer rose to 30·341 inches at 9 a.m. of Monday (wind, E.) and fell to 29·436 inches at 11 p.m. of Friday (wind, S.S.E.). On Wednesday the thermometer fell to 48·1° in the screen, on Thursday it rose to 71·9°. The rainfall was ·070 inch on Friday only. The prevalent winds were E. and S.E.

The rainfall in Dublin during the five months ending May 31st amounted to 10·[illegible] inches on [illegible] days, compared with 12·709 inches on [illegible] days in 1894, 7·[illegible] inches on [illegible] days in 1893, 10·[illegible] inches on [illegible] days in 1892, only 5·[illegible] inches on [illegible] days in 1891, 11·[illegible] inches on 76 days in 1890, 10·[illegible] inches on [illegible] days in 1889, [illegible] inches on [illegible] days in 1888, [illegible] inches on [illegible] days in 1887, and a twenty-five years' average of 10·[illegible] inches on [illegible] days.

It may be remembered that on Saturday, May [illegible], 1892, [illegible] inches of rain were measured at this station, [illegible] inches having fallen within [illegible] hours, or at the rate of [illegible] inches in 24 hours. No such measurement had been recorded in Dublin since October [illegible], 1880, when [illegible] inches of rain fell. May [illegible], 1892, was only the third occasion within the past thirty years on which the rainfall exceeded [illegible] inches within 24 hours in Dublin.

At [illegible], Greystones, Co. Wicklow, the rainfall in May, 1895, was 0·[illegible] inch, distributed over only 4 days. Of this quantity ·100 inch fell on the 31st. The total fall since January 1st, 1895, equals 12·[illegible] inches on [illegible] days, compared with 13·[illegible] inches on [illegible] days in 1894, and [illegible] inches on 65 days in 1893.

At Cloneevin, Killiney, Co. Dublin, the rainfall in May was 0·12 inch on 3 days—·04 inch being measured on the 1st, 12th, and 31st respectively. The average rainfall in May at this station for the ten years, 1885–1894 inclusive, was [illegible] inches on 15 days. Five rainy days was the lowest number which had been observed in any month previously.

JUNE.—This was an exceptionally favourable month. Fair and quiet weather held until the 20th, but sunshine by day being often succeeded by calm cold nights, especially about the 15th, when severe frosts occurred in the inland districts of both Great Britain and Ireland. From the 22nd to the close, violent electrical disturbances took place and rain fell in abundance except in the South-east of England. This break-up of the fine weather and long-continued drought was preceded by a period of great warmth, particularly in Ireland.

In Dublin the arithmetical mean temperature ([illegible]°) was above the average ([illegible]°), by [illegible]°; the mean dry bulb readings at 9 a.m. and 9 p.m. were [illegible]°. In the thirty years ending with 1894, June was coldest in 1882 (M. T.=[illegible]°), and in 1879 (the "cold year") (M. T.=[illegible]°). It was warmest in 1887 (M. T.=[illegible]°), in 1868 (M. T.=[illegible]°), and in [illegible] (the "warm year") (M. T.=[illegible]°). In 1888 the M. T. was [illegible]°; in 1889, [illegible]°; in 1890, [illegible]°; in 1891, [illegible]°; in 1892, [illegible]°; in 1893, [illegible]°; and in 1894, 57·0°.

The mean height of the barometer was 30·084 inches, or 0·167 inch above the corrected average value for June—namely, 29·917 inches. The mercury rose to 30·466 inches at 9 a.m. of the 14th, and fell to 29·557 inches at 9 p.m. of the 30th. The observed range of atmospheric pressure was, therefore, 0·909 inch—that is, a little more than nine-tenths of an inch.

The mean temperature deduced from daily readings of the dry bulb thermometer at 9 a.m. and 9 p.m. was [illegible]°, or [illegible]° above the value for May, 1895. Using the formula, *Mean Temp.=Min.+(max.—min.×·465)*, the value was also [illegible]°, or [illegible]° above the average mean temperature for June, calculated in the same way, in the twenty-five years, 1865–89, inclusive ([illegible]°). The arithmetical mean of the maximal and minimal readings was [illegible]°, compared with a twenty-five years' average of [illegible]°. On the [illegible] the thermometer in the screen rose to [illegible]°—wind, E.S.E.; on the 14th the temperature fell to [illegible]°—wind, [illegible]. The minimum on the grass was [illegible]°, also on the 14th.

The rainfall amounted to 1·[illegible] inches, distributed over 13 days. The average rainfall for June in the twenty-five years, 1865–89, inclusive, was 1·817 inches, and the average number of rainy days was [illegible]. The rainfall was, therefore, slightly above, while the rainy days were more decidedly below the average. In 1878 the rainfall in June was very large—5·[illegible] inches on [illegible] days; in 1879 also [illegible] inches fell on 24 days. On the other hand, in [illegible], only ·100 inch was measured on 8 days; in 1887, the rainfall was only [illegible] inch, distributed over only [illegible] days; in 1874 only [illegible] inch was measured on [illegible] days; and in 1868 only ·677 inch fell on but [illegible] days. In 1889 the rainfall was as much as [illegible] inches, distributed over as many as 18 days. In 1890 it was 1·930 inches on 16 days; in 1891, [illegible] inches on 14 days; in 1892, 1·[illegible] inches on 17 days; in 1893, 1·[illegible] inches on [illegible] days; and in 1894, 1·[illegible] inches on 16 days.

High winds were noted on only [illegible] days, and the force of a gale was never attained. Temperature reached or exceeded 70° in the screen on 7 days; compared with 17 days in 1887, only 1 day in 1888, 10 days in 1889, only [illegible] days in 1890, [illegible] days in 1891, [illegible] days in 1892, [illegible] days in 1893, and only [illegible] days in 1894. Hail fell on the [illegible] and [illegible]. Solar halos were observed on the 2nd, [illegible], 11th, [illegible], and 23rd. Thunderstorms occurred on the [illegible], [illegible], and 30th.

Saturday, the 1st, was a *fair bright day*, with a pleasant and fresh breeze from S. to S.E. and E.S.E.

Splendid summerlike weather prevailed during the greater part of the week ended Saturday the 8th. After Sunday the distribution of atmospheric pressure over the British Isles was anticyclonic—the highest pressure of all being found over Ireland on and after Tuesday. At 8 a.m. of Sunday a depression, in which the barometer was down to [illegible] inches, was found near the Scilly Islands; another, with readings of about [illegible] inches, lay off the Lincolnshire coast. The latter disturbance had already caused a heavy fall of rain at Spurn Head (·[illegible] inch) and York (1·24 inches) and a thunderstorm at the latter place. Thunder and lightning had also occurred at the North Foreland and Cambridge. In Dublin the day was fine and warm, but cloudy at times. The depression soon dispersed and a general increase of pressure took place. Monday was fair and bright until evening, when clouds came up from N. and rain fell heavily in Dublin for a time (·100 inch). The downpour was local and resembled an [illegible] thunderstorm. Light evaporation showers fell on Tuesday, but the rainfall measurement was scarcely perceptible. A spell of brilliant, calm, warm weather followed, lasting until Saturday, when clouds increased and the sky began to wear a less settled appearance.

as depressions appeared in the far North. At 1.30 p.m. on this day a well-defined solar halo appeared. During the fair spell, light easterly sea breezes came in daily along the east coast, tempering the burning rays of an unclouded summer sun. On Thursday evening Venus and Mars were seen in conjunction to W.N.W., and Jupiter and Mercury also in conjunction to N.W. In Dublin the mean height of the barometer was 30·263 inches, pressure ranging between 29·919 inches at 9 a.m. of Sunday (wind, N.E.) and 30·430 inches at 9 a.m. of Thursday (wind, E.N.E.). The corrected mean temperature was 55·7°. The mean dry bulb temperature at 9 a.m. and 9 p.m. was 59·9°. On Wednesday the screened thermometers fell to 47·7°, on Friday they rose to 70·7°. The rainfall was ·107 inch, ·103 inch being measured on Monday—the only "rainy day." The prevailing winds were N.N.W. and E.N.E.

Although changeable at times, the weather of the week ended Saturday, the 15th, was generally seasonable and propitious. As a rule the barometer stood highest over Ireland while it was relatively low both over Northern Europe and in the Mediterranean Basin. At no time, however, were gradients steep and so the force of the wind was never great. With the spreading southwards of north-westerly winds early in the week came a remarkable reduction of temperature, and the thermometer readings by night in Scotland and Ireland were unusually low after Monday—at Wick, for example, the minima in the screen were 53°, 43°, 43°, 37°, 37°, 41°, and 34°; even in the city of Dublin, they were as low as 51·6°, 51·9°, 49·0°, 45·5°, 42·9°, 46·0°, and 43·5°. At Edenfel (Omagh) and Markree (Co. Sligo) the sheltered thermometer fell to 30° on Thursday, the 13th. The grass minimum was 24° at Edenfel, on the same night. On Friday night the thermometer fell to 33° in the screen and to 23° on the grass at Loughborough. In Dublin, heavy showers fell on Tuesday and Wednesday, largely in consequence of a rapid evaporation and the coldness of the air leading to subsequent condensation. Hail fell on Wednesday. On Thursday and Friday a shallow depression passed eastwards along the south coast of Ireland and across the south of England. It produced an abundant rainfall in Munster and along the English coast. At this time, beautiful bright weather with cool, easterly sea breezes prevailed in the neighbourhood of Dublin. The mean atmospheric pressure in this city was 30·123 inches, the barometer being observed to range from 29·898 inches at 9 a.m. of Tuesday (wind, W.N.W.) to 30·337 inches at 9 a.m. of Saturday (wind, E.). The corrected mean temperature was 54·8°. The mean dry bulb reading at 9 a.m. and 9 p.m. was 55·8°. On Monday the screened thermometers rose to 68·0°, on Saturday they fell to 41·5°. The rainfall was ·313 inch on two days, ·191 inch being registered on Wednesday. The prevalent winds were first N.W., afterwards E.

Although far from settled, the weather of the week ended Saturday, the 22nd, was generally favourable, and at the end of the week a rapid and considerable rise of temperature took place. The first two days were fair—clear, cold nights were succeeded by brilliant sunshine by day, the heat of the sun being tempered meanwhile by sea breezes along the Irish coasts. During this time the barometer was gradually falling and on Tuesday morning a large area of comparatively low pressure lay over the British Isles, the North Sea, and the Bay of Biscay. Within this area at least three minima existed, and the weather therefore fell into a rainy, thundery state. In Dublin a grateful fall of rain took place between 7 and 10 a.m. on Tuesday, but the measurement was only ·040 inch. The changes in atmospheric pressure were slight and irregular until Wednesday evening, when the depressions began to fill up or disperse. On Thursday morning areas of high pressure were found over Scandinavia and the Peninsula, while the barometer was relatively low in the intervening regions. A good deal of electrical disturbance was the result. Subsequently the Spanish anticyclone spread northwards and the weather became very fine and warm, as the south-westerly winds passed over Ireland. In Dublin the mean height of the barometer was 30·011 inches, pressure ranging between 29·891 inches at 4.30 p.m. of Tuesday (wind, W.) and 30·313 inches at 9 p.m. of Saturday (wind, W.S.W.). The corrected mean temperature was 56·3°. The mean dry bulb temperature at 9 a.m. and 9 p.m. was 58·4°. On Monday the screened thermometers fell to 44·0°; on Saturday they rose to 75·1°. The rainfall was ·114 inch on four days, ·052 inch being measured on Thursday as the result of heavy electrical showers ushered in by a dangerous S.W. squall at 6.30 p.m. The prevailing winds were N.W. and S.W.

As first dry and hot in the week ending Saturday, the 29th, the weather broke on Wednesday, with severe thunderstorms in most parts of the British Islands, and remained unsettled, showery and thundery to the close of the week. In the period from Sunday to Tuesday inclusive an atmospheric depression was passing in an east-south-easterly direction across Scandinavia and the Baltic to Poland. This system caused considerable rains, northerly gales, and a great fall in temperature all over Northern Europe, but fine weather was general throughout the British Isles, although it was cool in Scotland and the North of England. In Ireland and the South of England summer heat prevailed, the sheltered thermometer rising to 85° in London on Sunday and at Parsonstown on Monday. On Tuesday the barometer stood above 30·3 inches in a ridge extending southwards from the N.E. of Scotland to the neighbourhood of Paris. Off the West of Ireland pressure was slightly lower (30·3 inches) and was giving way. At night the weather became thundery in the last named district, and on Wednesday violent thunderstorms occurred in Ireland, in central and northern England, and in Scotland. In the S.E. of England the weather remained for the most part fine and dry until Friday, when showers fell locally. In Dublin the mean height of the barometer was 30·044 inches, pressure decreasing from 30·285 inches at 9 a.m. of Monday (wind, E.) to 29·560 inches at 9 p.m. of Saturday (wind, W.). The corrected mean temperature was 65·1°. The mean dry bulb reading at 9 a.m. and 9 p.m. was 63·0°. On five days the maximal temperature exceeded 70° in the screen, the highest reading of all being 77·6° on Wednesday. The minimum was 51·0° on Saturday. The rainfall was ·437 inch on four days, ·263 inch being registered on Wednesday. Hail fell on Saturday, when thunder also was heard. The prevalent winds were at first E., then S.W.

On Sunday, the 30th, a succession of thunderstorms passed over Dublin from S. to N. and rain fell in torrents at frequent intervals, the total measurement being ·641 inch.

The rainfall in Dublin during the six months ending June 30th amounted to 12·620 inches on 80 days, compared with 14·201 inches on 102 days in 1894, 9·684 inches on 78 days in 1893, 11·770 inches on 97 days in 1892, 8·749 inches on 77 days in 1891, 12·613 inches on 94 days in 1890, 10·578 inches on 97 days in 1889, 13·118 inches on 87 days in 1888, 8·741 inches on 67 days in 1887, and a twenty-five years' average of 12·313 inches on 95·6 days.

At Knockdolian, Greystones, Co. Wicklow, the rainfall in June, 1895, was 1·423 inches, distributed over 9 days. Of this quantity ·393 inch fell on the 25th, and ·255 on the 27th. The total fall since January 1 has been 14·670 inches on 67 days, compared with 17·681 inches on 96 days in the first six months of 1894, and 11·776 inches on 75 days during the corresponding period in 1893.

The rainfall at Cloneevin, Killiney, Co. Dublin, amounted to 1·94 inches on 12 days. The greatest fall in 24 hours was ·35 inch on the 25th. The average rainfall for June in 10 years was 1·620 inches on 11·0 days. Since January 1, 1895, 13·84 inches of rain have fallen at this station on 81 days.

July.—A very changeable, showery, and windy as well as a cool month, with a large rainfall at the beginning and close, and a decided prevalence of winds from westerly points—N.W., W., and S.W.

In Dublin the arithmetical mean temperature (59·2°) was markedly below the average (60·6°); the mean dry bulb readings at 9 a.m. and 9 p.m. were 58·0°. In the thirty years ending with 1894, July was coldest in 1879 (the "cold year") (M.T. = 57·2°). It was warmest in 1887 (M.T. = 63·7°), and in 1868 (the "warm year") (M.T. = 63·5°). In 1885 the M.T. was 61·0°; in 1888 it was as low as 57·3°; in 1889 it was 58·7°; in 1890, 58·1°; in 1891, 59·0°; in 1892, 57·8°; in 1893, 61·6°; and in 1894, 60·2°. From this, July, 1887, proves to have been the warmest since the present records commenced, whilst July, 1879, was the coldest.

The mean height of the barometer was 29·837 inches, or 0·078 inch below the corrected average value for July—namely, 29·915 inches. The mercury marked 30·281 inches at 9 a.m. of the 6th, and fell to 29·341 inches at 9 a.m. of the 31st. The observed range of atmospheric pressure was, therefore, 0·940 inch—that is, a little more than nine-tenths of an inch.

The mean temperature deduced from daily readings of the dry bulb thermometer at 9 a.m. and 9 p.m. was 58·0°, or 0·0 below the value for June, 1895. Using the formula, *Mean Temp.* = *Min.* + (*max.* − *min.* × ·465), the value was 58·7°, or 1·5° below the average mean temperature for July, calculated in the same way, in the twenty-five years, 1865–89, inclusive (60·2°). The arithmetical mean of the maximal and minimal readings was 59·2°, compared with a twenty-five years' average of 60·6°. On the 6th the thermometer in the screen rose to 73·5°—wind, S.W.; on the 4th the temperature fell to 46·1°—wind, N.W. The minimum on the grass was 44·5°, also on the 4th.

The rainfall was 4·503 inches, distributed over 16 days. The average rainfall for July in the twenty-five years, 1865–89, inclusive, was 2·420 inches, and the average number of rainy days was 17·2. The rainfall, therefore, was considerably above—in fact, nearly twice—the average, while the rainy days were somewhat below it. In 1880 the rainfall in July was very large—6·087 inches on 24 days; in 1871, also, 4·391 inches fell on 20 days. On the other hand, in 1870, only ·539 inch was measured on 8 days; in 1869 the fall was only ·739 inch on 9 days; and in 1885 only ·761 inch fell on but 5 days. In 1893, 1·959 inches fell on 13 days; in 1893, 3·043 inches on 18 days; and in 1894, 3·779 inches on 21 days.

High winds were noted on as many as 13 days, but attained the force of a gale on only two occasions—the 12th and 14th. Temperature reached or exceeded 70° in the screen on only 2 days—the 6th and 7th. In July, 1887, temperature reached or exceeded 70° in the screen on no fewer than 17 days. In 1888, the maximum for July was only 68·7°. In 1891 and 1894, maxima of 70° were reached on only 3 days, and in 1892, on only 2 days; but in 1893, 70° was reached on 5 days in the month. Electrical disturbances were frequent on the 19th and 31st. Hail fell on the 12th.

The weather of the period ended Saturday, the 6th, proved the converse of that of the previous week, being at first broken, with thunderstorms and heavy rains, but afterwards becoming fine, dry, and exceedingly very warm. During the first three days the weather in the British Isles was controlled by a cyclonic system which travelled slowly along the S. coasts of Ireland, to North Wales, thence across the N. of England and the North Sea to the South of Sweden, where it was found on Thursday morning. Its passage was attended by clouded skies, heavy rains, and in many places thunder and lightning, as well as by low temperature for the season. On Thursday an anticyclone spread in over Ireland and England from the westward, causing a return of fine, dry weather, which culminated in great warmth on Saturday. On this day the high pressure system "backed" towards S.E., causing a warm S.W. wind to blow over Ireland. In Dublin pressure increased from a minimum of 29·401 inches at 1 30 p.m. of Monday (wind, E.) to a maximum of 30·281 inches at 9 a.m. of Thursday (wind, N.W.). On Thursday the minimum in the screen was 46·1°; on Saturday the maximum was 73·5°. Rain fell on the first two days to the amount of ·757 inch, ·666 inch being measured on Monday. The prevalent wind was north-westerly.

Changeable, but not unfavourable, weather held throughout the week ended Saturday, the 13th. The distribution of atmospheric pressure was cyclonic in the British Islands and Scandinavia, anticyclonic for the most part over France and Germany, as well as in the South of England up to Tuesday. Gradients for south-westerly winds were steep over Ireland until Wednesday morning, when a depression of some depth and intensity was found with its centre between the Shetlands and the S.W. coast of Norway. This disturbance caused strong winds—and gales at exposed stations—from W. and N.W., in connection with it rain fell heavily in the N.W. of Ireland, the Hebrides and Shetlands. Scarcely had that system passed away when another and more anxious depression approached Ireland from the Atlantic, producing copious rains in places and squally S.W., veering to N.W. winds. On Thursday night it blew a moderate gale in both Dublin and Liverpool. Friday proved fair and bright in the rear of the depression, the centre of which lay over Denmark at 8 a.m. On Saturday the barometer fell again, and the wind freshened from W. with a quickly rising temperature. Very warm, even hot, weather was experienced in England up to Friday—the maxima in London were 80°, 83°, 79°, 77°, and 76° respectively. In Dublin the mean height of the barometer was 29·918 inches, pressure ranging from 30·116 inches at 9 a.m. of Sunday (wind, S.S.W.) to 29·641 inches at 9 p.m. of Thursday (wind, N.W.). The corrected mean temperature was 60·1°. The mean dry bulb reading at 9 a.m. and 9 p.m. was 59·7°. On Sunday the thermometer rose to 71·8° in the screen, on Friday it fell to 49·0°. The rainfall amounted to ·148 inch, on two days, ·122 inch being measured on Thursday. The prevailing winds were at first S.W., afterwards N.W., blowing from both quarters with considerable force.

As the week ended Saturday, the 20th, advanced, the weather fell into a very changeable, showery condition, and the strong winds of the previous week gave place to variable breezes from southerly quarters. Thunder-showers occurred on Friday and Saturday. At the beginning of the period a deep trough of low atmospheric pressure stretched from W. to E. across the southern part of Scandinavia and the Baltic Sea. Baric gradients for N.W. winds were steep over the British Isles, and moderate gales from the quarter named blew at many stations on Sunday and Monday, which were otherwise fine and dry days in most places. On Monday night a new disturbance advanced to the N.W. of Ireland from the Atlantic. It caused heavy rain in Munster and a temporary rise of temperature. During the remainder of the week the barometer fell intermittently as area after area of low pressure developed or arrived over the British Isles and their neighbourhood. On Friday and Saturday torrential showers of rain and hail, accompanied in some instances by thunder and lightning, occurred in many places, and the week closed with a generally unsettled appearance. In Dublin the mean height of the barometer was 29·703 inches, pressure ranging from 30·017 inches at 9 a.m. of Monday (wind, W.N.W.) to 29·411 inches at 9 a.m. of Saturday (wind, S.E.). The corrected mean temperature was 59·2°. The mean dry bulb temperature at 9 a.m. and 9 p.m. was 57·7°. On Sunday the sheltered thermometers fell to 51·7°; on Tuesday they rose to 68·1°. Rain fell on six days to the amount of ·748 inch, ·238 inch being measured on Thursday and ·203 inch on Friday. Thunder and hail occurred on Friday. The prevalent winds were N.W. and S.W.

A torrential rainfall in many parts of Ireland and England was the leading feature in the weather of the week ended Saturday, the 27th. Atmospheric pressure ruled low throughout, and it frequently happened that several minima developed within a wide-spreading barometric depression. The result was the commingling of opposing warm and cold-air currents, light variable winds, and an abundant precipitation. In the 24 hours ending 8 a.m. of Monday 1·33 inches of rain fell at Brixton in the south of London. In Dublin, the measurement at 9 a.m. of Wednesday was 1·016 inches, while that of the succeeding 24 hours was 1·236 inches—2·270 inches in two days. At Killiney, Greystones, and Fassaroe (Co. Wicklow) the downpour was not so heavy—1½ inches being registered. Friday and Saturday were fair days in and near Dublin, but thunderstorms and very heavy rains continued to prevail in many parts of Great Britain. On Sunday much thunder and lightning occurred in Ireland and Wales—a life was lost by lightning in the Co. Carlow and another in Brecknockshire. In Dublin the mean height of the barometer was 29·664 inches, pressure ranging between 29·341 inches at 9 a.m. of Sunday (wind, S.S.W.) and 29·907 inches at 9 a.m. of Tuesday (wind, W.N.W.). The corrected mean temperature was 57·7°. The mean dry bulb temperature was 57·1°. On Friday the screened thermometers rose to 63·7°, whereas on Wednesday they fell to 50·3°. The rainfall was 2·753 inches on six days, 1·236 inches being measured on Thursday and 1·016 inches on Wednesday. The prevalent winds were W.N.W. and S.S.E.

During the period from Sunday the 28th, to Wednesday the 31st, inclusive, no rain fell in Dublin. The weather was cloudy and cool, but otherwise favourable, with moderate N.W. winds. In London Sunday was gloomy and very wet, owing to the passage across the S.E. of England of a small depression embraced within the limits of a large area of low atmospheric pressure over Great Britain and the North Sea. As this disturbance passed away the barometer rose slowly in most districts and the weather became fine and dry, although the sky remained cloudy and the air was cool. On Tuesday and Wednesday a shallow area of low pressure moved eastwards across France. This system caused N.E. winds, and bright, cool weather in England. In Ireland the sky remained cloudy. In Dublin the barometer rose from 29·735 inches at 9 a.m. of Sunday (wind, W.N.W.) to 30·117 inches at 9 a.m. of Wednesday (wind, N.). On Monday the screened thermometer fell to 51·0°, on Wednesday it rose to 65·6°.

The rainfall in Dublin during the seven months ending July 31st amounted to 14·784 inches on 86 days, compared with 18·183 inches on 130 days in the corresponding period in 1894, 11·058 inches on 82 days in 1893, 13·782 inches on 109 days in 1892, 10·835 inches on 93 days in 1891, 16·457 inches on 118 days in 1890, 13·146 inches on 117 days in 1889, 15·894 inches on 109 days in 1888, 7·658 inches on 80 days in 1887, and a twenty-five years' average of 14·723 inches on 115·6 days.

At Knockdolian, Greystones, Co. Wicklow, the rainfall in July was 3·680 inches on 16 days, compared with 3·605 inches on 19 days in 1894, 1·920 inches on 16 days in 1893, 1·975 inches on only 10 days in 1892, 1·734 inches on 18 days in 1891, and 1·459 inches, distributed over 18 days, in 1890. Of the total rainfall 1·040 inches fell on the 24th and ·600 inch on the 25th. The total fall since January 1 has been 17·960 inches on 83 days, compared with 21·136 inches on 119 days in 1894, 10·054 inches on 80 days in 1893, and 16·708 inches on 80 days in 1892.

At Clonsevin, Killiney, Co. Dublin, the rainfall in July was 3·68 inches on 17 days, compared with a ten years' average of 3·025 inches on 13·9 days. On the 24th the rainfall was 1·08 inches. In July, 1894, 4·09 inches fell on 22 days, the maximum being 1·17 inches on the 24th, as in the present year. On the day named 1·700 inches fell at Fassaroe, Co. Wicklow. Since January 1, 1895, 18·67 inches of rain have fallen on 93 days at this station (Clonsevin).

AUGUST.—Like August, 1894, this month was very rainy. In Dublin rain was measured on as many as 27 days, and the total fall was nearly three-quarters of an inch in excess of the average. Unlike August, 1894, however, the month was fairly warm—the mean temperature being slightly above the average. This was due to comparative warmth by night—the mean minimum temperature being 51·3° compared with the average 50·5°, while the mean maximum was exactly the average—namely, 65·6°. There was an overwhelming prevalence of S.W. and W. winds, S. and N.W. being the next most frequent quarters from which the wind blew. Two-thirds of the sky was clouded throughout the month, compared with three-fourths in August, 1894.

In Dublin the arithmetical mean temperature (60·0°) was slightly above the average (59·7°); the mean dry bulb readings at 9 a.m. and 9 p.m. were 59·8°. In the thirty years ending with 1894, August was coldest in 1881 (M. T.=57·0°), and warmest in 1893 (M. T.=63·0°). In 1881, the M. T. was only 57·1°; in 1879 (the "cold year"), it was 57·7°; in 1887, 60·5°; in 1888, 58·4°; in 1889, 58·6°; in 1890, only 57·8°; in 1891, 58·1°; in 1892, 60·0°; in 1893, 63·0°; and in 1894, 57·9°.

The mean height of the barometer was 29·818 inches, or 0·079 inch below the corrected average value for August—namely, 29·897 inches. The mercury marked 30·210 inches at 9 a.m. of the 25th and fell to 29·247 inches at 9 a.m. of the 11th. The observed range of atmospheric pressure was therefore ·963 inch—that is, a little less than an inch.

The mean temperature deduced from daily readings of the dry bulb thermometer at 9 a.m. and 9 p.m. was 59·8°, or 1·9° above the value in August, 1894. It was also 0·3° above the value for July, 1895. Using the formula, *Mean Temp.* = *Min.* + (*max.* — *min.* × ·47), the mean temperature was 58·7°, or 0·4° above the average mean temperature for August, calculated in the same way, in the twenty-five years, 1865–89, inclusive (58·3°). The arithmetical mean of the maximal and minimal readings was 60·0°, compared with a twenty-five years' average of 59·7°. On the 7th the thermometer in the screen rose to 71·7°—wind, W.S.W.; on the 25th the temperature fell to 46·3°—wind, N.W. to W.N.W. The minimum on the grass was 41·6°, also on the 25th.

The rainfall was 3·348 inches, distributed over 27 days. The average rainfall for August in the twenty-five years, 1865–89, inclusive, was 2·625 inches, and the average number of rainy days was 15·6. The rainfall, therefore, and also the rainy days were considerably in excess of the average. In 1874, the rainfall in August was very large—4·940 inches on 18 days; and in 1868 also 4·743 inches fell on, however, only 13 days; but the heaviest downpour in August occurred in 1868, when 5·747 inches were registered on 23 days. On the other hand, in 1881, only ·777 inch was measured on 8 days. In 1887, 1·890 inches of rain fell on 16 days; in 1888, 1·270 inches on 12 days; in 1890, 2·720 inches on 19 days; in 1891, 4·053 inches on 25 days; in 1892, 3·117 inches on 22 days, in 1893, 2·713 inches on 16 days; and in 1894, 3·730 inches on 18 days.

High winds were noted on as many as 8 days, but did not attain the force of a gale on any occasion in Dublin. A thunderstorm occurred on the 11th, and lightning was seen on the 10th. Temperature reached 70° in the screen on 4 days. The atmosphere was foggy on the 15th.

The weather was broken during the first three days. On Thursday, the 1st, a considerable and tolerably brisk fall of the barometer set in, as a new series of low pressure systems approached the British Islands from the Atlantic. At 7 45 p.m. heavy rain fell in Dublin, and the wind freshened from the southward. Next day (Friday) thundershowers occurred in many districts, and hail was reported from Cambridge. Saturday was dull and chiefly wet in England. In the evening and at night rain fell in torrents in many places. The barometer fell to 29·23 inches at 8 a.m. at Stornoway. In Dublin it fell to 29·291 inches at 9 p.m. of Saturday (wind, W.). On Friday the screened thermometer rose to 65·5. Rain was measured on all three days to the amount of ·687 inch, ·440 inch falling on Saturday. The prevailing wind was S.W.

The record for the week ended Saturday, the 10th, is again one of unsettled, showery weather. The type of distribution of atmospheric pressure was throughout cyclonic. On Sunday a large area of low barometer covered the British Isles, the absolute minimum (29·24 inches) being logged at 8 a.m. at Spurn Head in Yorkshire. During the day heavy thunder showers occurred in the S.E. of England and also in the Co. Wicklow. At Greystones the fall of rain and hail amounted almost to an inch and the thunder and lightning were exceptionally violent. On Monday another depression advanced across Ireland from W.S.W., causing a renewed rainfall, particularly over the southern half of this country as well as in Wales and the S. and E. of England. During the next two days heavy showers fell at intervals, being accompanied by thunder in the Thames valley and along the E. coast of England. At 8 a.m. of Thursday another depression had arrived off the N.W. of Ireland, whence it travelled towards N.N.E., accompanied by renewed rain or passing showers. On Saturday again a depression passed across Ireland, so that the weather was kept in a changeable state to the very close of the week. In Dublin the mean height of the barometer was 29·[illegible] inches, pressure varying between 29·318 inches at 9 a.m. of Sunday (wind, W.N.W.) and 29·[illegible] inches at 9 p.m. of Wednesday (wind also W.N.W.). The corrected mean temperature was 57·9°. The mean dry bulb reading at 9 a.m. and 9 p.m. was 57·1°. On Thursday the thermometer in the screen fell to 48·0°, on Friday it rose to 69·6°. Rain fell daily to the amount of 1·116 inches, ·145 inch being measured on Sunday and ·700 inch on Saturday. The prevalent winds were once more N.W. and S.W. Sheet lightning was seen on Saturday evening.

The unsettled, changeable, showery weather observed in previous weeks continued throughout the week ended Saturday, the 17th. After Monday, however, the rains were not so heavy—at least near Dublin—and there was a decided advance in temperature. The week opened with a well-marked cyclonic system lying over Ireland and travelling northwards. At midnight of the 10–11th a rainstorm passed over Dublin from the southward, accompanied by vivid lightning and distant thunder. At Holyhead no less than 2·68 inches of rain fell in this storm. On Sunday, Monday, and Tuesday heavy showers fell at intervals in connection with the same disturbance, the centre of which passed directly over Dublin about 11 a.m. on Sunday, when the wind suddenly shifted from E.S.E. to W.N.W. At 8 a.m. of Monday the depression was central over the Hebrides and in its rear the barometer was rising generally throughout England and Ireland. During Tuesday a secondary system of low pressure passed up the English Channel, reaching the Netherlands on Wednesday morning and Eastern Prussia 24 hours later. This disturbance caused very heavy rains in the S. and E. of England, and afterwards in Germany. At 8 a.m. of Wednesday the rainfall measurements were—in London ·81 inch, at Cambridge 1·08 inches, and at Yarmouth 1·49 inches. With the passing away of this depression conditions improved, except in Scotland and the N.W. of Ireland, and on Friday morning an anticyclone lay over England, Wales, and France. On Saturday a large area of relatively low barometer was spreading eastwards across Ireland from the Atlantic, and the weather again fell into a showery condition. In Dublin the mean atmospheric pressure was 29·965 inches, the barometer ranging between 29·547 inches at 9 a.m. of Sunday (wind, E.S.E.) and 30·185 inches at 9 a.m. of Thursday (wind, N.). The corrected mean temperature was 60·3°. The mean dry bulb temperature at 9 a.m. and 9 p.m. was 59·0°. On Tuesday the screened thermometers sank to 51·7°; on Saturday they rose to 70·0°. The rainfall was ·885 inch on seven days, ·541 inch being recorded on Monday. The prevailing winds were W.S.W. and S.S.W. The air was foggy on Thursday evening.

During the earlier part of the week ended Saturday, the 24th, anticyclonic conditions held, the weather being warm and fine, except in the extreme West and North of our Islands, where the amount of cloud remained large and more or less rain fell daily. On Wednesday a very sudden change for the worse took place, the anticyclone retreated south-eastwards, and a shallow complex depression—with several minima—became developed over Ireland and England. As usually occurs under such circumstances, the atmosphere became close and oppressive, much sea-fog and cloud formed, and destructive thunderstorms broke out in the south of Ireland, over the greater part of England, and in Denmark. In Dublin a heavy downpour of rain occurred on Thursday, amounting to ·318 inch, but there was no thunderstorm. On Friday a V-shaped secondary depression passed eastwards to the southward of Ireland; this caused the wind to veer to N.W. or N. in this country, and the weather became at once colder, clearer, and finer. On Saturday, cumuli formed in the clear, cold atmosphere and heavy evaporation showers resulted. In London the thermometer rose to 81° in the shade on three days—Monday, Wednesday, and Thursday. In Dublin the mean height of the barometer was 29·939 inches, pressure ranging between 29·743 inches at 9 a.m. of Friday (wind, S.W.) and 30·181 inches at 9 p.m. of Saturday (wind, N.W.). The corrected mean temperature was 61·0°. The mean dry bulb reading at 9 a.m. and 9 p.m. was 59·5°. On Sunday the screened thermometers rose to 70·0°; on Saturday they fell to 49·0°. Rain fell on six days to the total amount of ·737 inch, ·318 inch being measured on Thursday. The prevalent winds were S.W. and N.W.

In the week ended Saturday, the 31st, the weather improved (except in the far North and North-west) as the week advanced, and became fine, warm, and breezy, having been at first dull, rainy and damp. As in many previous weeks, the distribution of atmospheric pressure was mainly anticyclonic in Central Europe, cyclonic over the Atlantic, the northern half of the British Isles, and in Scandinavia. Hence, the weather was comparatively fine in the South, blustering and rainy in the North. At the very beginning of the period, a remarkable dip in temperature occurred—the thermometer falling early on Sunday morning to 46° in Dublin, 45° at Aberdeen, 44° in London and at Parsonstown and Oxford, 43° at Cambridge and Loughborough, and 41° at Nairn. A dull, wet day followed, but temperature rose fast with a S.W. wind. Monday was also rainy in most places, the rainfall being heavy in Ireland, Wales, and Scotland and the North of England. A depression of great size and depth now passed northeastwards to Norway, causing S.W. gales at exposed stations, and squally S.W. to W. winds in many places. At 4.45 p.m. of Tuesday a brilliant double rainbow was seen in Dublin. The last four days of the week were warm, breezy, and changeable in Dublin; hot and fine in France and the S. of England; squally and showery or rainy in the N. of Ireland, Scotland, and Scandinavia. In Dublin the mean height of the barometer was 29·971 inches, atmospheric pressure ranging between 30·216 inches, at 9 a.m. of Sunday (wind, W.S.W.), and 29·640 inches at 9 a.m. of Tuesday (wind, W.). The corrected mean temperature was 60·4°. The mean dry bulb temperature at 9 a.m. and 9 p.m. was 59·6°. The shade thermometers rose to 71·7° on Wednesday, having fallen to 46·6° on Sunday. Rain fell on four days to the amount of ·443 inch, ·381 inch being measured on Monday. The prevalent winds were S.W. and W. At the close of the week temperature was low over Northern Europe.

The rainfall in Dublin during the eight months ending August 31st amounted to 20·323 inches on 128 days compared with 9·455 inches on 96 days during the same period in 1887, 17·884 inches on 131 days in 1888, 18·633 inches on 134 days in 1889, 19·384 inches on 127 days in 1890, 15·465 inches on 117 days in 1891, 17·379 inches on 131 days in 1892, 16·379 inches on 108 days in 1893, 21·459 inches on 145 days in 1894, and a twenty-five years' average of 17·435 inches on 129·1 days.

At Knockdolian, Greystones, Co. Wicklow, the rainfall in August, 1895, was 4·724 inches distributed over 16 days. Of this quantity 1·189 inches fell on the 10th, in addition to ·946 inch on the 4th. The total fall since January 1 amounts to 19·654 inches on 107 days, compared with 22·396 inches on 121 days in 1894, 16·961 inches on 105 days in 1893, and 21·394 inches on 108 days in 1892.

SEPTEMBER.—As in both 1893, and in 1894, September proved a favourable month throughout. The most remarkable feature in the month was the stability of an anticyclone over Central and Western Europe, while cyclonic conditions held in the far North and North-west, especially at the beginning. The high pressure system was accompanied by clear skies, quiet weather, and a there an extremely large diurnal range of temperature. In France and Germany tropical heat prevailed during the greater part of the month, and in England also the thermometer ranged unprecedentedly high. There were eight days on which the maximum in the shade recorded in London reached or exceeded 80°, the highest reading of all being 84° on the 24th. In Dublin the heat was tempered by a sea breeze, but the amount of bright sunshine was above the average, and the mean amount of cloud was only 42·3 per cent. Towards the close of the month heavy dews and dense night fogs became very prevalent.

The three warmest Septembers experienced in Dublin of late years have been—1865 (M.T. = 61·6°), 1880 (M. T. = 57·6°), and 1895 (M. T. = 59·1°).

In Dublin the arithmetical mean temperature (59·1°) was as much as 2·3° above the average (56·8°); the mean dry bulb readings at 9 a.m. and 9 p.m. were 57·5°. In the thirty years ending with 1894, September was coldest in 1882 and in 1883 (M. T. = [illegible]), and warmest in 1865 (M. T. = 61·6°). In 1893, the M. T. was as high as 55·6°; in 1879 (the "cold year"), it was 54·3°; in 1887, 54·0°; in 1885, 54·6°; in 1886, 56·6°, or exactly the average; in 1890, it was as high as 58·0°; in 1891, it was 57·6°; in 1892, 54·8°; in 1893, 55·9°; and in 1894, [illegible]. So warm a September as that of 1895 had not occurred for a quarter of a century, and this month was only half a degree (0·5°) cooler.

The mean height of the barometer was 30·102 inches, or 0·183 inch above the corrected average value for September—namely, 29·919 inches. The mercury rose to 30·430 inches at 9 a.m. of the 22nd, and fell to 29·401 inches at 9 p.m. of the 10th. The observed range of atmospheric pressure was, therefore, ·936 inch—that is, a little more than nine-tenths of an inch.

The mean temperature deduced from daily readings of the dry bulb thermometer at 9 a.m. and 9 p.m. was 57·5°, or only 1·2° below the value for August, 1895. Using the formula, *Mean Temp.* = *Min.* + (*max.* − *min.* × ·476), the mean temperature was 58·7°, or 3·2° above the average mean temperature for September, calculated in the same way, in the twenty-five years, 1865–89, inclusive (55·5°). The arithmetical mean of the maximal and minimal readings was 59·1°, compared with a twenty-five years' average of 55·8°. On the 2nd, the thermometer in the screen rose to 73·0°—wind, S.W.; on the 22nd the temperature fell to 45·0°—wind, calm. The minimum on the grass was 37·0°, also on the 22nd.

The rainfall was only ·548 inch, distributed over 7 days—the rainfall and rainy days were thus considerably below the average. The average rainfall for September in the twenty-five years, 1865–89, inclusive, was 2·174 inches, and the average number of rainy days was 14. In 1871, the rainfall was very large—4·048 inches on, however, only 13 days. On the other hand, in 1865, only ·056 inch was measured on but 2 days. In 1888, the rainfall was only ·729 inch on 10 days; in 1889, 1·043 inches fell on 12 days; in 1890, 1·440 inches on 14 days; in 1891, 2·137 inches on 18 days; in 1892, 2·631 inches on 13 days; in 1893, ·769 inch on 14 days; and in 1894, only ·643 inch on 3 days.

High winds were noted on seven days, and attained the force of a gale on two occasions in Dublin—the 10th and 11th. Lightning was seen on the 23rd. The atmosphere was foggy on the 2nd, 16th, 19th, 22nd, 23rd, 24th, 27th, 29th, and 30th.

During the week ended Saturday, the 7th, the weather was fine and hot on the Continent and in the South and East of England until Friday night, changeable in Ireland, Scotland, and the North of Europe generally. The heat became intense in France and Germany in the middle of the week—the thermometer rising in the shade to 94° in Paris on Tuesday, and to 91° in Berlin on Wednesday. On the night of this day a destructive thunderstorm accompanied with torrents of rain and hail (1·18 inches) passed over Lisbon (Portugal). A similar storm occurred on Friday, the rainfall being 1·58 inches. In London the daily maxima were 79°, 82°, 80°, 78°, 77°, and 76°—up to Friday inclusive. In Dublin Sunday and Monday were very fine days—the thermometer rose to 73° on Monday. Then followed a period of changeable, cloudy, and at times rainy weather lasting until Friday. Saturday proved beautifully fine—bright and warm. In the evening a lunar halo was visible. The distribution of atmospheric pressure which determined the weather just described was mainly anticyclonic over France, Germany, and the southern half of England, cyclonic to the northwestward of Ireland, in Scotland, and over Scandinavia. On Tuesday, however, a shallow thunderstorm depression passed northeastwards from the Bay of Biscay across Southern England to Denmark. It caused severe thunderstorms in England, but very little rain fell. On Friday night and Saturday morning violent thunderstorms and heavy rain prevailed over the S. and E. of England. In Dublin the mean height of the barometer was 29·973 inches, pressure decreasing to 29·619 inches at 9 a.m. of Monday (wind, S.W.), and increasing to 30·123 inches at 9 p.m. of Saturday (wind, W.). The corrected mean temperature was 63·3°. The mean dry bulb temperature at 9 a.m. and 9 p.m. was 57·8°. On Monday the screened thermometers rose to 73·0°; on Friday they sank to 50·9°. The rainfall was ·476 inch on five days, ·184 inch being measured on Wednesday and ·150 inch on Monday. The prevalent winds were S.W. and W.

Taken as a whole, the weather of the week ended Saturday, the 14th, was favourable. Until Monday evening an anticyclone stretched from Central Europe across England to the east of Ireland. There was, on Sunday morning, a baric maximum of slightly more than 30·20 inches over the greater part of England, and in that country a complete circulation of light anticyclonic winds existed. In Ireland the wind was moderate from S.S.E. and S. The thermometer rose to 76° in the shade in London and at Loughborough, to 76° at Parsonstown, and to 69° in Dublin. Monday was still warmer—the maxima being 82° in London, 83° at Loughborough, 80° at Oxford, 78° at Liverpool and Cambridge—in Dublin, 73°, the air being close and oppressive in the afternoon. Throughout Tuesday, the barometer fell fast in Ireland and Scotland as a deep depression approached the latter country from W.S.W. The centre of this system passed across the North of Scotland on Wednesday morning, the barometer falling to 28·80 inches at Nairn at 8 a.m. Fresh S.W. to N.W.

gales set in on the Irish and British coasts and temperature gave way, with falls of rain or passing showers. By Friday the barometer had entirely recovered from its depression, and another anticyclone was passing eastward over the southern half of the British Islands. At 8 a.m. its centre lay over the extreme S.E. of Ireland, the barometer reading 30·31 inches at Roche's Point, Cork Harbour. Fine, quiet, but at times cloudy weather held to the end of the week. In Dublin the mean height of the barometer was 30·010 inches, pressure ranging from 29·494 inches at 9 p.m. of Tuesday (wind, W.S.W.) to 30·305 inches at 9 p.m. of Saturday (wind, E.). The corrected mean temperature was 55·5°. The mean dry bulb reading at 9 a.m. and 9 p.m. was 57·7°. On Sunday the screened thermometers fell to 45·2°; on Monday they rose to 71·6°. The prevailing winds were at first S., afterwards W.N.W. Rain fell on two days to the amount of ·052 inch, ·039 inch being measured on Tuesday. Temperature was very low over Central England on Saturday morning—31° at Loughborough at 8 a.m.

During the week ended Saturday, the 21st, very fine weather prevailed for the most part in Ireland, England, and on the Continent. In Scotland and Scandinavia conditions were unsettled and a good deal of rain fell. At both the beginning and the close of the period an anticyclone of considerable intensity lay over England, Ireland, and France. These high-pressure systems were accompanied by fine, quiet, weather—temperature alone being unstable, rising very high by day and falling very low at night. In Paris on Thursday the minimum was 43°, the maximum 82°—range 39°. Heavy dews fell by night, and at times a good deal of fog hung about the coasts. On Tuesday a low pressure area skirted the N.W. of Ireland, passing northeastwards to Scotland and thence travelling eastward to the south of Sweden. This disturbance caused strong and squally S.W. winds as it approached, but in its rear the wind veered to N. and fell light, with a clearing sky. On Thursday much cloud covered England and drizzling rain fell tolerably widely over that country. In Ireland, however, the weather was fair and bright. Friday was brilliantly fine; on the morning of this day the isobar of 30·40 inches embraced the east of Ireland, the Irish Sea, and the central and eastern parts of England. The first frost of the season was reported from Sweden at this time, the thermometer falling to 30° in the screen at Haparanda. At Oxford the thermometer fell to 35° in the screen and to 31° on the grass. Saturday was fine, but cloud increased in Ireland, where the barometer was lower than on Friday. In Dublin the mean atmospheric pressure was 30·[illegible] inches, the extremes being highest, 30·[illegible] inches at 9 a.m. on Friday (wind, E.N.E.); lowest, 29·[illegible] inches at 9 a.m. of Wednesday (wind, W. by S.). The corrected mean temperature was 57·[illegible]°. The mean dry bulb reading at 9 a.m. and 9 p.m. was 55·[illegible]°. On Tuesday the thermometer rose to 67·[illegible]° in the shade, on Saturday it fell to 46·7°. A slight shower fell on Wednesday afternoon, but it yielded no measurable rainfall. The prevailing wind was westerly.

Splendid weather—dry, bright, and unusually warm—held throughout the week ended Saturday, the 28th. On Monday night, indeed, a severe thunderstorm passed northwards across the centre and west of Ireland from Roche's Point to Malin Head, but this electric disturbance caused no lasting break in the weather. A large anticyclone hung over Central Europe all through the period, and, as it were, a wave of high pressure swayed westwards across the British Isles and France from time to time. At the beginning of the week the air was calm and the sky was clear. Hence the diurnal range of temperature was extremely large—even in Dublin on Sunday the thermometer in the screen ranged from 43° to 64° and on Monday from 46° to 67°. But these variations fade into insignificance when compared with those recorded at Loughborough (Leicestershire). At that inland station the diurnal range was on Sunday from 33° to 74° and on Monday from 38° to 81°. On Tuesday the heat in England became intense, the thermometer rising to 85° in London and at Loughborough, and to 84° at Cambridge. Over England, as a whole, the maximum temperature of Monday was from 12° to 13° above the average for September and even this excess was outdone on Tuesday. A light southerly air-current was the bearer of this great heat, which had first shown itself in France. The nights were warm after Monday. A good deal of haze and fog hung about towards the close of the week, especially at the coast stations and over the sea-channels. The highest Irish temperatures recorded were 78° at Fermoy on Thursday and 77° on Friday. In Dublin the mean height of the barometer was 30·131 inches, pressure falling from 30·[illegible] inches at 9 a.m. of Sunday (wind, S.S.E.), to 30·104 inches at 9 p.m. of Tuesday (wind, S.S.W.), and rising again intermittently to 30·[illegible] inches at 9 a.m. of Saturday (wind, N.). The corrected mean temperature was 60·[illegible]°. The mean dry bulb reading at 9 a.m. and 9 p.m. was 59·[illegible]°. On Sunday the screened thermometers fell to 43·[illegible]°; on Thursday they rose to 70·[illegible]°. The prevalent wind was southerly. No rain fell in Dublin.

Sunday, the 29th, was at first calm, with heavy dew and a dense fog in Dublin. The weather afterwards became brilliant. Monday, the 30th, was also summerlike.

The rainfall in Dublin during the nine months ending September 30th amounted to 20·[illegible] inches on 150 days, compared with 10·[illegible] inches on 11[illegible] days during the same period in 1887, 17·[illegible] inches on 131 days in 1888, 16·[illegible] inches on 147 days in 1889, 20·[illegible] inches on 151 days in 1890, 16·[illegible] inches on 136 days in 1891, 19·910 inches on 140 days in 1892, 15·[illegible] inches on 1[illegible] days in 1893, 2[illegible] inches on 164 days in 1894, and a twenty-five years' average of 19·734 inches on 145·8 days.

At Knockdolian, Greystones, Co. Wicklow, the rainfall in September, 1895, was ·[illegible] inch, distributed over 10 days. Of this quantity ·375 inch fell on the 4th, and ·370 inch on the 2nd. At that station the rainfall since January 1, 1895, has been [illegible] inches on 117 days, compared with 23·[illegible] inches on 1[illegible] days in the same nine months of 1892, 17·[illegible] inches on 118 days in 1893, and 25·[illegible] inches on 137 days in 1894.

At Clonsevin, Killiney, Co. Dublin, the rainfall in August was [illegible] inches on [illegible] days (the maximal fall in 24 hours being 1·05 inches on the 10th), compared with a ten years' average of [illegible] inches on 1[illegible] days. In September only ·61 inch fell at Clonsevin on 7 days. The maximal fall in 24 hours was ·34 inch on the 2nd. On an average of ten years the September rainfall at this station has been 1·830 inches on 11·6 days. Since January 1, 1895, 21·44 inches of rain have fallen at Cloneevin on 129 days. The rainfall in the first nine months of 1894 at Cloneevin was 21·93 inches on 130 days.

At Claremont, Carrickmines, Co. Dublin, the rainfall in September was ·90 inch on 4 days. At this station 20·56 inches of rain have fallen since January 1.

OCTOBER.—A very cold October, with a great preponderance of north-westerly winds—both cyclonic and anti-cyclonic systems advancing generally from N.W., and crossing the British Islands towards S.E. The mean temperature was nearly 13° below that of September—the change from the unusual warmth of the end of that month being singularly abrupt and occurring as early as the morning of the 2nd. During the very cold period from the 21st to the 30th inclusive, thunder and lightning, and hail and sleet showers prevailed day after day over the Irish Sea, St. George's Channel, and the western half of the English Channel. The inland frosts of this cold spell were unusually severe both in Great Britain and in Ireland. Snow lay on the Dublin Mountains on the 2nd, and also from the 22nd to the end of the month.

In Dublin the arithmetical mean temperature (46·8°) was much below the average (49·7°); the mean dry bulb readings at 9 a.m. and 9 p.m. were 44·7°. In the thirty years ending with 1895, October was coldest in 1869 (M. T. = 44·6°), in 1880 (M. T. = 45·4°), and in 1883 (M. T. = 45·5°). It was warmest in 1876 (M. T. = 53·1°). In 1886, the M. T. was as high as 51·0°, in 1879 (the "cold year") it was 49·7°; in 1887 it was as low as 47·3°; in 1888, it was 49·1°; in 1889, 49·1°; in 1890, 51·7°; in 1891, 49·8°; and in 1893, 50·0°. October, 1895, beat the record for coldness.

The mean height of the barometer was 29·963 inches, or 0·023 inch above the corrected average value for October, namely, 29·940 inches. The mercury rose to 30·518 inches at 9 a.m. of the 17th, and fell to 29·077 inches at 9 a.m. of the 3rd. The observed range of atmospheric pressure was, therefore, as much as 1·441 inch—that is, a little less than an inch and a half.

The mean temperature deduced from daily readings of the dry bulb thermometer at 9 a.m. and 9 p.m. was 44·7°, or 13·[illegible]° below the value for September. The arithmetical mean of the maximal and minimal readings was 46·2°, compared with a twenty-five years' average of 49·7°. Using the formula, *Mean Temp.* = *Min.* + (max. — min. × ·465), the value was 46·0°, or 3·6° below the average mean temperature for October, calculated in the same way, in the twenty-five years, 1865–89, inclusive (49·6°). On the 1st the thermometer in the screen rose to 63·6°—wind, S.; on the 25th the temperature fell to 29·9°—wind, N.W. The minimum on the grass was 24·1°, also on the 25th. On five nights, the thermometer sank to or below 32° in the screen, and on twelve nights frost occurred on the grass.

The rainfall was 2·340 inches, distributed over 16 days—the rainfall and the rainy days were below the average. The average rainfall for October in the twenty-five years, 1865–89, inclusive, was 3·104 inches, and the average number of rainy days was 17·6. In 1880 the rainfall in October was very large—7·358 inches on 15 days. In 1875, also, 7·049 inches fell on 26 days. On the other hand, in 1890 only ·623 inch fell on but 11 days, in 1866 only ·574 inch on but 15 days, and in 1869 only ·836 inch on 13 days. In 1888, the rainfall was 1·257 inches on 16 days; in 1889, 4·653 inches fell on 22 days. In 1891, 5·350 inches fell on 18 days; in 1892, 7·635 inches on 17 days; in 1893, 1·083 inches on 16 days; and in 1894, 2·047 inches on 20 days. From these figures it will be seen that October, 1890, proved the driest October on record for more than a quarter of a century at least.

There was a thunderstorm on the morning of the 26th, and lightning was seen on the nights of the 25th, 27th and 28th. High winds were noted on 9 days, but attained the force of a gale on only two occasions—the 2nd and 3rd. The atmosphere was more or less foggy in Dublin on the 1st, 14th, 15th, 17th, 19th, 20th, and 31st. Hail fell on the 2nd, 4th, 21st, 22nd, 24th, 25th, 26th, and 31st; sleet on the 2nd, 22nd and 24th. A solar halo appeared on the 30th.

The period ended Saturday the 5th, witnessed the complete and final break-up of the warm, summer-like weather which had prevailed during the greater part of September. On Monday, September 30th, the barometer began to fall quickly all over Western Europe, and on Tuesday, the 1st, storm, rain, thunder and lightning, and a remarkable fall of temperature spread eastward across Ireland as a large and complex depression advanced from the Atlantic, its centre lying off the east coast of Scotland at 8 a.m. of Wednesday. This disturbance caused a complete break-up of the fine, warm weather, so that with the passing of September came a sharp plunge from summer into winter. Nearly six-tenths of an inch of rain fell in Dublin during the night of the 1st. Mount Leinster was snow-capped on the morning of the 2nd, which proved very inclement with heavy showers of sleety rain and hail, the thermometer in Dublin not rising above 49·1° in the screen and falling to 31·9° on the grass in the evening. A strong, tempestuous gale blew in the S.W. of England and on the Lancashire coasts, and this was renewed on Thursday. Dull rainy weather brought the period to a close. In Dublin the barometer ranged between 29·97 inches at 9 a.m. of Thursday (wind, W., blowing a gale) and 29·463 inches at 9 p.m. of Friday, (wind, W.). On Tuesday the screened thermometers rose to 63·6°, on Thursday they fell to 39·1°. The prevailing winds were W. and N.W. Rain fell on five days to the amount of ·931 inch, ·580 being registered on Tuesday, the 1st.

During the week ended Saturday, the 12th, except on Tuesday, which was a dull, rainy, cold day, favourable weather prevailed in Dublin, and indeed throughout the greater part of Ireland. In England and France conditions were unsettled and rain fell in large quantities. On Sunday a small atmospheric depression passed across the S. of England towards E.N.E., causing copious rain there and throughout the northern half of France, Belgium, and North Germany. Heavy showers fell on this day in the North of Ireland also. On Monday evening a new depression approached the Land's End from S.W. This system developed considerable intensity as it advanced across

England, and its centre lay over the E. and S.E. of that country at 8 a.m. of Wednesday. At the last named strong S. winds were blowing at Dungeness, the North Foreland, and Yarmouth, equally strong N. winds at stations in the meridian of Greenwich and to the westward of it. Very heavy rains accompanied the disturbance, the largest measurement of all being 4·41 inches at Nice. Squally N.W. winds held until the end of the week in the rear of this depression, the centre of which lay over the Christiania Fjord on Friday morning. At this time gradients were made steep by the advance of an anticyclone over Ireland from the Atlantic. In consequence the wind rose to a moderate gale on Friday night. Cloudy, breezy, mild weather brought the period to a close. In Dublin the mean height of the barometer was 29·739 inches, pressure falling to 29·068 inches at 9 a.m. of Tuesday (wind, N.E.) and rising to 30·180 inches at 9 p.m. of Saturday (wind, W.). The corrected mean temperature was 49·2°. The mean dry bulb temperature at 9 a.m. and 9 p.m. was 49·2°. On Saturday the screened thermometers rose to 57·6°; on Thursday they fell to 38·1°. The prevailing wind was N.W. Rain fell on two days to the amount of ·741 inch, ·170 inch being registered on Tuesday.

During the week ended Saturday, the 19th, fine autumnal weather ruled, except on Monday and Tuesday, when the British Isles were under the influence of shallow and irregular atmospheric depressions. These finally passed away or dispersed as a large anticyclone advanced from the north-westward on Tuesday and Wednesday. This fair-weather system governed the weather over Western Europe to the close of the week—the days being succeeded by quiet, clear, cold nights, with sharp frosts inland. Sunday was a dull, but fine, mild day. Heavy rains fell on Monday and Tuesday—the precipitation being especially large in parts of Ireland and the North of England—1·49 inches at Belmullet, 1·67 inches at Donaghadee, and 2·17 inches at Shields. As usually happens, slight but irregular barometric gradients and light variable winds, with unsteady temperature, led to these heavy rains. The principal downpour coincided with a rapid rise of the barometer, a setting in of N.E. and N. winds, and a brisk fall of temperature. On Thursday morning the isobar of 30·55 inches embraced the greater part of Great Britain and the N.E. and E. of Ireland. As the system of high pressure travelled south-eastwards, northerly winds set in over Ireland, temperature rose and the amount of cloud increased. Early on Friday morning sharp frost prevailed at the inland English stations, the minima in the screen being 27° at Cambridge, 28° at Leith, York and Oxford, 30° at Loughborough, and 34° in the Southern London district. At the coast stations temperature was much higher—thus, at 8 a.m. of Friday the thermometer read 51° at Yarmouth, but only 29° at Cambridge. In Dublin the mean height of the barometer was 30·228 inches, pressure receding to 29·670 inches at 9 a.m. of Tuesday (wind, S.E.) and rising to 30·518 inches at 9 a.m. of Thursday (wind, E.). The corrected mean temperature was 50·3°. The mean dry bulb reading at 9 a.m. and 9 p.m. was 49·8°. On Monday the screened thermometers rose to 61·8°, on Thursday they sank to 37·0°. The prevailing winds were E.N.E. and S.E. Rain fell on three days to the amount of ·476 inch, ·458 inch being measured on Monday.

A plunge into mid-winter was the main feature of the week ended Saturday, the 26th. On Sunday, the anticyclone, which had prevailed for several days, was fast breaking up, but the weather remained fine and the shade temperature in Dublin reached 56·0°. Monday broke dull and chilly, and a cold rain fell throughout the afternoon, followed by hailshowers in the evening. After midnight, a squally N.E. wind prevailed, with driving showers of cold rain, sleet, and hail. At dawn the Dublin and Wicklow mountains were snowcapped, and so they remained to the end of the week. Between Tuesday and Thursday a long trough of low atmospheric pressure stretched across the Peninsula and France to the south of Scandinavia. Polar winds consequently prevailed in the British Islands, where the weather became exceedingly cold for the time of year. On Wednesday the thermometer fell to 22° in the shade at Parsonstown; on Thursday the same low value was reached at Loughborough, the minimum on the grass being 16°. In Dublin heavy hail showers fell about 1 p.m. on both Thursday and Friday, and lightning was seen on the latter day both before dawn and after dark. About 9 a.m. of Saturday a storm of thunder, lightning and hail passed over the south-eastern coast of Dublin Bay, and this was soon followed by a fall of hail in the city itself. At Loughborough the minimum thermometer registered only 22° on Saturday morning. The mean height of the barometer in Dublin was 29·834 inches, pressure ranging between 30·249 inches at 9 a.m. of Sunday (wind, calm) and 29·321 inches at 9 a.m. of Thursday (wind, W.N.W.). The corrected mean temperature was 40·6°, the mean dry bulb reading at 9 a.m. and 9 p.m. being more than 1° lower—viz., 39·3°. On Sunday the shade maximum was as high as 54·6°, on Saturday the shade minimum was as low as 30·7°, the grass minimum being only 25·9°. The rainfall was ·731 inch, distributed over four days, ·520 inch being measured on Monday. The precipitation was chiefly in the form of hail and sleet. The prevalent wind was N.N.W.

During the earlier portion of the closing period—the 27th to the 31st inclusive—the weather was fair and cold on shore, but hail showers passed daily down the Irish Sea, St. George's Channel and across the mouth of the English Channel to the Channel Islands. These showers fell from massive cumuli and were accompanied by much thunder and lightning. On Wednesday the 30th, a depression advanced from N.W. across the British Isles, causing a rapid rise of temperature, much cloud and a heavy rainfall in many places. A fresh easterly wind was blowing as the month drew to a close.

The rainfall in Dublin during the ten months ending October 31st amounted to 23·716 inches on 148 days, compared with 17·364 inches on 123 days during the same period in 1887, 19·219 inches on 147 days in 1888, 24·789 inches on 169 days in 1889, 21·486 inches on 160 days in 1890, 22·710 inches on 148 days in 1891, 22·443 inches on 167 days in 1892, 16·141 inches on 135 days in 1893, 25·258 inches on 176 days in 1894, and a twenty-five years' average of 22·940 inches on 160·6 days.

At Knockdolian, Greystones, Co. Wicklow, the rainfall in October amounted to 2·605 inches on 14 days. Of this quantity ·675 inch fell on the 1st. The rainfall at Greystones in October, 1889, was no less than 4·235 inches on 20 days, or more than 11 times as great as the fall in

October, 1890, when only ·600 inch fell on 18 days. In 1891, 5·162 inches fell on 14 days, in 1892, 3·040 inches on 15 days, in 1893, ·710 inch on 15 days, and in 1894, 6·[illegible] inches on 17 days. From January 1st, 1895, up to October 31st, rain fell at Rathfarnham on 131 days to the total amount of 22·270 inches. In 1892, the rainfall of the corresponding ten months was 27·[illegible] inches on 160 days; in 1893, 17·601 inches on 133 days, and in 1894, 33·721 inches on 154 days.

At Clonsevin, Killiney, Co. Dublin, the rainfall in October, was 2·[illegible] inches on 14 days, compared with 3·040 inches on 17 days in 1892, ·710 inch on 14 days in 1893, 5·160 inches on 17 days in 1894, and a ten years' average of 3·737 inches on 17·4 days. On the 1st ·[illegible] inch fell. Since January 1, 1895, 24·23 inches of rain have fallen at this station on 148 days.

November, 1895, proved an open, dull, squally and rainy month in the neighbourhood of Dublin. It was perceptibly warmer than October, and no frost was recorded in the thermometer screen in the city. On the grass the thermometer fell to or below 32° on 6 nights only, compared with 13 nights in October. The range of pressure was great—nearly 2 inches. Only twice in the last thirty years has November been milder than in the present year—in 1881, when the mean temperature was as high as 50·0°, or 5·8° above the average, and in 1894, when the mean temperature was 47·8°, or 0·5° above that of the month now under review.

In Dublin the arithmetical mean temperature (47·0°) was decidedly above the average (44·7°); the mean dry bulb readings at 9 a.m. and 9 p.m. were 46·1°. In the thirty years ending with 1894, November was coldest in 1878 (M. T. = 39·3°), and in 1879 (M. T. = 4[illegible]°), warmest in 1881 (M. T. = 50·0°). In 1886, the M. T. was as high as 48·4°, in the year 1879 (the "cold year") it was 43·9°; in 1887, it was 42·6°, in 1888, 47·5°; in 1889, 46·4°; in 1890, 45·5°; in 1891, 45·[illegible]°; in 1892, 46·9°; in 1893, 43·[illegible]°; and in 1894, 47·8°.

The mean height of the barometer was 29·774 inches, or 0·086 inch below the corrected average value for November—namely, 29·860 inches. The mercury rose to 30·447 inches at 9 p.m. of the 26th, having fallen to 28·490 inches at 9·30 p.m. of the 10th. The observed range of atmospheric pressure was, therefore, 1·957 inches—that is, slightly less than two inches.

The mean temperature deduced from daily readings of the dry bulb thermometer at 9 a.m. and 9 p.m. was 46·1°, or 1·4° above the value for October, but 11·9° below that for September, 1895. The arithmetical mean of the maximal and minimal readings was 47·0°, compared with a twenty-five years' average of 44·7°. On the 15th the thermometer in the screen rose to 58·5°—wind, S.W.; on the 4th the temperature fell to 34·3°—wind, calm. The minimum on the grass was 29·8°, also on the 16th.

The rainfall was 3·563 inches, distributed over 21 days—the rainfall and the rainy days were considerably above the average. The average rainfall for November in the twenty-five years, 1865-89, inclusive, was 2·632 inches, and the average number of rainy days was 17·0. In 1878 the rainfall in November was large—5·016 inches on 20 days; in 1872, also, 5·411 inches fell on 24 days; in 1887, 3·019 inches fell on 16 days; in 1888, 6·349 inches fell on 26 days; in 1889, 4·212 inches fell on no less than 27 days; in 1891, 2·931 inches fell on 16 days; in 1892, 2·404 inches on 19 days. On the other hand, the rainfall in 1869 was only ·[illegible] inch on 8 days; in 1870, only 1·218 inches on 11 days; in 1879, 1·341 inches on 10 days; in 1882, 1·670 inches on 17 days; and in 1894, 1·452 inches on 16 days.

High winds were noted on 13 days, and attained the force of a gale on seven occasions—the 5th, 6th, 10th, 11th, 15th, 16th, and 19th. The atmosphere was more or less foggy in Dublin on the 3rd, 4th, 8th, 17th, 23rd, and 28th.

Lunar halos were seen on the 4th and 30th. Hail fell on the 16th.

The first two days of the month were quiet and fine, cloudy and mild, with a high barometer and moderate south-easterly winds. Much cirrus came up from S. on the afternoon of Saturday, the 2nd.

The weather was of the south-westerly and unsettled type throughout the week ended Saturday the 9th, and the distribution of atmospheric pressure was cyclonic—one depression of great intensity passing across the British Islands on Tuesday and Wednesday. At 6 p.m. of the former day the barometer was down to 28·47 inches at Belmullet, Co. Mayo, while it stood as high as 30·17 inches at Nice. This large difference of pressure was attended by fresh or strong south-westerly gales over the greater part of Western Europe, and rain fell freely in many districts. Before this disturbance arrived several shallow depressions existed, so that the weather was changeable. In Ireland, owing to slight baric gradients a good deal of fog formed and temperature became very low on Sunday night—the sheltered minima being 34° in Dublin and at Belmullet, 31° at Valentia Island, and 27° at Parsonstown. Temperature rose fast on Tuesday, as the deep cyclonic system approached, and remained above the average until Saturday, when a "chill" spread over Ireland from the westward. In South London the thermometer rose to 61° on Wednesday and 60° on Thursday. On Friday a secondary complex depression brought heavy rains to the S. and S.E. of England, but the weather improved in Ireland. In Dublin the mean height of the barometer was 29·617 inches, pressure ranging from 29·036 inches at 9 a.m. of Sunday (wind, S.E.) to 28·671 inches at 6 p.m. of Tuesday (wind, S.). The corrected mean temperature was 47·0°. The mean dry bulb reading at 9 a.m. and 9 p.m. was 45·6°. On Monday the screened thermometers fell to 34·6°, on Wednesday they rose to 56·7°. The prevailing wind was S.W. The rainfall measured ·971 inch on six days, ·500 inch being registered on Tuesday. On Friday the thermometer at Biarritz rose to 79° in the shade, and the temperature at that station at 8 a.m. of Saturday was 73°.

Cyclonic conditions and weather of the south-westerly type (that is, unsettled, rainy, squally, and with rapid alterations in temperature) held throughout Western and Northern Europe during the whole week ended Saturday the 16th. On Sunday a vast depression of great depth advanced rapidly towards the British Islands from S.W. Even in Dublin the barometer sank to 28·[illegible] inches

9·30 p.m., but much lower values were recorded in the extreme N.W. and N., and at 8 a.m. of Monday the reading of 28·23 inches was noted at Sumburgh Head in the Shetlands. The barometer had not been so low as 28·490 inches in Dublin since October 13, 1891, when it read 28·231 inches at 3·30 p.m. Severe S.W. gales resulted, and large quantities of rain fell over the whole kingdom. Monday was changeable owing to the approach of a secondary depression. At night lightning was seen in the South of Ireland, and from Prawle Point to the North Foreland in the South of England. At 9 a.m. of Tuesday the waning moon and the planet Venus were seen in bright sunshine. A beautiful conjunction of these bodies was well observed on Wednesday morning. Early on Thursday thunderstorms occurred both at Malin Head and at Roche's Point, accompanied by hail showers. On Friday a new series of deep depressions reached Ireland from the Atlantic, the barometer falling four-fifths of an inch in Dublin. Southerly gales and heavy rain occurred, while temperature rose to 58·8°. Early on Saturday morning a sudden "chill" succeeded this warmth in connection with a V-shaped secondary depression, and rain, hail and sleet fell abundantly, the Dublin and Wicklow Mountains becoming deeply covered with snow. At the same time the thermometer rose above 60° all over the South of England. In Dublin the mean height of the barometer was only 29·218 inches, pressure ranging from 28·490 inches at 3·30 p.m. of Sunday (wind, S.W.) to 29·821 inches at 9 p.m. of Thursday (wind, W.S.W.). The corrected mean temperature was 47·1°. The mean dry bulb reading at 9 a.m. and 9 p.m. was 48·8°. On Friday the screened thermometers rose to 58·8°; on Saturday they fell to 34·0°. The prevalent wind was S.W. Rain fell on six days to the amount of 1·288 inches, ·470 inch being registered on Friday.

During the week ended Saturday, the 23rd, the weather remained changeable, dull, open, and rainy, particularly on the east coast of Ireland. Sunday, no doubt, was a fine, even bright day, but the setting in, on Monday, of a decided southerly current of warm, moist air along the western face of a large anticyclone over the Continent brought dull skies and heavy frequent rainfalls to Ireland and the western half of Great Britain. In the east and south-east of England conditions were more favourable, and the weather, while dull, was comparatively dry. On Sunday morning the centre of a deep depression was found off the N.W. of Norway, where the barometer was below 28·70 inches—on the other hand, pressure exceeded 30·30 inches over Southern Germany, the S.E. of France and Italy. Strong S.W. and W. gales blew in Scandinavia, but the wind was moderating in the British Islands, with a quickly falling temperature. Early on Monday frost occurred over central England. The area of high pressure meanwhile moved northwards and developed, so that by Thursday the barometer rose above 30·70 inches in Sweden. A low pressure area at the same time arrived off the S.W. of Ireland, causing strong S.E. winds, gloom, and rain in this country. On Friday a complete reversal of these conditions took place—the barometer became high off the West of Ireland, and a complex depression passed southwards across the North Sea. The result was the setting in of northerly winds, with drier and colder weather in Ireland, but with falls of cold rain, sleet and hail in the sister country. In Dublin the mean height of the barometer was 30·026 inches, pressure ranging from 29·623 inches at 9 a.m. of Wednesday (wind, S.E.) to 30·307 inches at 9 p.m. of Saturday (wind, E.N.E.). The mean temperature was 47·3°. The mean dry bulb reading at 9 a.m. and 9 p.m. was 48·4°. On Thursday the screened thermometer rose to 55·6°; on Monday the minimum was 37·0°. Rain fell on five days to the amount of ·671 inch, ·370 inch being measured on Tuesday. The prevailing wind was S.S.E.

Except at the beginning of the week ended Saturday the 30th, when a brisk east wind was blowing, and at its close, when the wind was westerly, the weather was overcast and gloomy. Thursday and Friday were, in addition, very wet, damp days, with extreme thickness of the atmosphere. During the first three days of the period an anticyclone lay upon the North Sea between Scotland and Norway, while extensive areas of low pressure were found both over the extreme North of Europe and in the Mediterranean Basin and over the Peninsula. Strong westerly winds consequently prevailed in the far North, still stronger easterly and north-easterly winds in the South, while the atmosphere was calm in Scotland, and over the South of Scandinavia. Sharp cold prevailed at this time in the N.E. of Scotland—the thermometer falling at Nairn to 22° on Tuesday morning, but the weather was generally open in the British Isles. In Germany severe frost was felt—the minima at Munich being 21°, 21°, 27°, 19°, 13°, 23°, and 30°; at Berlin, 27°, 29°, 25°, 26°, 27°, 19°, and 16°. On the east coast of Ireland temperature was some 4° higher than at Holyhead during the easterly winds of the earlier part of the week. On Thursday, however, temperature became higher very generally, but rain at the same time set in, and a murky sky and extremely damp air lasted until Saturday, when the sky cleared with a bracing W. wind. In Dublin the mean height of the barometer was 29·999 inches, pressure ranging from 30·447 inches at 9 p.m. of Sunday (wind, E.) to 29·600 inches at 9 a.m. of Friday (wind, N.E.). The mean temperature was 46·1°. The mean dry bulb temperature at 9 a.m. and 9 p.m. was 46·8°. On Wednesday the screened thermometers fell to 41·7°, on Friday they rose to 50·6°. Rain fell on three days to the amount of ·467 inch, ·270 inch being registered on Thursday. Easterly winds prevailed until Saturday. The range of temperature was small—only 9·1°.

The rainfall in Dublin during the eleven months ending November 30th amounted to 27·136 inches on 167 days, compared with 16·375 inches on 141 days during the same period in 1887, 23·768 inches on 172 days in 1888, 25·716 inches on 178 days in 1889, 25·706 inches on 189 days in 1890, 24·531 inches on 163 days in 1891, 24·049 inches on 186 days in 1892, 18·011 inches on 155 days in 1893, 27·780 inches on 191 days in 1894, and a twenty-five years' average of 24·393 inches on 177·4 days.

At Knockdolian, Greystones, Co. Wicklow, the rainfall in November, 1895, was 5·443 inches distributed over 20 days. Of this quantity 1·140 inches fell on the 15th, ·750 inch on the 8th, and ·445 inch on the 19th. From January 1st, 1895, up to November 30th, rain fell at that station on 151 days, and to the total amount of 31·716 inches. The corresponding figures for 1893 were 19·348 inches on 150 days, and for 1894, 25·716 inches on 163 days.

At Clonsevin, Killiney, Co. Dublin, 5·43 inches of rain fell on 20 days, compared with a ten years' average of 3·068 inches on 15·7 days. The maximal fall in 24 hours was 1·01 inches on the 11th. Since January 1st, 1895, 29·65 inches of rain have fallen at this station on 165 days.

December.—A gloomy, wet, stormy, and generally inclement month. Fog also was often observed—the cold vapour fog of the 21st being especially noteworthy. Christmas week is memorable for a long continued south-easterly gale in Ireland, and downpours of rain in the south-east and south—at Roche's Point the rainfall measurement was 7 inches in the seven days ending 8 a.m. of Saturday, the 28th. A remarkable wave of warmth was passing over the extreme west of Europe at the close of the month.

In Dublin the arithmetical mean temperature (41·6°) was slightly above the average (41·3°); the mean dry bulb readings at 9 a.m. and 9 p.m. were 41·0°. In the thirty years ending with 1894, December was coldest in 1878 (M. T. = 33·6°), and in 1874 (M. T. = 35·6°), and warmest in 1865 (M. T. = 46·5°). In 1886 the M. T. was as low as 37·3°; in the year 1879 (the "cold year") it was also 37·3°. In 1887 the M. T. was 39·4°; in 1888 43·5°; in 1889 43·8°; in 1890 35·5°; in 1891, 43·0°; in 1892 38·6°; in 1893, 42·3°; and in 1894, 43·9°.

The mean height of the barometer was 29·723 inches, or 0·151 inch below the corrected average value for December—namely, 29·873 inches. The mercury rose to 30·290 inches at 9 a.m. of the 27th, and fell to 28·844 inches at 9 p.m. of the 13th. The observed range of atmospheric pressure was, therefore, 1·446 inches—that is, a little less than one inch and a half.

The mean temperature deduced from daily readings of the dry bulb thermometer at 9 a.m. and 9 p.m. was 41·0°, or 3·1° below the value for November, and 8·7° below that for October, 1895. Using the formula, *Mean Temp.* = *Min.* + (*max.* – *min.* × ·52), the value was 41·6°, or 0·3° above the average mean temperature for December, calculated in the same way, in the twenty-five years, 1865–89, inclusive (41·3°). The arithmetical mean of the maximal and minimal readings was 41·6°, compared with a twenty-five years' average of 41·3°. On the 30th the thermometer in the screen rose to 56·9°—wind, W.; on the 21st the temperature fell to 25·3°—wind, S.E. The minimum on the grass was 21·0° on the 8th. There were only 4 days of frost in the screen, and 10 days of frost on the grass.

The rainfall was 3·064 inches, distributed over as many as 27 days. The average rainfall for December in the twenty-five years, 1865–89, was 2·406 inches, and the average number of rainy days was 18·2. Both rainfall, therefore, and rainy days were considerably above the average. In 1876 the rainfall in December was very large—7·566 inches on 22 days. In 1872, [illegible] inches fell on as many as 24 days; and in 1868 (which was otherwise a fine and dry year) 4·740 inches fell on as many as 27 days. On the other hand, in 1867, only ·771 inch was measured on 13 days; and in 1871 only ·797 inch on 16 days. In 1885, only ·718 inch of rain was measured on but 10 days, but in 1886 the rainfall was 3·348 inches on 21 days. In 1887 (the "dry year"), the rainfall was 1·350 inches on 10 days; in 1888, 2·911 inches on 17 days; in 1889, 1·654 inches on 14 days; in 1890, 1·636 inches on 11 days; in 1891, 5·420 inches on 22 days; in 1892, only ·795 inch on 10 days; in 1893, 2·452 inches on 18 days; and in 1894, 1·611 inches on 15 days.

Lunar halos appeared on the 30th and 31st; a solar halo on the 31st. High winds were noted on 15 days, and attained the force of a gale on 7 occasions—the 4th, 5th, 11th, 13th, 22nd, 24th, and 26th. The atmosphere was more or less foggy in Dublin on the 5th, 10th, 11th, 17th, 19th, 20th 21st, 27th, 29th, and 31st. Snow or sleet fell in Dublin on the 6th, 7th, 12th, 13th, 15th, 24th, 25th and 26th. Hail fell on the 3rd, 6th and 12th. Thunder was heard on the 12th. Lightning occurred on the 13th. Faint aurora was seen on the 7th.

The most striking episode of the week ended Saturday the 7th, was the passage across North-western and Northern Europe, in the interval between Wednesday and Saturday, of an atmospheric depression, near the centre of which the barometer fell to 28 inches or less, at a time when pressure exceeded 30·40 inches over the Peninsula. The first three days were changeable, but generally favourable, with open weather and south-westerly or westerly winds. The barometer was low off the N. of Scotland and to the westward of Norway—29·60 inches on Sunday and Monday, 29 inches on Tuesday and Wednesday. During this time the barometer stood above 30 inches over France and Germany and was gradually rising in that region. Hence gradients became very steep over the British Isles and North Sea. On Wednesday a still further reduction of pressure took place over the Norwegian Sea, and at 8 a.m. of Thursday the barometer read only 27·84 inches at Christiansund in Norway, whereas it stood as high as 30·43 inches at Biarritz and Lisbon, and 30·48 inches at Ponta Delgada in the Azores. On Friday morning the reading at Madrid was 30·40 inches. Violent westerly gales raged over the North of France, Germany, the British Isles, and Scandinavia. Temperature rose in the S.—to 55° at Roche's Point, in London, and at the North Foreland, and to 53° at Cambridge; it fell fast to the N., and squalls of hail and snow, with thunder and lightning, swept over Scotland. A snow storm of much intensity subsequently extended to Ireland and England accompanied by lightning at many stations. On Thursday evening the barometer was down to 28 inches at Christiansund. In Dublin the mean atmospheric pressure was 29·201 inches, the range being from 28·[illegible] inches at 9 a.m. of Friday (wind, W.), to 30·014 inches at 9 p.m. of Saturday (wind, W.N.W.). The corrected mean temperature was 44·4°. On Thursday the screened thermometers rose to 54·5°; on Saturday they fell to 31·6°. The mean dry bulb temperature at 9 a.m. and 9 p.m. was 43·0°. Rain fell on five days to the amount of ·[illegible] inch, ·106 inch being measured on Friday. The greater part of this precipitation took place in the form of snow. The prevailing wind was W.

Cyclonic conditions persisted throughout the week ended Saturday, the 14th, and the weather was of a very unsettled, changeable type—the alternations in pressure and temperature being sudden and extreme. Rain, or sleet and snow fell almost daily in varying quantities, and thunder and lightning occurred in several parts of the United Kingdom in the course of Thursday. The week began with a frost prevailing in the rear of the great atmospheric depression of the closing period of the previous week. In and about Dublin the ground was covered with snow on Sunday, but a rapid thaw set in as the day advanced, and by Monday morning the air was quite mild, with a new depression central off the North of Scotland. In Dublin the thermometer stood 18 degrees higher at 8 a.m. of Monday than at 8 a.m. of Sunday. Tuesday was cold but fair. At night temperature rose again in Ireland, but sharp frost occurred in England, the thermometer sinking to 23° in the screen at both Oxford and Cambridge. Wednesday was a fine day, but at night the barometer fell fast, as a deep depression reached the North of Ireland and West of Scotland. This disturbance caused S.W. to N.W. gales, heavy rainfalls followed by showers of hail and sleet or snow. It was accompanied by thunder and lightning in some instances. In Dublin thunder was heard at 10.15 a.m. of Thursday. Friday was fine after some light snow showers, but at night the barometer again fell and temperature rose so that the thermometer stood 15·8° higher at 9 a.m. of Saturday than at 9 a.m. of Friday. The mean atmospheric pressure was, in Dublin, 29·700 inches, the barometer ranging from 30·135 inches at 9 a.m. of Sunday (wind, W.) to 29·160 inches about noon of Thursday (wind, W.S.W.). The corrected mean temperature was 40·6°. The mean dry bulb reading at 9 a.m. and 9 p.m. was 40·1°. On Sunday the screened thermometers fell to 30·2°; on Saturday they rose to 55·0°. Rainfall amounted to ·876 inch on six days, ·377 inch being measured on Thursday. The prevailing wind was westerly.

During the week ended Saturday, the 21st, the weather was changeable and cold—more steadily cold than in past weeks; but as uncertain as before with regard to atmospheric pressure, direction of the wind, and amount of cloud. On Sunday a large and deep depression was central over Ulster, Connaught, Leinster, and the Irish Sea, in which regions the barometer was below 29 inches. Temperature had risen fast in England, but fallen equally quickly in Ireland, at 8 a.m. the thermometer read 41° in London and at Cambridge; at 9 a.m. it stood at 38° in Dublin, where cold rain was soon followed by sleet and snow. Lightning was seen at night. At this time a high-pressure area (anticyclone) began to spread south-westwards over the North Sea and British Isles from the Baltic and Scandinavia, the result being that easterly and south-easterly winds set in on Tuesday, accompanied by fine, dry spells. In Dublin, however, showers fell on Tuesday evening and during Wednesday night, while Thursday proved gloomy and damp in the extreme at a time when a clear sky and sharp frost prevailed inland and in the S.W. of Ireland. At 8 a.m. of Thursday the thermometer was as low as 30° at Valentia Island and 29° at Parsonstown, the minima at these stations having been 27° and 26° respectively. On Friday an anticyclone of little intensity lay over Ireland, Scotland, and Wales. The air fell calm and a remarkable reduction of temperature occurred in Dublin, attended by a dense vapoury fog—by 3 p.m. the thermometer in the screen had sunk below 32° and during the following night a minimum of 24·3° was recorded. At Parsonstown the minimum was 21°. On Saturday a S.E. wind, connected with a new depression in the far S. and S.W., caused a rise of temperature in this neighbourhood. In Dublin the mean atmospheric pressure was 29·[illegible] inches, the lowest being 28·[illegible] inches at 9 p.m. of Sunday (wind, W.S.W.); the highest, 30·[illegible] inches at 9 a.m. of Friday (wind, W.N.W.). The corrected mean temperature was 35·[illegible]°. The mean dry bulb temperature at 9 a.m. and 9 p.m. was 37·1°. On Sunday the screened thermometers rose to 44·6°; on Saturday they fell to 24·6°. Westerly and easterly winds prevailed alternately. The rainfall was ·333 inch on six days, ·120 inch being recorded on Sunday, and ·131 inch on Saturday.

Weather of the most inclement description was experienced during the week ended Saturday, the 28th, in the S., S.E. and E. of Ireland. Day after day was gloomy, stormy, wet, and cold, and only on Saturday, when the wind at length veered from E. and S.E. to S.W., did more genial conditions prevail. In Dublin the sun remained invisible until Saturday forenoon, when it shone brightly for a few short intervals with the coming of the S.W. wind. The cause of the bad weather was the persistence of an area of high atmospheric pressure (anticyclone) over the Scandinavian Peninsula and the northern half of the North Sea, while a very large and deep depression swayed backwards and forwards off the extreme S.W. of Ireland. This distribution of pressure caused very steep gradients for S.E. winds, particularly in Ireland. Temperature was low except along the W. coast of France, over Cornwall, and in the S. and S.W. of Ireland, the result being that large quantities of rain fell along the line of commingling warm and cold-air currents, while the wind blew a fresh to whole gale from S.E. and E. in the same districts. At Roche's Point, Cork Harbour, the daily rainfalls up to 8 a.m. on Saturday were—1·15 inches, 1·60 inches, 1·60 inches, 0·80 inch, 1·30 inches, 0·10 inch, and 0·45 inch—in all, 7·00 inches. The gales were most severely felt in the E. and S.E. of Ireland, where the coasts were strewed with wrecks and a lamentable loss of life occurred on Christmas Eve. In Dublin the mean height of the barometer was 29·723 inches, pressure ranging between 29·[illegible] inches at 9 p.m. of Tuesday (wind, E.S.E.) and 30·250 inches at 9 p.m. of Friday (wind, S.E.). The corrected mean temperature was 40·6°. The mean dry bulb reading at 9 a.m. and 9 p.m. being 40·6°. On both Thursday and Friday the thermometer sank to 37·0° in the screen; on Saturday it rose to 53·6°. Rain or sleet fell daily to the amount of 3·300 inches, ·818 inch being registered on Sunday, ·444 inch on Monday, and ·855 inch on Tuesday. The prevalent wind was S.E.

The last three days of the month and of the year 1895 were singularly mild, but very changeable, cloudy and showery or rainy. On Monday, the 30th, the thermometer rose to 56·0° in the screen—the highest reading for the month. Lunar halos were seen on the 30th and 31st; a solar halo appeared on the 31st.

The rainfall in Dublin during 1895 amounted to 31·[illegible] inches on 194 days, compared with 29·[illegible] inches on 209 days in 1894, only 20·469 inches on 174 days in 1893, 26·[illegible] inches on 195 days in 1892, 27·[illegible] inches on 184 days in 1891, 27·[illegible] inches on 200 days in 1890, 31·[illegible] inches on 1[illegible] days in 1889, 22·[illegible] inches on 190 days in 1888, 18·[illegible] inches on 160 days in 1887, and a twenty-five years' average of 27·[illegible] inches on 191·3 days.

At Knockdolian, Greystones, Co. Wicklow, the rainfall in December, 1895, was 6·430 inches, distributed over 23 days. Of this quantity ·450 inch fell on the 24th, and ·260 inch on the 14th. From January 1st to December 31st, 1895, rain fell at Knockdolian on 174 days, and to the total amount of 35·165 inches. The corresponding figures for 1893 were 22·526 inches on 170 days, and for 1894, 28·776 inches on 184 days.

The rainfall at Clonsevin, Killiney, Co. Dublin, during December, 1895, was 4·19 inches on 27 days, compared with a ten years' average (1885–94) of 2·066 inches on 14·7 days. It was the wettest December of eleven years; 1886 comes next, with 3·67 inches on 20 days. The maximum fall in 24 hours was ·96 inch on the 23rd. Mr Robert O'Brien Furlong, M.A., Univ. Dub., reports that the total fall for 1895 at Clonsevin was 32·81 inches on 190 days. This was 7·264 inches in excess of the 10 years' average—viz., 25·546 inches, and is the highest recorded for 10 years—1885–94. The next highest annual fall was 32·64 inches in 1884, on 188 days.

In 1895 rain (including snow on 14 days) fell on 190 days, the average being 176·7 days.

---

Rainfall in 1896,

*At 40, Fitzwilliam-square, West, Dublin.*

*Rain Gauge:—Diameter of funnel, 8 in. Height of top—Above ground, 1 ft. 4 in.; above sea level, 50 ft.*

| Month. | Total Depth. | Greatest Fall in 24 hours. | | Number of Days on which ·01 or more fell. | Month. | Total Depth. | Greatest Fall in 24 hours. | | Number of Days on which ·01 or more fell. |
|---|---|---|---|---|---|---|---|---|---|
| | Inches. | Depth. | Date. | | | Inches. | Depth. | Date. | |
| January, | [illegible] | [illegible] | [illegible] | [illegible] | August, | [illegible] | [illegible] | [illegible] | [illegible] |
| February, | [illegible] | [illegible] | [illegible] | [illegible] | September, | [illegible] | [illegible] | [illegible] | [illegible] |
| March, | [illegible] | [illegible] | [illegible] | [illegible] | October, | [illegible] | [illegible] | [illegible] | [illegible] |
| April, | [illegible] | [illegible] | [illegible] | [illegible] | November, | [illegible] | [illegible] | [illegible] | [illegible] |
| May, | [illegible] | [illegible] | [illegible] | [illegible] | December, | [illegible] | [illegible] | [illegible] | [illegible] |
| June, | [illegible] | [illegible] | [illegible] | [illegible] | | | | | |
| July, | [illegible] | [illegible] | [illegible] | [illegible] | Total, | [illegible] | – | – | [illegible] |

The rainfall was 2·546 inches in excess of the average annual measurement of the twenty-five years, 1865–89, inclusive—viz., 27·626 inches.

It will be remembered that the rainfall in 1887 was very exceptionally small—16·601 inches, the only approach to this measurement in Dublin being in 1870, when only 20·816 inches fell, in 1864, when the measurement was 20·167 inches, and in 1882 with its rainfall of 20·463 inches. In seven of the twenty-five years in question the rainfall was less than 25 inches, and in 1885 it was 25·615 inches.

The scanty rainfall in 1887 was in marked contrast to the abundant downpour in 1886, when 33·264 inches—or as nearly as possible double the fall of 1887—fell on 250 days. Only twice since these records commenced has the rainfall in Dublin exceeded that of 1886—namely, in 1872, when 35·206 inches fell on 225 days, and in 1880, when 34·118 inches were measured on, however, only 187 days.

In 1896, there were 194 rainy days, or days upon which not less than ·005 inch of rain (five thousandths of an inch) was measured. This was almost exactly equal to the average number of rainy days, which was 195·9 in the twenty-five years, 1865–89, inclusive. In 1868 and 1887—the warm dry years of recent times—the rainy days were only 160, and in 1870 they were only 155. In 1868, however, the rainfall amounted to 24·935 inches, or more than 8 inches above the measurement in 1887, and even in 1870, 20·810 inches were recorded.

The rainfall in 24 hours from 9 a.m. to 9 a.m. exceeded one inch on two occasions in 1895—viz., May 28th (2·056 inches), and August 14th (1·310 inches). On no occasion in 1893 did one inch of rain fall on a given day in Dublin. In 1894, falls of upwards of an inch of rain in 24 hours were recorded on four occasions, viz., May 15th (1·230 inches); July 24th (1·480 inches); August 25th (1·059 inches); and October 23rd (1·049 inches). In 1893, 1·209 inches fell on January 12th; 1·014 inches on July 14th; and 1·226 on July 25th.

Included in the 194 rainy days in 1896 are 28 on which snow or sleet fell, and 40 on which there was hail. In January hail was observed on 10 days, in February and also in March on 6 days, in April on 2 days, in May, July, and November on 1 day, in June on 3 days, in October on 8 days, and on 3 days in December. Snow or sleet fell on 12 days in January, on 7 days in February, on 4 days in March, on 1 day in April and also in May, on 2 days in October, on 1 day in November, and on 2 days in December. Thunder occurred on 10 occasions during the year—twice in May, three times in June, twice in July, and once in August, October, and December. Lightning was also seen on three occasions in October, and once in January, March,

The rainfall in the first six months was [illegible] inches, on [illegible] days. The rainfall exceeded 6 inches in January (5·771), July (6·[illegible]), August ([illegible]), November ([illegible]), and December ([illegible]). In May it was only ·177 inch on 3 days.

Aurora borealis was observed on four occasions—namely, on March 13th, April 11th, May 2nd, and December 7th. More or less fog prevailed on 51 occasions—5 in January, 8 in February, 6 in March, 8 in May, 3 in August, 8 in September, 7 in October, 6 in November, and 10 in December. High winds were noted on 134 days—18 in January, 15 in February, 13 in March, 9 in April, 3 in May, 4 in June, 12 in July, 8 in August, 7 in September, 9 in October, 15 in November, and 13 in December. The high winds amounted to gales (force 7 or upwards according to the Beaufort scale) on 34 occasions—4 in January, 7 in February, 3 in March, 1 in May, 1 in July, 8 in September, 2 in October, 7 in November, and 7 in December.

The rainfall was distributed as follows:—9·084 inches fell on 52 days in the first quarter, [illegible] inches on [illegible] days in the second, 8·594 inches on 30 days in the third, 10·356 inches on 54 days in the fourth and last quarter.

---

*Abstract of Meteorological Observations taken at Dublin ([illegible] Fitzwilliam-square, West), during the Year 18[illegible].*

| Month. | Abs. Max. | Date. | Abs. Min. | Date. | Mean Daily Max. | Mean Daily Min. | Rainfall. | Rainy Days. | Mean Height of Barometer. | Highest Pressure. | Date. | Lowest Pressure. | Date. | Prevalent Winds. |
|---|---|---|---|---|---|---|---|---|---|---|---|---|---|---|
| | ° | | ° | | ° | ° | Ins. | | Ins. | Ins. | | Ins. | | |
| January, | [illegible] | [illegible] | [illegible] | [illegible] | [illegible] | [illegible] | [illegible] | [illegible] | [illegible] | [illegible] | [illegible] | [illegible] | [illegible] | [illegible] |
| February, | [illegible] | [illegible] | [illegible] | [illegible] | [illegible] | [illegible] | [illegible] | [illegible] | [illegible] | [illegible] | [illegible] | [illegible] | [illegible] | [illegible] |
| March, | [illegible] | [illegible] | [illegible] | [illegible] | [illegible] | [illegible] | [illegible] | [illegible] | [illegible] | [illegible] | [illegible] | [illegible] | [illegible] | [illegible] |
| April, | [illegible] | [illegible] | [illegible] | [illegible] | [illegible] | [illegible] | [illegible] | [illegible] | [illegible] | [illegible] | [illegible] | [illegible] | [illegible] | [illegible] |
| May, | [illegible] | [illegible] | [illegible] | [illegible] | [illegible] | [illegible] | [illegible] | [illegible] | [illegible] | [illegible] | [illegible] | [illegible] | [illegible] | [illegible] |
| June, | [illegible] | [illegible] | [illegible] | [illegible] | [illegible] | [illegible] | [illegible] | [illegible] | [illegible] | [illegible] | [illegible] | [illegible] | [illegible] | [illegible] |
| July, | [illegible] | [illegible] | [illegible] | [illegible] | [illegible] | [illegible] | [illegible] | [illegible] | [illegible] | [illegible] | [illegible] | [illegible] | [illegible] | [illegible] |
| August, | [illegible] | [illegible] | [illegible] | [illegible] | [illegible] | [illegible] | [illegible] | [illegible] | [illegible] | [illegible] | [illegible] | [illegible] | [illegible] | [illegible] |
| September, | [illegible] | [illegible] | [illegible] | [illegible] | [illegible] | [illegible] | [illegible] | [illegible] | [illegible] | [illegible] | [illegible] | [illegible] | [illegible] | [illegible] |
| October, | [illegible] | [illegible] | [illegible] | [illegible] | [illegible] | [illegible] | [illegible] | [illegible] | [illegible] | [illegible] | [illegible] | [illegible] | [illegible] | [illegible] |
| November, | [illegible] | [illegible] | [illegible] | [illegible] | [illegible] | [illegible] | [illegible] | [illegible] | [illegible] | [illegible] | [illegible] | [illegible] | [illegible] | [illegible] |
| December, | [illegible] | [illegible] | [illegible] | [illegible] | [illegible] | [illegible] | [illegible] | [illegible] | [illegible] | [illegible] | [illegible] | [illegible] | [illegible] | [illegible] |
| [illegible] | [illegible] | [illegible] | [illegible] | [illegible] | [illegible] | [illegible] | [illegible] | [illegible] | [illegible] | [illegible] | [illegible] | [illegible] | [illegible] | [illegible] |

[illegible]

[illegible]

[illegible]

| [illegible] |
| --- |
| [illegible] |

[illegible]

TABLE showing the Monthly and Yearly Rainfall at Dublin during the Twenty-one Years 1875 to 1895, inclusive; with the Means for the Twenty Years 1875 to 1894.

| Year. | January. | February. | March. | April. | May. | June. | July. | August. | September. | October. | November. | December. | Total. |
|---|---|---|---|---|---|---|---|---|---|---|---|---|---|
| | Inches. | Inches. | Inches. | Inches. | Inches. | Inches. | Inches. | Inches. | Inches. | Inches. | Inches. | Inches. | Inches. |
| [illegible] | [illegible] | [illegible] | [illegible] | [illegible] | [illegible] | [illegible] | [illegible] | [illegible] | [illegible] | [illegible] | [illegible] | [illegible] | [illegible] |
| [illegible] | [illegible] | [illegible] | [illegible] | [illegible] | [illegible] | [illegible] | [illegible] | [illegible] | [illegible] | [illegible] | [illegible] | [illegible] | [illegible] |
| [illegible] | [illegible] | [illegible] | [illegible] | [illegible] | [illegible] | [illegible] | [illegible] | [illegible] | [illegible] | [illegible] | [illegible] | [illegible] | [illegible] |
| [illegible] | [illegible] | [illegible] | [illegible] | [illegible] | [illegible] | [illegible] | [illegible] | [illegible] | [illegible] | [illegible] | [illegible] | [illegible] | [illegible] |
| [illegible] | [illegible] | [illegible] | [illegible] | [illegible] | [illegible] | [illegible] | [illegible] | [illegible] | [illegible] | [illegible] | [illegible] | [illegible] | [illegible] |
| [illegible] | [illegible] | [illegible] | [illegible] | [illegible] | [illegible] | [illegible] | [illegible] | [illegible] | [illegible] | [illegible] | [illegible] | [illegible] | [illegible] |
| [illegible] | [illegible] | [illegible] | [illegible] | [illegible] | [illegible] | [illegible] | [illegible] | [illegible] | [illegible] | [illegible] | [illegible] | [illegible] | [illegible] |
| [illegible] | [illegible] | [illegible] | [illegible] | [illegible] | [illegible] | [illegible] | [illegible] | [illegible] | [illegible] | [illegible] | [illegible] | [illegible] | [illegible] |
| [illegible] | [illegible] | [illegible] | [illegible] | [illegible] | [illegible] | [illegible] | [illegible] | [illegible] | [illegible] | [illegible] | [illegible] | [illegible] | [illegible] |
| [illegible] | [illegible] | [illegible] | [illegible] | [illegible] | [illegible] | [illegible] | [illegible] | [illegible] | [illegible] | [illegible] | [illegible] | [illegible] | [illegible] |
| [illegible] | [illegible] | [illegible] | [illegible] | [illegible] | [illegible] | [illegible] | [illegible] | [illegible] | [illegible] | [illegible] | [illegible] | [illegible] | [illegible] |
| [illegible] | [illegible] | [illegible] | [illegible] | [illegible] | [illegible] | [illegible] | [illegible] | [illegible] | [illegible] | [illegible] | [illegible] | [illegible] | [illegible] |
| [illegible] | [illegible] | [illegible] | [illegible] | [illegible] | [illegible] | [illegible] | [illegible] | [illegible] | [illegible] | [illegible] | [illegible] | [illegible] | [illegible] |
| [illegible] | [illegible] | [illegible] | [illegible] | [illegible] | [illegible] | [illegible] | [illegible] | [illegible] | [illegible] | [illegible] | [illegible] | [illegible] | [illegible] |
| [illegible] | [illegible] | [illegible] | [illegible] | [illegible] | [illegible] | [illegible] | [illegible] | [illegible] | [illegible] | [illegible] | [illegible] | [illegible] | [illegible] |
| [illegible] | [illegible] | [illegible] | [illegible] | [illegible] | [illegible] | [illegible] | [illegible] | [illegible] | [illegible] | [illegible] | [illegible] | [illegible] | [illegible] |
| [illegible] | [illegible] | [illegible] | [illegible] | [illegible] | [illegible] | [illegible] | [illegible] | [illegible] | [illegible] | [illegible] | [illegible] | [illegible] | [illegible] |
| [illegible] | [illegible] | [illegible] | [illegible] | [illegible] | [illegible] | [illegible] | [illegible] | [illegible] | [illegible] | [illegible] | [illegible] | [illegible] | [illegible] |
| [illegible] | [illegible] | [illegible] | [illegible] | [illegible] | [illegible] | [illegible] | [illegible] | [illegible] | [illegible] | [illegible] | [illegible] | [illegible] | [illegible] |
| [illegible] | [illegible] | [illegible] | [illegible] | [illegible] | [illegible] | [illegible] | [illegible] | [illegible] | [illegible] | [illegible] | [illegible] | [illegible] | [illegible] |
| Means, | [illegible] | [illegible] | [illegible] | [illegible] | [illegible] | [illegible] | [illegible] | [illegible] | [illegible] | [illegible] | [illegible] | [illegible] | [illegible] |
| [illegible] | [illegible] | [illegible] | [illegible] | [illegible] | [illegible] | [illegible] | [illegible] | [illegible] | [illegible] | [illegible] | [illegible] | [illegible] | [illegible] |

* [illegible]
† [illegible]
‡ [illegible]
§ [illegible]

TABLE showing the Monthly and Yearly Number of Rainy Days* at Dublin during the Twenty-one Years 1875 to 1895, inclusive; with the Means for the Twenty Years 1875 to 1894.

| Year. | January. | February. | March. | April. | May. | June. | July. | August. | September. | October. | November. | December. | Total Rainy Days. |
|---|---|---|---|---|---|---|---|---|---|---|---|---|---|
| [illegible] | [illegible] | [illegible] | [illegible] | [illegible] | [illegible] | [illegible] | [illegible] | [illegible] | [illegible] | [illegible] | [illegible] | [illegible] | [illegible] |
| [illegible] | [illegible] | [illegible] | [illegible] | [illegible] | [illegible] | [illegible] | [illegible] | [illegible] | [illegible] | [illegible] | [illegible] | [illegible] | [illegible] |
| [illegible] | [illegible] | [illegible] | [illegible] | [illegible] | [illegible] | [illegible] | [illegible] | [illegible] | [illegible] | [illegible] | [illegible] | [illegible] | [illegible] |
| [illegible] | [illegible] | [illegible] | [illegible] | [illegible] | [illegible] | [illegible] | [illegible] | [illegible] | [illegible] | [illegible] | [illegible] | [illegible] | [illegible] |
| [illegible] | [illegible] | [illegible] | [illegible] | [illegible] | [illegible] | [illegible] | [illegible] | [illegible] | [illegible] | [illegible] | [illegible] | [illegible] | [illegible] |
| [illegible] | [illegible] | [illegible] | [illegible] | [illegible] | [illegible] | [illegible] | [illegible] | [illegible] | [illegible] | [illegible] | [illegible] | [illegible] | [illegible] |
| [illegible] | [illegible] | [illegible] | [illegible] | [illegible] | [illegible] | [illegible] | [illegible] | [illegible] | [illegible] | [illegible] | [illegible] | [illegible] | [illegible] |
| [illegible] | [illegible] | [illegible] | [illegible] | [illegible] | [illegible] | [illegible] | [illegible] | [illegible] | [illegible] | [illegible] | [illegible] | [illegible] | [illegible] |
| [illegible] | [illegible] | [illegible] | [illegible] | [illegible] | [illegible] | [illegible] | [illegible] | [illegible] | [illegible] | [illegible] | [illegible] | [illegible] | [illegible] |
| [illegible] | [illegible] | [illegible] | [illegible] | [illegible] | [illegible] | [illegible] | [illegible] | [illegible] | [illegible] | [illegible] | [illegible] | [illegible] | [illegible] |
| [illegible] | [illegible] | [illegible] | [illegible] | [illegible] | [illegible] | [illegible] | [illegible] | [illegible] | [illegible] | [illegible] | [illegible] | [illegible] | [illegible] |
| [illegible] | [illegible] | [illegible] | [illegible] | [illegible] | [illegible] | [illegible] | [illegible] | [illegible] | [illegible] | [illegible] | [illegible] | [illegible] | [illegible] |
| [illegible] | [illegible] | [illegible] | [illegible] | [illegible] | [illegible] | [illegible] | [illegible] | [illegible] | [illegible] | [illegible] | [illegible] | [illegible] | [illegible] |
| [illegible] | [illegible] | [illegible] | [illegible] | [illegible] | [illegible] | [illegible] | [illegible] | [illegible] | [illegible] | [illegible] | [illegible] | [illegible] | [illegible] |
| [illegible] | [illegible] | [illegible] | [illegible] | [illegible] | [illegible] | [illegible] | [illegible] | [illegible] | [illegible] | [illegible] | [illegible] | [illegible] | [illegible] |
| [illegible] | [illegible] | [illegible] | [illegible] | [illegible] | [illegible] | [illegible] | [illegible] | [illegible] | [illegible] | [illegible] | [illegible] | [illegible] | [illegible] |
| [illegible] | [illegible] | [illegible] | [illegible] | [illegible] | [illegible] | [illegible] | [illegible] | [illegible] | [illegible] | [illegible] | [illegible] | [illegible] | [illegible] |
| [illegible] | [illegible] | [illegible] | [illegible] | [illegible] | [illegible] | [illegible] | [illegible] | [illegible] | [illegible] | [illegible] | [illegible] | [illegible] | [illegible] |
| [illegible] | [illegible] | [illegible] | [illegible] | [illegible] | [illegible] | [illegible] | [illegible] | [illegible] | [illegible] | [illegible] | [illegible] | [illegible] | [illegible] |
| [illegible] | [illegible] | [illegible] | [illegible] | [illegible] | [illegible] | [illegible] | [illegible] | [illegible] | [illegible] | [illegible] | [illegible] | [illegible] | [illegible] |
| Means, | [illegible] | [illegible] | [illegible] | [illegible] | [illegible] | [illegible] | [illegible] | [illegible] | [illegible] | [illegible] | [illegible] | [illegible] | [illegible] |
| [illegible] | [illegible] | [illegible] | [illegible] | [illegible] | [illegible] | [illegible] | [illegible] | [illegible] | [illegible] | [illegible] | [illegible] | [illegible] | [illegible] |

TABLE showing the Temperature of the Air in Dublin in the Twenty-one Years 1875–1895, and the Average Temperature for the Twenty Years 1875 to 1894, inclusive, as recorded by Dr. J. W. Moore.

| Year. | January. | February. | March. | April. | May. | June. | July. | August. | September. | October. | November. | December. | Year. |
|---|---|---|---|---|---|---|---|---|---|---|---|---|---|
| 1875, . . . | [illegible] | [illegible] | [illegible] | [illegible] | [illegible] | [illegible] | [illegible] | [illegible] | [illegible] | [illegible] | [illegible] | [illegible] | [illegible] |
| 1876, . . . | [illegible] | [illegible] | [illegible] | [illegible] | [illegible] | [illegible] | [illegible] | [illegible] | [illegible] | [illegible] | [illegible] | [illegible] | [illegible] |
| 1877, . . . | [illegible] | [illegible] | [illegible] | [illegible] | [illegible] | [illegible] | [illegible] | [illegible] | [illegible] | [illegible] | [illegible] | [illegible] | [illegible] |
| 1878, . . . | [illegible] | [illegible] | [illegible] | [illegible] | [illegible] | [illegible] | [illegible] | [illegible] | [illegible] | [illegible] | [illegible] | [illegible] | [illegible] |
| 1879, . . . | [illegible] | [illegible] | [illegible] | [illegible] | [illegible] | [illegible] | [illegible] | [illegible] | [illegible] | [illegible] | [illegible] | [illegible] | [illegible] |
| 1880, . . . | [illegible] | [illegible] | [illegible] | [illegible] | [illegible] | [illegible] | [illegible] | [illegible] | [illegible] | [illegible] | [illegible] | [illegible] | [illegible] |
| 1881, . . . | [illegible] | [illegible] | [illegible] | [illegible] | [illegible] | [illegible] | [illegible] | [illegible] | [illegible] | [illegible] | [illegible] | [illegible] | [illegible] |
| 1882, . . . | [illegible] | [illegible] | [illegible] | [illegible] | [illegible] | [illegible] | [illegible] | [illegible] | [illegible] | [illegible] | [illegible] | [illegible] | [illegible] |
| 1883, . . . | [illegible] | [illegible] | [illegible] | [illegible] | [illegible] | [illegible] | [illegible] | [illegible] | [illegible] | [illegible] | [illegible] | [illegible] | [illegible] |
| 1884, . . . | [illegible] | [illegible] | [illegible] | [illegible] | [illegible] | [illegible] | [illegible] | [illegible] | [illegible] | [illegible] | [illegible] | [illegible] | [illegible] |
| 1885, . . . | [illegible] | [illegible] | [illegible] | [illegible] | [illegible] | [illegible] | [illegible] | [illegible] | [illegible] | [illegible] | [illegible] | [illegible] | [illegible] |
| 1886, . . . | [illegible] | [illegible] | [illegible] | [illegible] | [illegible] | [illegible] | [illegible] | [illegible] | [illegible] | [illegible] | [illegible] | [illegible] | [illegible] |
| 1887, . . . | [illegible] | [illegible] | [illegible] | [illegible] | [illegible] | [illegible] | [illegible] | [illegible] | [illegible] | [illegible] | [illegible] | [illegible] | [illegible] |
| 1888, . . . | [illegible] | [illegible] | [illegible] | [illegible] | [illegible] | [illegible] | [illegible] | [illegible] | [illegible] | [illegible] | [illegible] | [illegible] | [illegible] |
| 1889, . . . | [illegible] | [illegible] | [illegible] | [illegible] | [illegible] | [illegible] | [illegible] | [illegible] | [illegible] | [illegible] | [illegible] | [illegible] | [illegible] |
| 1890, . . . | [illegible] | [illegible] | [illegible] | [illegible] | [illegible] | [illegible] | [illegible] | [illegible] | [illegible] | [illegible] | [illegible] | [illegible] | [illegible] |
| 1891, . . . | [illegible] | [illegible] | [illegible] | [illegible] | [illegible] | [illegible] | [illegible] | [illegible] | [illegible] | [illegible] | [illegible] | [illegible] | [illegible] |
| 1892, . . . | [illegible] | [illegible] | [illegible] | [illegible] | [illegible] | [illegible] | [illegible] | [illegible] | [illegible] | [illegible] | [illegible] | [illegible] | [illegible] |
| 1893, . . . | [illegible] | [illegible] | [illegible] | [illegible] | [illegible] | [illegible] | [illegible] | [illegible] | [illegible] | [illegible] | [illegible] | [illegible] | [illegible] |
| 1894, . . . | [illegible] | [illegible] | [illegible] | [illegible] | [illegible] | [illegible] | [illegible] | [illegible] | [illegible] | [illegible] | [illegible] | [illegible] | [illegible] |
| Average, . | [illegible] | [illegible] | [illegible] | [illegible] | [illegible] | [illegible] | [illegible] | [illegible] | [illegible] | [illegible] | [illegible] | [illegible] | [illegible] |
| 1895, . . . | [illegible] | [illegible] | [illegible] | [illegible] | [illegible] | [illegible] | [illegible] | [illegible] | [illegible] | [illegible] | [illegible] | [illegible] | [illegible] |

Dublin Castle,

18th June, 1896.

Sir,

I have to acknowledge the receipt of your letter of the 16th instant, forwarding, for submission to His Excellency the Lord Lieutenant, the Agricultural Statistics of Ireland, with detailed Report on Agriculture, for the Year 1895.

I am, Sir,

Your obedient servant,

D. HARREL.

The Registrar-General,

Charlemont House,

Rutland Square,

Dublin.

www.ingramcontent.com/pod-product-compliance
Lightning Source LLC
Chambersburg PA
CBHW021815190326
41518CB00007B/603
* 9 7 8 3 7 4 1 1 9 6 5 9 1 *